TWO HUNDRED YEARS

OF

AMERICAN FOREIGN POLICY

Two Hundred Years
of
American Foreign Policy

Edited by
WILLIAM P. BUNDY

A Council on Foreign Relations Book
Published by
New York University Press · New York · 1977

Copyright © 1977 by Council on Foreign Relations, Inc.
Library of Congress Catalog Card Number: 76-49699
ISBN: 0-8147-0990-7

Library of Congress Cataloging in Publication Data
Main entry under title:

Two hundred years of American foreign policy.

Includes bibliographical references.
1. United States—Foreign relations—Addresses,
essays, lectures. I. Bundy, William P., 1917-
E183.7.T9   327.73   76-49699
ISBN 0-8147-0990-7

Manufactured in the United States of America

Contents

[v]

Introduction

This book started as a way for *Foreign Affairs* magazine (and its parent organization, the Council on Foreign Relations in New York City) to commemorate the American Bicentennial in a way that would be neither froth nor pomposity. A series of historical essays on key themes in American foreign policy seemed to meet this need, provided that we could find qualified authors possessing the critical spirit, and turn them loose to tell the story and to distill in their own way whatever lessons and implications for the future they found.

The model was already at hand. In the spring of 1975 Alastair Buchan of Oxford University, formerly head of the (then) Institute for Strategic Studies in London, had suggested that he write for our July 1976 issue an analysis of the British-American relationship since 1776. He proposed not only to trace its ups and downs, from war to intimate collaboration, but to argue the thesis that excessive reliance on Britain had stunted the development of an independent American foreign policy for more than a century, while, in turn, Britain's undue reliance on its "special relationship" since 1945 had inhibited the British from striking out on the new paths their postwar situation should have dictated. It seemed a challenging and important interpretation, for which the time was ripe.

In seeking other writers capable of the same kind of rethinking, we were fortunate to find our first choices uniformly interested and willing. For readers already familiar with the field and with writers in it, the individual names alone may suffice to attest the importance of the book. Felix Gilbert's *To the Farewell Address* has been for fifteen years a recognized classic on that precise subject; now he broadens his canvas to look at the whole framework of thinking the Founding Fathers left to their successors. Gordon Craig's writings on Nazi Germany and (with Gilbert) on the diplomacy of the interwar years admirably qualify him to dissect the role of America in the European balance of power. Abraham Lowenthal stands at the very top among the younger men who have transformed earlier ways of thinking about America's relationship to Latin America. John Davies' ouster from the Foreign Service in 1954, on charges that could only have been taken seriously in the era of Joseph McCarthy, removed from the ranks of American policy-makers one who was not only expert on East Asia but gifted with an extraordinary capacity to see the world in historical perspective. And George Kennan and Charles Kindleberger are recognized deans in the historical interpretation of Soviet foreign policy and world economic history, respectively.

Yet it may be noted that none of the final group of seven has devoted his career to the history of American foreign policy. Gilbert and Craig are lifelong professional historians, but overwhelmingly focused on Europe; Kennan, Davies and Kindleberger were longtime practitioners of diplomacy and practical economics before writing selectively on American history, and Abraham Lowenthal (like Buchan) is primarily an analyst and critic of contemporary policy. In addition to the negative virtue of having no established positions to defend, all seven shared to the fullest the capacity to look beneath the surface of events, to find central unifying themes, and to write clearly and vigorously.

The result is most certainly a distinguished collection of essays. But it is, we think, a little more than that. For there was in 1976 in America—and in the minds of its best critics and friends here and abroad—a sense of change and of the legacy of the past that may have made this a peculiarly fruitful time for the writing of just this kind of essay.

To grasp the extent of change in America's perception of herself and her role in the world, one may recall that prior to World War II one of the greatest of American diplomatic historians, Samuel Flagg Bemis, used to insist to his students that the United States in its whole foreign policy history had never committed any major error or moral wrong. At the time it seemed to some of these students that this thesis involved a fairly tortured interpretation of the Mexican War of 1846. The questioning tended to stop there.

Perhaps World War II and the early postwar years would not have shaken the faith of those many (perhaps most) Americans who shared the Bemis thesis in its essentials. But the belief that America was uniquely good and innocent came under increasing strain in the 1950s, and in the 1960s and 1970s collapsed completely under the impact of events culminating in the Vietnam War and Watergate. In the process there developed, especially among younger historians, a "revisionist" school sharply challenging the basic course of policy after (and in some cases during) World War II. Moreover, in many geographic areas, notably East Asia and Latin America, the revisionist critique reached back far into the past. Embattled attacks were in some cases countered by equally embattled defenses, particularly concerning the post-war period itself, and sometimes the deeper roots of policy were ignored or shortchanged.

It would be an oversimplification to say that the essays in this volume represent the synthesis between a thesis of praise and an antithesis of denigration of American performance in the world. Similarly, they do not prove that the acts of the present were foreordained by the past. But there is a thread common to all seven essays, of finding much to criticize in what the United States has done (and thought), of finding much in the past that does help to explain the present, and of finding the benevolent and malevolent intermingled, often inextricably. With the possible exception of John Davies' devastating critique of the American experience in East Asia, the authors picture an American foreign policy with, in the phrase of Justice Holmes, the qualities of its defects, or vice-versa. Idealistic, self-righteous, often selfish at root, and by these tokens occasionally capable of enlightened and constructive behavior and occasionally of the reverse. If, as some say, America has in the past few years lost its innocence, these essays reflect that mood fairly.

It is a mood, one would argue, likely to endure. My colleague at the Council on Foreign Relations, Bayless Manning, has suggested that American foreign policy has passed in its two hundred years from the simplicity of the Doric column (up to 1900), to the somewhat more intricate pattern of the Ionic (from 1900 until the 1950s, when the United States was involved in the world selectively), and finally today to a totally complex Corinthian design.* Some of the earlier themes persist today—notably those of power and national entities—but the emerging agenda is one of concrete world problems that call for new forms of international action. In such a world, the United States may persist in the simplified

---

* "246 Years of American Foreign Policy: Doric, Ionic—and Corinthian?" in *The Americans: 1976*, Volume II in the series sponsored by Critical Choices for Americans, Lexington, Mass.: D. C. Heath and Company, pp. 253-292.

attitudes of the past, but probably only for brief periods and in a diminishing way, for it is neither dominant nor unique to the degree it was, or tended to see itself, at periods of the past. Abe Lowenthal's essay on Latin America and the end of American hegemony catches this point acutely. But it is present in all the others.

Hence, it may not be presumptuous to suggest that these essays are likely to remain important for some time to come. They express thoughtful views of the American past, at a time of much greater maturity in national attitudes toward that past. And they project those views into the future, with a full sense of how complex that future may be. This is living history, and 1976 turned out to be the right time to get it.

I close on a note of personal sadness. In early 1976, just as he had finished his manuscript, Alastair Buchan—the originator of this series—died. To express our deep sense of loss, the editors of *Foreign Affairs* dedicated the original articles to his memory. We renew that dedication with this book.

William P. Bundy
Editor, *Foreign Affairs*

[ONE]

Bicentennial Reflections

Felix Gilbert

"The best that history can give us is to arouse our enthusi-asm"—Goethe's famous reflection on the value of history has found little favor with historical scholars who can rightly claim that a careful analysis of past events and of the structure of the society of other times can help us to understand the complex character of the world in which we live. Yet if we consider the impact of history in more general and more primitive terms, there is much truth in Goethe's statement. The re-evocation of outstanding national achievements and of a nation's great leaders reinforces social coherence and creates pride and confidence in the future. The commemoration of victories, the observance of the anniversaries of crucial years in the history of a nation—as much as such celebrations have the danger of

Felix Gilbert is Professor Emeritus and a member of the School of Historical Studies at the Institute for Advanced Study, Princeton. He is the author of *To the Farewell Address* and other works, and co-editor with Gordon A. Craig of *The Diplomats, 1919-1939*.

[1]

stimulating the worst instead of the best in the national character—have a justification in revealing the values on which a society was built and in strengthening the bonds that hold it together. When Machiavelli stated that, from time to time, every society must return to its beginnings, "its principles," he gave a conscious formulation to that which every country has practiced in the past and will continue to practice in the future.

Even if we accept that such observances are inherent in the nature of political life, it must be recognized that the celebration of great events of the past has special characteristics and peculiar dangers in the United States. If the message of the past in the great European countries, which, in their long and extended history, have undergone many changes and revolutions, has been rather indistinct and might be summed up as enthusiasm, such celebrations have a much more precise meaning in the United States, still relatively close to the years of its emergence as an independent power. They contain an appeal to return to the principles on which the new state was founded. If the present world does not fulfill the original expectations, the reason is a conscious or unconscious deviation from the wisdom of the Founding Fathers. The beliefs and convictions which are thought to have inspired the organization of the early republic still have validity and applicability, and national celebrations serve to remind the American people of the true character of the republic and of the excellence of its institutions. America still lives under the constitution which was established in the eighteenth century. As far as internal developments are concerned, all changes that have taken place have emerged from the framework set up at the beginning. There is meaning in considering the principles which inspired the original establishment, for they provide the criteria against which the political life of the present might be measured.

But it is something entirely different if the same authority is assigned to the doctrines which determined the thinking on foreign affairs in the young republic. For in a democracy, the internal organization of the political society lies in the hands of the citizens, and they can build on the basis which was laid, according to their will. An equal freedom of choice, of direction, an equal amount of self-determination does not exist in the area of foreign affairs. Foreign policy takes place in an arena which only to small extent can be shaped by the national will; other powers and external factors play their part in its formation. Accordingly, the influence which can be exerted on changes in the constellations of foreign policy is limited. There are dangers, therefore, in extending to foreign affairs a belief in the permanent validity and authority of the principles which guided the first steps of the young republic. Yet such views have been tenuously held; even if it is realized that the world in which we now live is widely different from the world that was, there is still an inclination to cling to the assumptions and prejudices which colored the attitude toward foreign affairs in the past. The celebration of the bicentenary gives reason to reflect on what the ideas and actions of the Founding Fathers in the field of foreign affairs actually were and what they have meant in the course of our history.

II

The constellation under which the British colonies in North America became an independent sovereign state was unique. With the French surrender of Canada and the weakening of the power of Spain in the south, foreign nations no longer represented a threat to the narrow stretch of settlements along the Eastern Atlantic coast. Their expansion toward the west had always been a task taken on by the settlers themselves rather than by the military forces of England. The colonies on the North American continent were not regarded as more—perhaps even as less—valuable than other British possessions such as the sugar islands of the West Indies. For the British, the American colonies were useful chiefly as a market for manufactured goods, and unavoidably the question arose whether the protection which Britain offered was worth the disadvantages of the restrictions which were implied in the colonial relationship and which hampered the commercial development of the colonies. All this is known, but it needs to be mentioned because it explains why freedom of commerce and freedom of navigation appeared as the most essential element of sovereignty and the most fundamental aim of foreign policy when the new nation was founded.

Yet the demand for a new regulation of the relations between England and the American colonies arose at a moment—and that was the most significant factor in the unique constellation existing at the time of the birth of the United States—when the entire system of European politics had come under heavy criticism, when the ruling classes seemed to disregard and suppress those groups and interests which represented the most vital forces in society. In this period, the middle classes, as the driving forces in the expansion of commerce and the promotion of industrial activities, felt strong enough to challenge the monopoly of power, and the privileges, possessed by a ruling class rooted in the traditions of a feudal past. This tension created the climate for the accusations which the *philosophes* of the Enlightenment raised against the oppressive and irrational institutions and mores of the Ancien Régime. A particular target was the conduct of foreign policy. The partitions of Poland, by which a whole nation was rubbed off the map as a result of the arbitrary decisions of three despots, were seen as a prime example of the criminality of the foreign policy of the Ancien Régime. Voltaire's haunting description of a battlefield in *Candide* was intended to show the senselessness of wars and the contemptuous disregard of rulers for the lives of their subjects. If rulers would only follow the dictates of reason and reasonableness, peace would reign.

But the rejection of war, of military triumphs and territorial expansion, also implied criticism of the entire scale of values from which the activities of power politics arose. Manly prowess, honor, heroic behavior—these were virtues of a class formed in the age of feudalism. They were not the virtues which the bourgeoisie esteemed and cultivated. Their actions and the success of their actions were based on prudence, on rational calculation, on a reputation of reliability, on recognition of reciprocity of interests. Transferred into the field of foreign affairs, the true methods and aims of foreign policy became willingness to compromise; the interest of an individual nation was regarded as inextricably bound up with the common interest of all nations, the general interest. The aim of foreign policy was the establishment and maintenance of peace. The gist of these ideas can be found in a famous eighteenth-century comedy, Sédaine's *Philosophe sans le savoir;* there the modest and prudent merchant emerges as a person far superior to all the elegant figures of aristocratic society. By pursuing his trade, which extends to the farthest corners of the world, he serves the interest of all nations and ties the entire globe together in peaceful cooperation. Sédaine's comedy expresses the belief, widely held by the intellectuals of the eighteenth century, that the era in which feudal values had dominated was at its end and that a new era— a *novus ordo seclorum*—was beginning.

The people who were the personal embodiment of the amorality of the politics of the Ancien Régime were the men who served the despots in carrying out their sinister plans in foreign policy: the diplomats. The *philosophes* spoke of them in most biting terms. They were "competitors in grimaces," they were the practitioners of an "obscure art, which hides itself in the folds of deceit, which fears to let itself be seen and believes it can succeed only in the darkness of mystery." Secrecy, incitement of hatred, deception and fraud—these were the characteristics of diplomacy. Diplomats constructed complicated systems of alliance, but lightheartedly broke commitments whenever it seemed convenient. They insisted on strict observance of complicated rules of etiquette although such rules were meaningless and ridiculous. They pretended that diplomacy was a science, based on concepts like "reason of state" and "balance of power." Actually, such notions achieve only to "please both the ignorance and the laziness of the ministers, ambassadors and clercs." And the idea of "balance of power," which the diplomats pretend to be an instrument to secure peace, in fact is dangerous, even disastrous, because "the system of balance of power is a system of resistance, consequently of disturbance, of shocks and of explosions."

The Ancien Régime—its institutions and attitudes—had not crossed the ocean or taken roots in the alien soil of North America, certainly not in New England. If "the new man" existed anywhere, it was there. And more important, it was also that the belief in the coming of a new world order touched a deep religious vein. Although much had changed since the pilgrim fathers had set out to escape from the tyranny of a catholicizing church and monarchy, there remained a strong feeling that their aim ought to be the building of an ideal society: they had not abandoned the dream of "the city on the hill."

It follows that the thinking of the leaders of the new nation, as far as foreign affairs were concerned, would be patterned by the criticisms which the system of the power politics of the Ancien Régime and its diplomacy had provoked. It is less clear, however, what these general assumptions meant for the concrete course which the new republic should pursue in its foreign policy. European corruptness and amorality might lead to the conclusion that it would be best to consider the ocean as a wall which ought to separate the European from the American world and to withdraw as far as possible from contacts with the European nations. Such an inclination was reinforced by the English ties of the colonists. Since the Hanoverians had ascended the English throne and their concern for the interests of their continental fiefdom had become a factor in British foreign policy, a public debate had been engendered in England about the appropriateness for Britain to conclude alliances with continental powers and to become involved in continental wars. Some of the political pamphleteers argued that "treaties of commerce are Bonds that we ought to contract with our neighbors," but all other continental connections and involvements were dangerous and in contrast to the true interest of England: "Nature has separated us from the continent ... no man ought to endeavour to join what God Almighty has separated." Therefore, England's foreign policy ought to be guided by *"principes isolés."*

But if religious belief and echoes of disputes in England recommended to the colonists the breaking of all ties with Europe, the same feeling of opposition and hostility toward the Ancien Régime might also lead to a different course: to take the lead in terminating a system that trampled on the rights of humanity, and to assume an active role in establishing a new and better world order, in which there would be peace and prosperity through commerce. Eighteenth-century optimistic trust in progress easily combined with a feeling of religious duty: the Enlightenment's conviction of the perfectibility of humanity reinforced the missionary element in Protestantism. There was also considerable realism in this view of the task of the new nation. Its organization took the form of a republic, and as such it was an outsider in the world of monarchies; it could be argued that, in order to survive, a republic would have to destroy the system of monarchical absolutism which held sway in Europe. With the outbreak of the French Revolution, this issue became a matter of practical decision.

A confusing array of interrelated but also contradictory ideas and suggestions for the course of American foreign policy was contained in the discussions and writings of English radicals and enlightened *philosophes*, to whom the colonists felt a natural affinity and whom they considered as natural allies. Peace and unrestricted commerce seemed the basic aims and exigencies of a new world order. The corruption and amorality of the Ancien Régime made withdrawal from the European world an appropriate attitude, but did not such separation require a thorough change and a novel organization of economic life, and was it not incompatible with the development of commerce which appeared to be the natural instrument for developing the resources of the new nation? And did a move toward isolation and separation not mean acting against the prescripts of God and Nature? Was it not a duty to take an active part in creating a new world order, which, as many signs seemed to indicate, was the next and final stage of development of history and near attainment?

Moreover, decision about the road to be taken could not be based on purely theoretical considerations. Possibilities and choices were limited and restricted by the need to attain and secure the independence of the new nation in a world which was still ruled by the principles and notions of power politics, balance of power and reason of state.

Divided opinions about aims and actions dictated by the needs for survival during the early years of the American republic resulted in a wavering course, and sometimes produced a lack of frankness which was hardly compatible with the ideas and ideals of a new diplomacy. Examples are the negotiations about French support in the war of independence, and later those about peace with England. Certainly, the representatives sent to France received as instruction a "Model Treaty" which restricted any connection with France to trade and precluded preference to particular nations; commerce ought to be entirely free. When the treaty was concluded, however, it contained not only commercial but also political arrangements; it was a traditional political alliance. Restriction of diplomatic agreements to treaties securing complete freedom of trade remained the American ideal, but such agreements were concluded only with a country like Prussia which was barely involved in trade on the Atlantic Ocean.

In the peace negotiations with England, the representatives of the United States proceeded behind the back of their French ally, and if such behavior was successful, it hardly corresponded to what one would expect from the protagonists of a new morality in foreign affairs. But if the wavering course of American foreign policy revealed not only the difficulties which a novel and idealistic approach in foreign policy encountered in practice, it also reflected the uncertainties in the minds of the leading American statesmen about the right course; they themselves wavered and shifted in their views.

III

When the United States became independent, John Adams and Jefferson were leading advocates of a new diplomacy. In the early months of 1776, Adams set down his views on the relations which an independent America should establish with other powers; he emphasized that they ought to be neither of a political nor a military character, but entirely limited to "commercial connections." He himself drafted for the American mission to France the "Model Treaty" which formulated these ideas about the need for a new approach in relations among nations. When he was sent to Paris, he reported with lively approval the criticism which the men of the Enlightenment uttered "against the practice of lying, chicanery and finessing in negotiations," and emphasized that he was a diplomat in a new key. He told the French Foreign Minister that "the dignity of North America does not consist in diplomatic ceremonies or any of the subtleties of etiquette; it consists solely in reason, justice, truth, the right of mankind and the interests of the nations of Europe." But when he became involved in the conduct of the peace negotiations, he was almost more distrustful of the intentions of the French allies than the skeptical diplomats of the old school would have been, and he was not incapable of a certain amount of deception. In his later years he became convinced of the need for alliances, particularly with Great Britain, in order to guarantee the security of the United States; he even began to recognize the usefulness of an "equilibrium, a balance of power."

In the case of Adams, the evolution from an idealistic to a realistic concept of foreign affairs probably corresponds to his general development. The young radical became a conservative in his later years; in this, he is a more interesting and richer mirror of his time than the television hero holding with cantankerous obstinacy to the simple virtues of his youth.

In contrast to Adams, there is in the case of Jefferson less an evolution of thought than a lifelong adherence to different, even divergent, strains of thinking. Originally, Jefferson had been the most extreme advocate of a complete separation from Europe; he saw in commerce the great danger of luxury and corruption and regarded an agrarian society as the form of life most appropriate to America because, as an agrarian country, she could exist by herself, independent of contacts with the outside world for the fulfillment of her material needs. Even when Jefferson was forced to admit that this was not the route the Americans were traveling, he considered the maintenance of diplomatic relations with other powers—and that meant the existence of an American diplomatic corps—as superfluous and dangerous for peace; a few consuls at centers of trade ought to suffice. Jefferson also fervently believed in the coming of a new and better world order, and wanted the United States to use its influence and strength to support those movements and nations which struggled for this aim against the powers of the Ancien Régime. The notion that the United States had to set an example and had a mission to fulfill—to bring about the end of war, power politics and old-style diplomacy—was firmly fixed in Jefferson's mind. This view is reflected in the sympathy which he felt for the French Revolution and its leaders. But when the situation demanded, he could threaten war or pursue an expansionist policy for the United States.

There was one figure on the American scene who never shifted or felt hesitations, who had only contempt for the missionary approach to foreign policy and who believed that the United States should become one state among others: that was Alexander Hamilton. He found nothing concrete or substantial in the "idle theories which have amused us with promises of an exception from the imperfection, weaknesses and evils incident to society in every shape. Is it not time to awaken from the deceitful dream of a golden age and to adopt as a practical maxim for the direction of our political conduct that we, as well as the other inhabitants of the globe, are yet remote from the happy empire of perfect wisdom and perfect virtue?" Hamilton had no doubt that the United States would have to follow a course of power politics. If he ever made any concession to the demand for keeping the American and European worlds apart, it consisted in envisaging a restriction of American power politics primarily to the Western Hemisphere: the United States ought to aim at "an ascent in the American system." But Hamilton was an exceptional figure; in domestic affairs, as well, he was inclined to favor centralized institutions directed from above; his authoritarian and aristocratic tendencies show that he was a man of old Europe rather than of the New World.

In comparison to Hamilton's clear and decided attitude, the wavering between a variety of aims and methods by the other leaders of the new nation leaves the impression of uncertainty and weakness. But it ought to be recognized that what might appear as indecision was an almost necessary consequence of the political constellation into which the American republic arrived. A new state will always meet opposition before it is accepted as an independent equal, and it will have to feel its way tentatively and cautiously to a place in the existing state system. For the United States, this task was all the more difficult because the state system itself was in crisis and every step could mean involvement in the conflicts which were developing.

Of course, the main conflicts in the young republic were over domestic issues, but with the outbreak of the French Revolution, foreign policy was unavoidably drawn into the struggle. The questions whether the United States ought to withdraw into a completely neutral position, whether it should tolerate the British blockade of France and thereby reconstruct a special relationship with England on a new basis, or whether it should support the French attempt to set political life in a new framework, were deeply connected with issues of economic interest and of social organization. A pro-French versus a pro-British attitude almost became the crucial and divisive issue in American party politics.

It is well known that an important motif in the composition of Washington's Farewell Address was the President's fear that the divisions over foreign policy might be fatal to national union. But his conciliatory purpose could not be achieved if he pronounced for one side in this conflict. It is characteristic that leaders of the two opposing factions, Madison and Hamilton, had a hand in drafting the Farewell Address, and, indeed, the most influential part of the Farewell Address, the section on foreign policy, was an attempt to embody the various strands of the thinking on foreign policy and to synthesize them.

Emphasis is placed on the separation of America from Europe; and the view of the distinctiveness of these two continents is expressed in terms of the doctrine of the interests of the state, popular with writers and diplomats of the Ancien Régime: "Europe has a set of primary interests, which to us have none or a very remote relation." In accordance with the foreign policy practiced in the Ancien Régime, Washington acknowledged the necessity of alliances although he preferred them to be "temporary alliances for extraordinary emergen-

[12]

cies." The dislike of traditional diplomacy, which this limitation to temporary alliances suggests, was then directly expressed in the contemptuous way in which Washington spoke of "the toils of European ambition, Rivalship, Interest, Humour or Caprice." Washington rejected the immorality of the diplomacy of the Ancien Régime; he demanded that the United States should not accept the view that the interests of a nation are sufficient reason to disregard the moral code and to practice deception and infidelity: "I hold the maxim no less applicable to public than to private affairs that honesty is the best policy." The wish that the United States enter upon a new kind of diplomacy is implied in the "great rule" with which this section begins: it is necessary "in extending our commercial relations to have [with foreign nations] as little political connection as possible." At the end it is then hinted that if commerce is left free, following "a natural course of things," then a better age might be reached, in which there will be "harmony and a liberal intercourse with all nations." All the various themes that had been raised in the discussion on foreign policy are here interwoven into a whole. Jefferson, remaining convinced of the need to get rid of the entire system of diplomacy, could take up a single theme of the Farewell Address in his warning against "entangling alliances," and John Quincy Adams, in drafting the document that became the Monroe Doctrine, could enlarge on Washington's distinction between a European and an American system.

IV

Whereas, in the light of the intellectual trends prevailing at the time when the United States entered upon the political scene, the substance and impact of the Farewell Address can be easily understood, it needs to be explained why the meaning of Washington's message was primarily seen as a recommendation of isolationism, and why Washington's advice was raised to a dogma which was assumed to possess validity for all future times. In the eighteenth century, many rulers and statesmen composed documents—political testaments—in which they expressed what they considered to be the "permanent maxim" of their state, but most of these recommendations fell into oblivion as soon as the author had died. What gave Washington's "political testament" superior and more lasting authority?

In the United States, an almost binding force on all future generations was ascribed to the pronouncements of the Founding Fathers, partly at least to emphasize unity, coherence and continuity and to counter the dangers of disintegration. Washington's "great rule" shared the esteem enjoyed by all the pronouncements of the Founding Fathers. But this is not the only, and probably not the decisive, reason for the authority which the section of the Farewell Address on foreign policy acquired. Just as the thinking about the direction which the foreign policy of the young republic ought to take was linked to the particular intellectual and political constellation existing at the end of the eighteenth century, so also the fact that the Farewell Address gained the character of a dogma and its content became reduced to a recommendation of isolationism was determined by the political constellation which emerged in the nineteenth century. After the upheavals of the French Revolution and the Napoleonic era, Europe entered upon a period of restoration and reaction. This was no time for a missionary idealistic policy based on the belief in the coming of a new age of peace and democracy. The United States turned westward, whereas Europe, when it emerged from the stillness of reaction, became occupied with the tensions and fights accompanying the creation of national states in Central Europe. Although there were disputes over the northern borders of the United States, over European interference in Mexico or the continuous problem of the freedom of the sea, these tensions were ephemeral episodes that did not alter the main fact: during most of the nineteenth century, as far as foreign policy was concerned, Europe and the United States lived in different worlds.

At the end of the nineteenth century, in the age of imperialism, there was a twilight zone, when the American government could not withstand the temptation to expand in the Caribbean and the Pacific Ocean by accelerating the demise of the Spanish Empire, and when America's interest in extending her influence into other parts of the world was concealed under the slogan of an open-door policy. The United States was no longer an island remote from the rest of the world. The First World War put an end to views which indeed had become illusionary.

It is striking, however, that even then the policy of cooperation with a group of powers was presented and justified as an attempt to realize the aims and traditions of the Founding Fathers. Wilson saw the entry of the United States into the war as a step toward the establishment of permanent peace. The beginning of a new era in foreign policy and diplomacy was to be secured by the creation of a League of Nations in which democracy would extend into the area of foreign policy: great and small powers would have the same vote; the policy of special alliances, of a balance of power among great powers, dominating the smaller ones, would no longer be possible. The rational and liberal ideas of the Enlightenment had a strong hold over Wilson's mind; something of the internationalist spirit and the missionary zeal of these years lived in him. In abandoning isolationism and embracing internationalism, he felt sure that he was striving for the same goals the Founding Fathers had pursued.

However, Wilson's opponents, by emphasizing the ambiguities which his program contained and by making full use of the mistakes which had been made, returned to the doctrines of nonentanglement and isolationism as representing the true American tradition in foreign policy. Thus began a debate which lasted through the 1920s and 1930s and up to the beginning of the Second World War.

It was a consequence of this debate that when Roosevelt slowly and gradually moved toward support of the powers fighting Hitler, he played down the idealistic element which, in the war against the Nazi dictatorship, undoubtedly had a justified appeal, and instead emphasized the idea of "national security." When this concept entered political consciousness it became clear how remote from the present the concepts of isolationism and internationalism had become. In looking back to the 1930s, the debate about isolationism versus internationalism which then patterned so much of the thinking on foreign policy has a ghostlike character. The relevance of the great pronouncements on foreign policy from the early years of the republic has ended; they have become history. The world is no longer divided into different political spheres; the United States has become part of an interconnected global system. Although an all-embracing world organization exists, it is based neither on common values, identical constitutional forms nor an unimpeded flow of trade. There are blocs in which the great powers lead; there is no full equality between large and small states. In the constellation in which the foreign policy of the United States must now operate the prescriptions of the past are no longer applicable.

V

There remains the question, however, whether, although the pronouncements of the Founding Fathers can no longer be regarded as authoritative, the attitude that lay behind them has also disappeared. The answer to this question surely must be negative. In American opinion on the significance of diplomats and diplomacy, in the strongly moralistic element which permeates all considerations of foreign policy, in the assumptions about the leading role of the United States in the world, we find beliefs and hopes similar to those which inspired the thinking on foreign affairs in the early years of the republic.

Of course, such views and attitudes are not unique or peculiar to the United States. This is a democratic country, and distrust of diplomacy, an inclination to view political questions as moral questions and the notion of a special national mission are features in the attitude of all democratic nations. Diplomats, accredited to courts or governments, moving in the upper strata of society and charged with expensive representative duties requiring a high personal income, are suspected, in almost all democratic countries, of being remnants of a monarchical age and tending to authoritarian or autocratic forms of government. Nor can the assent of the people be gained to actions which might involve material losses, personal risks and even the sacrifice of life, if they are not convinced of the righteousness of the course and the special and unique value of the existence of their nation for the world. The need for a wider consensus in foreign policy forms a desirable, almost necessary obstacle to the dangers which arbitrary or emotional reaction might bring about.

The paradox of the present situation is that, if the need for an ideological consensus leads to caution and deliberateness before taking action, in our world of opposing ideologies it also increases the tension between nations. But this is not the place for a discussion of the complex connection between ideology and power politics in the twentieth century. The question is whether the preservation of feelings which dominated the thinking on foreign affairs in the early years of the republic has magnified and intensified the problems inherent in the foreign policy of a democratic country and has created difficulties and been a burden in the conduct of American foreign policy.

The attitude of the American people to diplomacy contains

elements of an eighteenth-century belief that misunderstandings and conflicts among nations are the fault of governments which prevent direct communication from people to people. There is distrust, therefore, of the views of diplomats, who are servants of the governments and whose business is with the governments of other nations. The knowledge of a businessman who has spent some time in financial negotiations in another country, or of a military man who has talked to a few generals of a foreign country, inspires more confidence than the views of a professional diplomat who has observed developments in these countries for years. It is striking that in the United States—probably more than in any other country—important diplomatic missions are entrusted to people who are not professional diplomats. The weaknesses and limitations of the diplomatic profession are obvious, but in the United States it is frequently forgotten that it is a profession which is needed and has virtues.

However, the most outstanding feature of American foreign policy is its extremely moralistic character. Actions taken to adjust to new developments are explained as determined by the need to maintain principles basic to a moral world order; Washington's statement of the "great rule" and the proclamation of the Monroe Doctrine have been patterns for various presidential "doctrines" justifying recent actions of American foreign policy. The aura of moral philosophy, bestowed on contingency measures, imparts to American foreign policy a rigidity unsuited to the rapid changes in the political scene of the twentieth century. Wars in which the United States becomes involved are "crusades"—a notion which requires complete victory; it prejudices negotiation and compromise. The moralistic approach to foreign policy produces the almost intuitive assumption that, when the policy of the United States meets resistance, it is because its opponents are evil. To consider politics as a fight of good against evil makes it easy to believe that interference in the internal affairs of another state in favor of one party against another is permissible, even a duty. This disregard of the sovereignty of other states has been a source of deep resentment against the United States.

But the most perilous legacy which has come down to us from the eighteenth century is the American claim to world leadership. Certainly, the United States is one of the super-powers, one of the decisive forces in the world of today. But this is not identical with the idea that it is the *one* leading power, superior to all others. It is this notion, however, deeply ingrained in American thought, which is still strongly held and which we find in the speeches of politicians and statesmen. World leadership is a dangerous term, for it has a vagueness which invites almost limitless application; it has been presented as implying that the United States must be the most powerful, the economically strongest, the militarily best-equipped power. If leadership is weighed in material and quantitative terms only, it seems a means to justify domination and control rather than an appeal to cooperation; it becomes an impediment to what must be the paramount aim of foreign policy in the nuclear age: the preservation of peace. Perhaps the most valuable lesson which the Bicentennial can impart to American foreign policy is that world leadership is not a possession which can be inherited, but a privilege, for which every generation must strive anew.

[TWO]

Mothers and Daughters (Or Greeks and Romans)

Alastair Buchan

Social scientists write many books and papers nowadays about the development of "transnationalism"—meaning the impact on interstate relations of unofficial contacts and communications—as if this were something new on the face of the earth.

Until his untimely death in February 1976, Alastair Buchan was Montague Burton Professor of International Relations at Oxford. He had been Commandant of the Royal College of Defence Studies, London, 1970–72, and Director of the (then) Institute for Strategic Studies, London, 1958–69; and is the author of *Power and Equilibrium in the 70s* and other works.

Professor Buchan had completed the manuscript for this article before his death. Minor revisions and editing were completed by his close friend, Herbert G. Nicholas, Rhodes Professor of American History and Institutions at Oxford since 1969, and the author of *The United States and Britain* and other works.

[20]

Actually, over the long reach of history, it is the autarkic state or society that is the rarity. Certainly no interstate relationship has been more permeated or effectively influenced by transnational factors than that between Britain and the United States. No two societies have had a more profound impact upon each other, in terms of racial stock, political and juridical concepts, culture in all its meanings. And personal dealings have repeatedly affected specific historical events since American independence—for example, British banking houses largely financed the Louisiana Purchase, while private messages between Richard Cobden and Charles Sumner defused an imminent confrontation between the two governments over the *Trent* affair in 1861.

This interpenetration is a palpable fact and will, I have no doubt, be explored in depth in many different places during 1976. There is also no dispute about the fact that over the past hundred years the relationship has swung through an arc of 180 degrees, that the economic and cultural dominance of Britain over America in broadly the first century gave way to a position of increasing American dominance—first economic, later strategic, political and in many ways intellectual—over Britain as the second century advanced. There have been periods of marked alienation in the relations of the two countries, notably just after the Civil War and even more markedly between the world wars, but there has never been any serious discontinuity in political and economic relations, except briefly in the war of 1812-14; no equivalent of the Gaullist "ice age," the long estrangement between the United States and China, or the wars with Germany and Japan.

Has this continuous and pervasive contact which has swelled in volume in the past generation damaged or strengthened the two countries? Has the one society been able to prevent the other from making serious mistakes or to contribute to its learning process? Have the two countries lured each other into needless adventures, inspired a false sense of confidence in

[21]

each other, distorted the other's perspective; or has the relationship been as benign as much Bicentennial oratory will no doubt maintain?

II

One way of reexamining the first century of the Anglo-American relationship is to think of it in terms of the first "adversary partnership" that the republic had to manage. This phrase too comes out of the social science jargon of the past decade, applied primarily to contemporary Soviet-American relations. At first sight there seems no useful analogy between the relations of the young United States, still not in full possession of its own half-continent, with the powerful mercantile state from which it had hived off, and the relations of an enormously powerful America having both to confront and cooperate with a Soviet Union almost entirely foreign in political and social values, both armed with a vast stock of long-range nuclear weapons. But if one inverts the partners one can see the similarity: to early nineteenth-century Britain, still an aristocratic polity and fearful or skeptical about democracy, the young United States had many of the characteristics of a revolutionary society (though, of course, the role of major challenger was initially reserved for France). More than that, Britain as the conservative world power with a global navy—exerting a policy of containment from its bases in Canada, the Caribbean and Central America—must have seemed to many Americans as the postwar United States has looked to Russians.

Above all, Canada had an almost identical role in their relations to that of Western Europe in the postwar era: to some Americans it represented a British Trojan horse on North American soil, just as the American postwar military presence in Europe was seen in Moscow as intrusive and aggressive until the solution of the German problem. But also, to successive American Administrations from the early nineteenth century to the settlement of the Alaskan boundary dispute in 1903, Canada represented a hostage to British good behavior, just as Khrushchev once described Western Europe as his hostage.

It is true that, after Yorktown, it was clear that Britain could never again attempt to conquer the United States even if she had wished to. Conversely, the United States has had no motive, except in moments of anger, for declaring war on Britain (though both powers had war plans for armed confrontations with each other until well into the twentieth century). In other words, they were in strategic terms mutually deterred, so that the credibility of the British commitment to Canada was never fully tested any more than that of the United States to Europe has been; the historical difference was that there was nothing like the force of technological change to bedevil political confidence. On the other hand, the extent to which American soil could be used as a base for the subversion of Canada—as it was with the rebellion of 1837 in the days of Jacksonian radicalism, and in the Fenian raids of 1866 and the Riel Red River rebellion of 1870, in the heyday of Republican radicalism—together with the whole cult of Manifest Destiny, bore a certain resemblance, making allowance for scale, to the impact of Lenin's dicta about the inevitable victory of communism or to Khrushchev's espousal of wars of national liberation.

The essential point is that throughout much of the nineteenth century the relationship *was* partly an adversarial one— on questions of territory, or tariffs, or freedom of the seas—but with an increasing perception of common interests. Castlereagh said it first in 1820: "There are no two states whose friendly relations are of more practical value to each other and whose hostility so inevitably and so immediately entails upon both the most serious mischiefs ... [than] the British and American nations." This dual character was properly exemplified in the Monroe Doctrine, adversarial in appearance, cooperative in essence. Under James Monroe and John Quincy Adams, the prickly young republic rejected Canning's's attempt to formulate their common interest in keeping the rivalries of the continental European powers out of the Americas as being too maternalistic; "mother and daughter" standing "together against the world." Instead, it posted a "hands-off" sign outwardly as applicable to the British as to anyone else. But although the Monroe Doctrine was a unilateral declaration, it would have been meaningless without the concurrence of the British and the dominance of their fleet.

But day-to-day diplomacy had to battle with a more hostile climate of mutual dislike and incomprehension between arrogant John and avaricious Jonathan. Trade policy had a great deal to do with it; the interest of the young United States as primarily an exporter of cotton and other raw materials had originally been in free trade while Britain was still mercantilist. But America became more protectionist as she industrialized—and long after—while Britain's espousal of free trade became dogmatic and remained so until the twentieth century. Rivalry in the North Atlantic was a persistent factor, especially where New England's interests were involved. Britain and the United States were natural competitors here—in the carrying trade, in doing business with the enemy (when there was one), in recruitment for their merchant marines and navies. This was what the War of 1812 was largely about, as were the isthmus disputes, the *Trent* affair, the *Alabama* claim, etc. For each country this was *their* ocean, to the mutual exclusion of a third party.

If a common ocean bred disputes, a shared culture could nourish animosities. Scabrous comments on each other's societies became an increasing source of friction as books and newspapers circulated more widely. James Fenimore Cooper in 1826 talked of English maidservants as being in "less enviable condition than Asiatic slaves." To Bronson Alcott in 1842 every Englishman was a "fortification. Organized of blood he finds necessity for spilling it." And Horace Greeley wrote in 1851 that "the British are not in manner a winning people. Their self-conceit is the principal reason." [1] These were typical reactions, even though Emerson, Hawthorne and even Henry Adams might paint a different picture.

American critics met their match in Mrs. Trollope and Dickens, but the relationship has never been symmetrical and a succession of British visitors were as much intrigued as they were repelled by the new form of society, especially the frontier. (The most biting British critics of American society, Kipling, Wells, G. K. Chesterton, belong to a later period, to the era of the trusts and the big city machines.) American contempt for British complacency and class consciousness, British highminded condemnation of slavery and corruption: this was the leitmotiv of much of the nineteenth century. But in the words of a British historian: "In America it was a case of an Anglophile minority and an Anglophobe majority; in Britain of anti-American and pro-American minorities and an indifferent majority. But as the cause of democracy triumphed, so did popular awareness of America and her increasing power grow. . . ." [2]

For a full century after 1776 it was politically very easy to whip up anti-British sentiment. Even as the older animosities faded, the Irish began to flood in. In this situation, the various Canadian border settlements were a triumph of what we now call "arms control." The Rush-Bagot Agreement of 1817 on the demilitarization of the Great Lakes, which held through the Civil War and other periods of high tension, was an explicit recognition that Anglo-American relations were not a zero sum game, and a triumph for what Harold Nicholson later described as the British tradition of "civilian" diplomacy.[3] And the Ashburton-Webster Treaty of 1842, which not only settled the Maine boundary but the axis of the border as far as the Lake of the Woods and thence across the continent, was negotiated in a situation in which both Congress and the

Canadian legislatures were voting war credits. Like the negotiation of SALT I in 1972, the principal achievement of both Daniel Webster and Lord Ashburton lay in persuading their own governments rather than in reaching agreement between themselves. And in 1846 the settlement of the Oregon boundary dispute, at the other end of the continent, was remarkable for being achieved despite the bellicosity of President Polk and the "54.40 or fight" emotion that he played upon: it showed, as later negotiations have, how a sensible Secretary of State, Buchanan, could sort matters out if given some discretion.

Meanwhile, in the hostage country, Canada, there was a running debate—about the credibility of its guarantor, about whether its own interests might be sacrificed in the process of détente that followed the Civil War—analogous in many ways to what we have witnessed in Western Europe in the 1970s. The Canadian leaders identified their interests more with Britain than with the United States, but they knew that some British politicians like Cobden, Bright and Gladstone expected that eventually the new Dominion of 1867 might become part of the United States, might become "Americanized"; and that in the last instance they must look after themselves. Here too the parallel may be instructive.

There is another aspect of the old Anglo-American adversary partnership that is more disquieting if it should have the force of precedent or parallel today. In the first hundred years, peace in the successive crises was preserved largely because the older power with the more complex interests was prepared to give way to the dynamic regional one, not only over the border, but over Texas, over navigation on the Columbia, over the *Alabama*, because it had so much at stake elsewhere in the world.

III

A new age of Anglo-American relations opened after the Civil War, and between the Centennial and the First World War something like an entente developed. The old arguments over slavery or the Canadian border were disposed of. The United States had found that it could organize its fast-growing manpower and industry in such a way as to become a serious military power. By 1850 its population had surpassed that of Britain; by 1880 at the latest it had a larger economy. Writing in 1879, Gladstone considered that "it is she [the United States] alone who, at a coming time, can and probably will wrest from us our commercial supremacy. . . . We have no more title against her than Venice or Genoa or Holland has had against us." [4] This was the era of transnational equilibrium when American companies and gadgets flowed into Britain, and British capital into the United States. This was the time in which Henry James aspired "to write in such a way that it would be impossible to an outsider to say whether I am . . . an American writing about England or an Englishman writing about America." [5] On the one hand, American heiresses fought for the hands of English lords but, on the other, the volume of British emigration to America was still running high, enough to create a multiplicity of personal relationships (assisted by a special cheap postal rate). It was the epoch of burgeoning intellectual and political friendships, spreading out from the intimacy between Ralph Waldo Emerson and John Stuart Mill to John Morley, Leslie Stephen and Matthew Arnold on the one side, William James, Henry Adams and William Dean Howells on the other. British intellectuals and liberals came to the United States to discuss the social and political implications of the democracy that was rapidly evolving in their own country. Their American counterparts, still primarily of British stock, crossed the Atlantic to share in a widened circle of comment and discussion in London, Oxford or Cambridge. And the Reverend Endicott Peabody embarked on the education of potential American statesmen at Groton in the manner of Thomas Arnold at Rugby a generation earlier.

This was the era in which James Bryce wrote *The American Commonwealth* (1888), which was for many years regarded by Americans as being the authoritative account of their own political system. In it he unconsciously put his finger on the reason for this placid relationship, the absence of diplomatic controversies: "We have hitherto found no occasion to refer to them [foreign relations] save in describing the functions of the Senate; and I mention them now as the traveller did the snakes in Ireland, only to note their absence...." [6] Only the Venezuela incident of 1895 and the grumbling issue of the American desire for dominance over Central America, which the issue of the Panama Canal elicited, seriously disturbed relations between London and Washington. At the turn of the century, men as different as Joseph Chamberlain, Andrew Carnegie, A. V. Dicey (the British constitutional historian), and W. T. Stead were advocating one form or another of Anglo-American union.

Ironically, in view of later attitudes, the period of late nineteenth-century expansion in both countries excited very little criticism in the other. "As a partner in the white man's burden," as Herbert Nicholas has written recently, "the USA was indulgent, in a quite novel degree, to British colonial aspirations." [7] The Boer War and the annexation of the Philippines created internal divisions within each country, but not between them. The Open Door in China, the subject nowadays of such fierce revisionist attack, was essentially an Anglo-American policy, though, like the Monroe Doctrine, unilaterally American in its official formulation.

One reason for this mutual compliance, one reason why Alfred Thayer Mahan was feted in London in the 1890s, was the growth of the German navy which, if it proved a direct threat to British isolationism and security, could also be seen as an eventual threat to American autonomy and isolation. It was in an American magazine, *McClure's*, that Rudyard Kipling first published his "White Man's Burden," and its injunction was addressed in the first instance to the North American branch of the White Man's missionary church. It struck answering chords in the missionary breast of many an American: William McKinley, John Hay and Teddy Roosevelt most obviously, but "Marse" Henry Watterson, Walter Hines Page and Brooks Adams as well.

IV

This gilded age might have ended in any case with the growing political influence of Irish- and German-Americans. But 1914 snapped it shut by resurrecting an issue that had traveled beneath the surface of Anglo-American relationships for nearly a century and a half, that of belligerent and neutral rights in time of war. There is no analogy between American behavior in the First and Second World Wars. In 1914 no leading American suggested, in public at any rate, that the war could involve the United States. Though Colonel House found much more in common with Edward Grey, during his diplomatic exploration of the belligerent capitals in 1915, than he did with Bethmann-Hollweg—indeed the germ of the League sprang from the Grey-House conversations, though the idea has a much longer ancestry—Wilson saw himself as a mediator until the end of 1916. There were by then powerful economic interests in the United States behind the victory of the Allies, from J. P. Morgan and Co., which had floated massive loans to Britain and France, to the steel, the engineering and the nascent aircraft industries; and there was a growing awareness of a potential threat to America of a

[29]

German-dominated Western Europe. Yet these had to a large extent been politically neutralized by the effect of the Easter rising in Ireland and the strength of the German-American vote. Had the Allies rebuffed, and had Germany accepted, Wilson's peace appeal of December 1916, the United States would, as Wilson admitted to House, have found itself fighting at Germany's side.[8] As it was, the German Admiralty, taking a gamble on the necessity for a quick victory, announced the opening of unrestricted submarine warfare and the Germans started making overtures to Mexico. Just 59 years ago the United States entered its first European war.

When peace came, there was little understanding and no mutual respect between Wilson and Lloyd George, and a high degree of mutual hostility between articulate opinion in both countries. What the Hearst press gave, the Beaverbrook press returned. In the circumstances, it is remarkable that the Anglo-American treaty of guarantee of the French-German border should have got as far as the floor of the Senate and been defeated by only ten votes; if it had passed it might have completely changed the course of world history. Given the lack of real confidence between London and Washington, certainly at the top, the extent to which the Versailles settlement, in Eastern as well as Western Europe, bore an Anglo-American rather than an Anglo-French imprint was a sign of how relatively easily international lawyers and diplomats in each country communicated with each other below the surface of political suspicion.

Gladstone's perception of 40 years earlier that the United States was destined to replace Britain as *the* great industrial power had proved correct. Much greater respect was paid in London to American views. But British policy became increasingly affected by American policy at a time when there was little wisdom in Washington and Britain was still powerful enough to sustain a global foreign policy of her own. After the Senate's rejection of the League of Nations,

America's absence became a frequent excuse for tentative and half-hearted British policy in its councils. American isolationism fostered British isolationism and vice versa. The isolationists in America were matched in the 1920s and 1930s by what D. C. Watt well calls "the irresponsibles" in Britain, who displayed, in particular, "an almost criminal neglect of Anglo-American relations." [9] The old symbiosis that had led to mutual condonement of expansion asserted itself in a different form.

Moreover, though Britain still had by far the larger navy, fear of an immense American postwar naval buildup program (for which Congress would have been unlikely to vote the funds) led Britain to become interested in an Anglo-American naval limitation treaty. And, when the American price proved to be the abrogation of the Anglo-Japanese alliance of 1902, in which both Britain and Japan had invested considerable diplomatic capital, Britain gave way to American (and Canadian) worry about Japan, at a time when she still had greater economic interests in the Far East than did the United States. Both, in their eagerness in 1922 and again in 1930 to balance each other's strength on the high seas to achieve "parity," did so with little consideration of world order as a whole.

As the interwar years progressed, Japan's rancor at this formal ratifiction of her secondary status (there were other irritants as well) increased, while the actual disposition of American and British naval power, in fact, offered her a free hand in East Asia and the southern and western Pacific. Neither the Hoover Administration nor the British National government had any serious intention of bringing Japan to book over her invasion of Manchuria, though a good deal of diplomatic energy was expended on each side to create such an illusion. Later under Roosevelt, when the "Manchuria incident" was succeeded by the war with China, and both a British and an American gunboat were sunk by the Japanese, the United States would entertain no idea of a joint protest.

[31]

The interwar years witnessed other causes of alienation between the two countries, despite the fact that the problems they faced in the 1930s, recession and unemployment, were very similar. One was the whole issue of war debts; the United States, now the strongest economy in the world, refused to acknowledge the centrality of its position and persisted in the habits of a debtor nation, demanding repayment of both debts and reparations which London, in effect, became responsible for collecting. Repayment was made particularly difficult by the Fordney-McCumber Tariff of 1922, while the Hawley-Smoot Tariff of 1930 was a major factor in Britain's development of the imperial preference system at the Ottawa Imperial Congress of 1932. At the transnational level, the virtual end of American immigration in the early 1920s meant the weakening of personal ties, while prohibition on the one hand, and the rise of figures like Al Capone and Huey Long on the other, made it easy to mock American society. Each country turned inward to brood upon its own troubles.

British and American politicians had little to do with each other, despite the work of the Inter-Parliamentary Union which, for instance, brought James Byrnes to Europe for the first time in 1937. There were only three resident British journalists in Washington in the latter 1930s and, though there was a larger and more distinguished group of American journalists in London, their parish was Europe as a whole and not just Britain. The foreign services of the two countries tended for the most part to patronize each other. And what was true of diplomacy was even more true of the armed services. The two navies, which had been friendly in World War I, developed a cordial dislike of each other, largely as a consequence of the Naval Agreements, exemplified later on the American side by the views and personalities of Admirals King and Leahy. The two armies had very little contact, partly because the U.S. Army led an isolated existence even in its own country. Only the two air forces were on terms of friendship, partly because their environment imposed a common language on them, partly because the U.S. Army Air Force (as it then was) looked to the Royal Air Force as a model and exemplar in establishing its right to be a separate service.

Moreover, the intellectual communities of the two countries had only intermittent links, despite the growing admiration of students of the 1930s for the achievements of the New Deal. A few British writers and historians, John Buchan and Harold Nicolson in one generation, John Wheeler-Bennett in the next, knew the United States well, and Denis Brogan was an Americanist in the great tradition of Tocqueville and Bryce. Moreover, few American intellectuals knew Britain well or appreciated her social accomplishments. Unfortunately the British authors who enjoyed the largest readership in the United States were far removed from the earlier tradition of the novel as a vehicle of social realism; they were satirists like Huxley or sentimentalists like Galsworthy. Conversely, though these were the years when the British public took to its heart the new American realism of Hemingway, Sinclair Lewis and Faulkner, these were in the main the apostles of disillusionment whose picture of America was drenched in their own bitterness and frustration. Significantly it was in Paris, not London, that the expatriates among them found spiritual refuge.

Harvard and Oxford, Columbia and London had an established tradition of hospitality to each other's scholars, and figures like Samuel Morison, Allan Nevins or Wallace Notestein were well-known in Britain. But the two scholarship schemes that had been founded to strengthen links between the two countries had not yet produced many figures of significant influence within their own countries. Ironically, the most influential ex-Rhodes scholar was Stanley Hornbeck, head of the Far Eastern division of the State Department, who was passionately committed to the resurrection of China as a great power and as strongly committed to the end of the European empires in Asia. Ernest K. Lindley, Roosevelt's favorite journalist, and Clarence Streit, whose *Union Now* made a powerful impression on my generation of British and American students, were also Rhodes scholars. The Commonwealth fellowships, founded by Edward Harkness to enable British graduates to travel widely in the United States, had by the war produced only three men of influence: William Penney, the nuclear physicist and engineer; Geoffrey Crowther, Bagehot's greatest successor as editor of *The Economist;* and a young Cambridge-educated Lancastrian who was making a reputation in the new techniques of radio reporting, Alistair Cooke.

Only three communities of interests in each country had any tradition of continuous communication with each other. One was that of the law, for though the United States was not then a member of the International Court, British and American lawyers had long been interested in the development of each other's common and statute law; since lawyers are even more influential in American public life than in British politics, this was an important contribution to communication. A second community was the merchant or investment banking fraternity in Wall Street and the City. Despite his distrust for Wall Street, FDR had always been clear that, if war came, he would have to draw on its talent, and his recruitment of figures like James Forrestal, Paul Nitze, and many others brought in a group of men to whom London was a familiar place. The third Anglo-American community was the entertainment industry: actors, singers, producers. But to judge what role Noel Coward, Bob Hope, Douglas Fairbanks, Leslie Howard, Sir C. Aubrey Smith, Vivien Leigh, or Gary Cooper played in the evolution of mutual "images" that permitted a close wartime and postwar relationship would take one into a realm of sociological speculation for which, alas, the field work has never been done.

V

Behind these limitations on each country's perception of the other lay a deep-seated difference in their view of the international community and their role in relation to it. In 1920 the United States had opted out of the evil "balance of power" problems of Europe and had left the task entirely to Britain and France. This opting-out, in turn, represented the retention by the United States of an evangelical and somewhat above-the-battle attitude to the more grubby problems of power, while British thinking, however "contractionist," as it generally was in the era of appeasement, was nonetheless habituated to the issues of power and maneuver.

It is worth stressing this basic factor—the alienation of the interwar years—so as to underline the magnitude of the change in the nature of the Anglo-American relationship that occurred during 1941 and the four years thereafter. The change was not accomplished easily; for, though Roosevelt never sought to don Wilson's mantle of the mediator, once his tentative effort at diplomatic intervention in early 1938 had been rebuffed by Chamberlain—"it is always best and safest to count on nothing from the Americans but words"—he was hemmed in by a powerful structure of neutrality legislation which had been constructed by Congress. The way in which Roosevelt gradually dismantled it, including first "cash-and-carry," then the destroyers-for-bases deal which satisfied a long-felt aspiration of the U.S. Navy, and finally Lend-Lease is well-known. What is still unclear is whether, if the United States had not been attacked by Japan and if Hitler had not then declared war in consequence, FDR would have led the country into full belligerency on the side of Britain. Despite the extraordinary grass-roots success of William Allen White's Committee to Defend America by Aiding the Allies, despite the sympathetic reporting of the bearing of the British people under adversity, despite the much greater threat to

American security that Hitler's victory would have posed in contrast with the Kaiser's, despite his easy-going relationship with Churchill, Roosevelt himself seemed repeatedly a victim in 1940–41 to a kind of paralysis of decision, as if waiting for events to make his mind up for him. Of course stubborn isolationist resistance in Congress was a factor never to be underestimated, but one senses in FDR's phases of irresolution something more—an awareness of what Woodrow Wilson had meant when he said, "It is a fearful thing to lead this country into war."

Nevertheless, the period of what Robert Sherwood called "the common law alliance"—the months of 1940 and 1941 when soldiers and sailors hammered out common tactical and strategic concepts, when officials resolved differing practices—laid the groundwork at levels far below the summit for the extraordinarily rapid growth of the joint war machine once the United States was formally committed.

Much has been written about the relationship between Churchill and Roosevelt, and it was indeed a remarkable accident of history that two such experienced, self-confident and masterful individuals should have risen to the leadership of the two countries at that particular moment in history; suppose it had been Wallace and Baldwin, or even Willkie and Halifax. Their friendship was the most significant intimacy since the end of the dynastic era. It was they who took all the major decisions, but even more remarkable was the system of combined chiefs of staff, field commands and combined boards that they imposed, so that there was a miniature Whitehall of 9,000 British officials in Washington at the peak of the war, and its counterpart in London. Much of the success of this was due to individuals: on the military side to George Marshall and John Dill, to Eisenhower and Tedder and Spaatz; on the civil side to Maynard Keynes, Averell Harriman, James Byrnes and many, many others. And it was they and their juniors who carried the legacy of mutual affection, knowledge and respect into the postwar years—with consequences that were not necessarily as beneficial as such virtues might suggest. And below this level there were hundreds of thousands of personal contacts: American servicemen training for Normandy in Britain, British aircrews training in the United States, combined forces fighting the Germans in Italy; scientists, engineers and intelligence experts.

But beneath the achievement of combined command and procurement which led to victory in Europe, and contributed to it in Asia, to the occupation of Germany, and the founding of the United Nations, there smoldered a number of resentments and frustrations on one side or the other. First and foremost, the wartime relationship had been, like earlier ones, asymmetrical. Not only had the United States been the "arsenal of democracy," which meant that the British services became increasingly dependent on American equipment, but, even though the United States achieved this by mobilizing only a portion of its manpower (and unlike Britain not conscripting women), the fact that it had a population over three times as large meant that the United States could put larger forces in the air, on the ground and in the water. Yet Britain was the unsinkable aircraft carrier without which the United States could not attack continental Europe. This fact that each ally had a stranglehold over the other contributed to the bitterness of the military debate about a Second Front in 1942 and 1943. It was not difficult to start an argument that the Americans were prepared to fight to the last Englishman, or that the British were using American forces in the Mediterranean to prop up the remains of the British Empire. At times, this suspicion of each other's motives reached the level of paranoia, as General Marshall once ruefully recalled:

> On one occasion our people brought in an objection to something the British wanted. I didn't see anything wrong with the British proposal, but our planners

explained that there was an ulterior purpose in this thing. . . . Later [Air Chief Marshal Sir Charles] Portal said that he had drafted the proposal and that it was taken from a memorandum of ours. And it was a fact; he showed it to me. . . . Our own paragraph was the key to our own objections.[10]

In the immediate postwar period, there was a sense of apprehension in Britain that Roosevelt's insistence at Teheran and Yalta that American troops would be withdrawn from Europe two years after the war (a decision which Truman did not reverse at Potsdam) meant that the task of developing a balance with the Soviet Union in Europe would fall primarily on British shoulders. "Such a task would be far beyond our strength," wrote Churchill.[11] Living, as their predecessors had done throughout Britain's history, cheek by jowl with the European continent, Churchill and his wartime team thought instinctively about what balance of power would be left across the Channel when victory had been won.

It took four years of erosion of American optimism about Russian intentions before this gap between British and American attitudes closed. The revulsion that Hull felt in 1943 at Churchill's percentage deal with Stalin in the Balkans was typically American. Writers like Walter Lippmann, whose *U.S. Foreign Policy: Shield of the Republic* was a bestseller in 1943, might argue the necessity for a postwar Anglo-American alliance; officials in the Pentagon might encourage continuing military cooperation with Britain (there was a discreet meeting of British and American military planners in late 1945 under the guise of a conference on military history). But official American policy remained concentrated on the United Nations and on Four Power machinery for the control of Germany, or on such pieces of paper as the Declaration of Liberated Europe. Western Europe was Britain's affair, and this view was expressed even more forcibly by the radicals of the American Right and Left (such as Henry Wallace) in the ensuing year.

Throughout the latter half of the war the British government had felt trapped between an American assumption that America could devolve her own responsibility for European security onto the proposed world security organization, and persistent American opposition to any attempt by Britain to fill the vacuum this would leave. This was, and had been throughout the war, particularly evident in the American attitude toward France, which Roosevelt and Stalin at Teheran had decided to treat almost as an enemy country. "The President suspected," in the words of an American historian, "that Churchill's interest in seeing France restored as a military power was part of the Prime Minister's misguided infatuation with the discredited principle of the European balance of power." [12] As early as May 1944, the U.S. Joint Chiefs had warned the State Department of the dangers of a European balance in which Britain was much weaker than Russia and which would lead to a new European war in which the United States would get sucked in on Britain's side.

One issue on which the bureaucracy in Washington was as hostile to Britain and as suspicious of British intentions as the White House, was that of the future of the British Empire and of colonialism in general. "One thing we are *not* fighting for is to hold the British Empire together," declared *Life* in October 1942. A few weeks later Wendell Willkie's call from Chungking for an end to imperialism and Roosevelt's endorsement of the statement gave rise to Churchill's famous remark: "I have not become the King's First Minister in order to preside over the dissolution of the British Empire."

The first phase of the battle between London and Washington centered on the future of India in which Roosevelt appeared to be trying to edge himself into the position of a mediator between Britain and the Congress Party. But attempts to confront Churchill with the issue led to such scorching rows that by the end of 1943 Roosevelt had decided to drop the subject. Instead, he used the more devious tactic of privately discussing the future of the colonial empires first with Chiang Kai-shek at Cairo and then with Stalin at Teheran at the end of 1943. The former was in fact FDR's trump card in dealing with Churchill on colonial questions, and the fact that Chiang was a bitter critic of British policy in India and elsewhere in Asia was one of the reasons why Churchill so distrusted Roosevelt's continuous effort to elevate China to the status of a great power. Though there were American opponents of the Administration's position on India, they were mostly academic and, if Clement Attlee had not unilaterally defused the Indian issue by granting independence in 1947, it would have been difficult to sustain any intimate Anglo-American relationship in the postwar era.

On the general issue of U.N. trusteeship for colonial territories, too, there was a good deal of British resistance to what was regarded as American libertarian high-pressuring—e.g., on the issue of whether "self-government" (the British preference) or "independence" (the American preference) should be held out as the eventual U.N. goal. The argument was further sharpened by the ambivalence of U.S. positions—on the one hand, "liberation" for all subject peoples, on the other, U.S. insistence that some of its own requirements for overseas bases should be met by the creation of "strategic trusteeships" placed under the Security Council, where the American veto would apply to keep meddlesome third parties from interfering.

The relationship between the Foreign Office and the State Department, which was one of close collaboration on the appraisal of Soviet policy as it had been of Japanese, was one of ill-concealed hostility where the Middle East was concerned. Though the Middle East was, under the rough division of responsibility drawn up after American entry into the war, a British sphere, the United States early established an independent relationship with Iran. The principal focus of Anglo-American hostility was Saudi Arabia where, during the war, the two ministers in Jidda accused each other of double-dealing, and to which the United States attached great importance because in the mid-1940s the Department of the Interior had convinced itself that American domestic oil reserves were running out. It was only in 1944, after some two years of internecine strife, that an agreement to respect each other's oil concessions was negotiated by two of the toughest characters on either side of the Atlantic, Harold Ickes and Lord Beaverbrook.

But it was in Palestine that the real seeds of Anglo-American trouble lay. The trusteeship formula might give the U.S. Navy satisfactory control of the Pacific Islands, but it provided no relief from the responsibility for Palestine which Britain had assumed in 1920 when her relative strength was much greater. Roosevelt, impressed by his conversation with Ibn Saud on his way back from Yalta, had inclined toward the Arab case in the last months of his life. But as Germany went down to defeat, with Allied troops uncovering the full horrors of Nazi treatment of the Jews, a wave of public pressure for the mass emigration of at least 100,000 European Jews into Palestine struck President Truman, pressure to which he reacted like an ordinary humane man and not as a statesman. In August 1945, the British—their plan to divide the area into a Jewish state, a Jerusalem state under international protection, and a trans-Jordan compensated and enlarged by fusion with the southern part of Syria, knocked sideways—suggested that the United States bear responsibility for its policy by participating in an Anglo-American Commission of Enquiry; it is just 30 years since its report was issued favoring the continuation of a mixed Palestinian state.

The fourth source of postwar conflict was the complex and sorry muddle over atomic energy. In the course of the first year of peacetime, the Administration appeared, in contemporary British eyes at least, to tear up two wartime agreements on postwar cooperation and to distort the meaning of the Anglo-American-Canadian agreement of November 1945, for the sake of a piece of legislation, the McMahon Act, that would ensure civilian control. In fact, it has become clear that British handling of the question left a great deal to be desired; that at the very point when British research was moved from the United Kingdom to the United States in 1941 there was a choice between a cooperative and a combined operation (as with other industrial projects) and that the former was mistakenly preferred; that Churchill had no real appreciation of the extent to which the threads of policy on this subject were not in the hands of Roosevelt; that key figures around Truman, notably James Byrnes, had been determined from an early date that the United States would not share military nuclear technology with anyone; and that the Attlee government made a serious diplomatic mistake in concentrating its efforts on bilateral and trilateral agreements with the United States and Canada rather than making a constructive contribution to the problem of international control, that is, relations with the Soviet Union, which was the Administration's real preoccupation. At the same time, the Administration thought that Britain was trying to cling to a cooperative arrangement for commercial reasons, when in fact security was the issue. In part, it was a bureaucratic muddle in both capitals, since influential legislators or officials knew little or nothing of the wartime story. But it was also a clear indication of how little bargaining power Britain now had in Washington, other than her control of certain uranium supplies, and even these brought a diminishing return as American access to uranium expanded.[13]

Finally, there was the acidulous debate over the future of global economic relations, the intellectual duel between Maynard Keynes and Harry Dexter White at Bretton Woods in 1944, the battle fought by Will Clayton against imperial preference, the precipitate cut-off of Lend-Lease in 1945, and the stringent terms of the British loan negotiated in the latter months of that year. Some Englishmen had seen this coming for a long time and in an article for *Foreign Affairs* written some months before America entered the war, Geoffrey Crowther warned his countrymen of the gathering weight of American opinion against preferential and bilateral trade agreements.[14] As the war progressed, more and more of them came to see the force of this argument and that Britain would profit from an open trading system. The real difference concerned timing: the British government, conscious of the profound weakness of the economy, its industries run down, its work force tired, its external assets exhausted, envisaged a long transitional period before the application of full multi-lateralism, during which the maximum assistance would be needed to regenerate the British economy. The Administration believed otherwise—that if the moment of postwar convalescence was not exploited to refashion the international economic order, deep-rooted national habits of protectionism would reassert themselves in all the industrial countries—and the stronger power won.

In consequence, the British had to swallow the considerable pride in their wartime achievements, accept a final settlement of Lend-Lease which was generous by American terms but still left Britain with a debt of $650 million to repay, and above all to negotiate a loan of $3.75 billion; though this had a low interest rate, early convertibility of the pound was its central condition. If one wishes to plumb the depths of postwar mutual suspicion, one has only to turn up the Commons debate of December 13, 1945, in which only just over half the votes were cast in favor of the loan, or the much larger congressional hearing and debates of the next few months, with their evocative refrain that once again Uncle Sam was being asked to pull Britain's chestnuts—Socialist chestnuts this time—out of the fire.

In July 1947, *Foreign Affairs* printed an article by the Director of the Institute of World Economics and Politics in Moscow. Its gist was that:

> [Anglo-American] relations, viewed in perspective, appear a peculiar combination of antagonism and cooperation, as a result of which the United States is constantly gaining ascendancy over Britain, reducing her more and more to the status of a second-rate power in both economic and political respects. This process began nearly a century ago, but owing to the different effect of the war on the economies of the two countries it has been immensely speeded up.[15]

At this point many Englishmen of the Right as well as the Left would have agreed with him. But bitter necessity left them little choice, except to retreat into an austerity as severe as that which the Soviet Union had experienced in the interwar years.

VI

It was not unnatural that the term "the special relationship" should first surface in Churchill's speech at Fulton, Missouri, on March 5, 1946, which also contained the famous phrase, "From Stettin in the Baltic to Trieste in the Adriatic, an iron curtain has descended across the continent." This is not to argue that Churchill or anyone else in Britain deliberately exaggerated the Soviet threat in order to mitigate the pains of American economic hegemony, or draw the United States back into Europe. But during the war Churchill, and after it Ernest Bevin, the Churchill of the Labour Party, were generally more skeptical of Soviet intentions than Roosevelt had been and Truman, Byrnes and Marshall initially were. Indeed, in the early meetings of the Security Council in 1946,

Byrnes found himself often mediating between Bevin and Molotov over Indonesia, Greece and the Middle East. Despite continuous explanations to Stalin and Molotov by American emissaries from 1942 onward that the "Anglo-Saxons" did not form a bloc in world politics—explanations that were received with polite skepticism in Moscow—despite the American desire for a free hand in refashioning an international order of which she was now the core power, the preceptions of London and Washington on the issues of 1946 such as Germany, Iran or the Dardanelles, were much closer to each other than they were to those of any other country (Canada, perhaps, excepted).

More than that, as the cold European winter of 1946–47 demonstrated how fragile all the West European economies were, it became necessary, on the one hand, to consider a broader rejuvenation of them than simply bilateral commercial loans; on the other, it also became clear that, if the United States were to exert the direct leverage of military confrontation against the Soviet Union in Europe, it was only Britain who possessed the facilities to do so.

The Truman Doctrine of March 1947 was the result of an abdication of power by an economically beleaguered Britain which caught the United States unprepared. America had never grasped the extent to which Britain was overextended, nor faced up to the implications for American policy of a British withdrawal in the eastern Mediterranean. Indeed, even after Truman had accepted the consequences in principle, American successfully pressed Britain to keep troops in Greece until the beginning of 1950.

As Acheson's memoirs make plain, the success of the Marshall Plan, by contrast, owes much to the speed and imagination with which Britain under Ernest Bevin picked up and developed the American initiative of June 1947. Here, thanks to the intimate cooperation of Bevin, Acheson and Bidault, the plan became an instrument for the rehabilitation

[45]

not just of Britain but of Western Europe as a whole. Although the British and French postwar loans were running out like quicksands, the countries that were politically in most urgent need of economic assistance were Germany and Italy. The development of the Committee for European Economic Cooperation in Paris, and the stimulus to European trade that the Marshall Plan was designed to provide, were remarkable, not only for eliciting a great deal of both European and American enthusiasm for European integration and even political unification, but as the first moment in the 170 years of Anglo-American relations in which the United States treated Britain as an integral element of Western Europe rather than as a particular island off its shores, "anchored" as Emerson had said "at the side of Europe." (Documents on strategic planning, however, continued to differentiate the two until the early 1950s and perhaps later.) Churchill and Smuts had floated the balloon of a West European "Commonwealth" during the war, only to have it sharply punctured by the American doctrine of universal interests; now it was revived under a different name by products of the British connection like William Fulbright and Walt Rostow, Charles Bonesteel, George A. Lincoln and Lincoln Gordon.

What created a "special" Anglo-American relationship between 1947 and 1952 within the broader and later strategic nexus between the United States and Western Europe were three factors in particular. One was a change in the British style or technique of dealing with the United States. As long as the British considered themselves a great power, or as long as the United States considered Britain one, it was almost as natural to transact significant business in London as in Washington. Thus, John Winant, Averell Harriman and Lewis Douglas, the wartime and postwar American ambassadors in London, had been nearly as important links in the chain of diplomatic interchange as Lords Lothian, Halifax and Inverchapel, their counterparts in Washington between 1939 and 1947. But with Britain greatly weakened and London therefore less important, with the process of American policymaking becoming more complex as a Republican Congress demanded a powerful voice and the bureaucracy expanded, Washington clearly became the place where serious business must be transacted. Misunderstandings over atomic energy had been a fearful warning of the consequences of not mastering, and indeed influencing, the American executive-legislative relationship.

Thus it occurred that the imitation Virginian manor house on Massachusetts Avenue that is the British Embassy was converted into a powerhouse of British official talent under the leadership of a tall, calm philosopher, Oliver Franks, who had played the leading role in organizing the distribution and provision of Marshall aid. The quality of the Franks Embassy can be measured at the diplomatic level by the fact that almost every First Secretary retired as a very senior ambassador or its counterpart during the early 1970s, and at the military level by the fact that the ambassador's advisers were full-ranking generals and admirals, with a marshal of the RAF in the person of Tedder as an active participant for a good deal of the time. More than that, there was a unique coincidence of temperament and outlook between Franks and Dean Acheson. Franks may have read Castlereagh's advice to the outgoing British Minister to Washington in 1819: "The first precept which I will recommend is to transact your business with the American government as far as possible by personal intercourse with the Secretary of State rather than by writing notes. . . ." But in fact there was no need to press the point, for Acheson and Franks became such intimate interlocutors that it was hard to say where the one man's train of thought ended and the other's began. "No comparable relationship," Acheson's first biographer has written, "between a Secretary of State and an ambassador can be found in American history." [16]

The second element in the original postwar intimacy

resulted from the growing militarization of the East-West balance of power in Europe in the late 1940s. The Soviet rape of Czechoslovakia in February 1948 and the beginnings of the Berlin blockade that summer undermined—rightly or wrongly—the assumption that what was at issue was a diplomatic and political confrontation with the Soviet Union in central and southern Europe. If it became necessary to organize collective security in Europe, Britain had unique assets. By reason of the differing rates of demobilization and its continuance of conscription, Britain was nearly as strong a military power, in terms of force in being, as the United States, though not yet possessing nuclear weapons and with much of its army still dotted about the imperial map. By reason of the war, British senior officers and officials had experience of working with Americans in combined staffs and commands which France, the only other major European military power, lacked. And by reason of geography Americans had, as a Yale political scientist had expressed it during the war, "an additional stake in Britain's island base because it offers a unique opportunity for American power to make itself felt on the other side of the ocean." [17] This first became evident in peacetime through the move of three B-29 squadrons to East Anglia during the Berlin blockade; it became increasingly significant as American military strategy turned from one of defense to one of deterrence. Moreover, the ethnic groups in the United States that had traditionally been hostile to any Grand Alliance with Britain—the Irish and the Germans— were even more hostile to communism.

Bevin, moreover, had already laid the groundwork of a European collective security system, first by negotiating the Treaty of Dunkirk with France, a 50-year treaty of full mutual support in the event of hostilities with Germany, and a year later the Brussels Treaty which embraced the Benelux countries. Britain had for the first time in many generations got involved in permanent European commitments in time of peace; what the British could do, so could the Americans. Britain had created the core of the system and it merely required the cooperation of certain small countries such as Portugal and Iceland—what the position papers of the time called "stepping-stone countries"—to convert a collective security system into an American command and reinforcement system, as happened some 20 months after the signature of the North American Treaty in the wake of the alarm caused by the Korean War. Contemporary American writers like Lippmann argued that the British had been pressing for an American alliance through much of the twentieth century. This was not quite accurate; Britain had been trying to get the United States to play a role in maintaining a European power balance; with NATO this seemed to have been achieved.

The third reason for the original "special relationship" was that the United States, as the only great, undamaged power after the Second World War, found it extremely difficult to set limits on American influence and presence. Acheson and Forrestal tried to limit American commitments or to argue that American interests were concentrated primarily on Western and Southern Europe, Iran and Japan. But for a country of the resources of the United States, private as well as official, the gravitational power exerted by the international system as a whole was irresistible. In consequence, Washington—which had had only a rudimentary intelligence service before the war, a high-powered but amateur operation, OSS, during it and thereafter a CIA that had very limited resources until the Korean War lifted the lid of government expenditure—found a desperate need to understand and be informed about areas and places that had hitherto been visited only by stray American botanists or anthropologists. Later this gap was filled by a dramatic increase in the scope of the major American universities, but in the first instance Washington relied heavily on the knowledge of the old imperial powers, principally Britain. British military technology, especially on aircraft and carrier design, was imported by the United States. Ideas flowed in both directions also, for it is generally acknowledged that the concept of nuclear deterrence in the sense of a bomber fleet in being, capable of instant and massive retaliation, originated with Sir John Slessor, the British Chief of the Air Staff.

This does not mean that the Truman years were plain sailing for the Anglo-American relationship. Its intimacy was primarily between officials, not legislators, still less the general public in either country. It encompassed the quarrel over Iranian oil, a grumbling argument over atomic energy, the refusal of the British government to participate in the European Coal and Steel Community, and, above all, conflicts of policy over China. The last-named was the most serious for it aroused the strongest passions in American opinion.

Britain had acquiesced in American dominance over the occupation of Japan and American postwar attempts to mediate single-handed in the Chinese civil war, despite Australian misgivings, for lack of resource to do otherwise. But the Attlee government saw no reason to depart from its policy of de facto recognition when the Chinese Communist regime became established in Peking in 1949, whereas American policy responded to public pressure and withheld it. Moreover, Britain had solid commercial interests in the Far East which she refused to relinquish (except for strategic goods) when a Communist regime took over, exposing herself to accusations of trading with the enemy on the part of Senator Knowland, Representative Judd, and the old China lobby. The breach was not between Bevin and Acheson but between British and American public opinion.

The Korean War accentuated those problems, not because Britain did not support the principle of U.N. action to resist aggression but for three reasons in particular. First, the high-handed conduct of the war by MacArthur, coupled with the onset of McCarthyism, seriously weakened British public confidence in the quality of American public policy. (I can remember, as the correspondent of a London paper in Washington in those years, being badgered by an editor deeply sympathetic to the United States for some good news instead of bad.) This reached its nadir, getting entangled with another old quarrel, when President Truman on November 30, 1950, made an incautious statement at a press conference that implied the possible use of American nuclear weapons in Korea, leading to Attlee's agitated flight to Washington. A second reason was the skeptical, even cynical, American attitude toward the validity of the Commonwealth relationship which the war brought to the surface. The Attlee government took a proprietary pride in the new Commonwealth, embracing India, Pakistan and Ceylon, as well as the older white dominions, and when the Indian government's accurate reports of developments on Chinese policy were ignored in Washington, there was a grinding of teeth in London as well as in Delhi, confirming simultaneously Britain's distrust for Washington's handling of the war and regret that the voice of emancipated India should be so little regarded. The third reason was the American insistence on German rearmament after September 1950, which was less of a body blow to Britain than to France, but was still difficult to accept for a country that had been unique in fighting the Second World War from the first day to the last.

Although I, like many of my compatriots, feel that the easy entree which London has enjoyed in Washington over the past 30 years has distorted British perspectives, it is not easy to find fault with this postwar "era of good feelings." Britain was a seriously weakened country in the postwar years; the threat of Soviet power loomed large over Europe in Stalin's day and in Bevin's eyes; although the Commonwealth was still an association of considerable vitality, there was much to be said for helping the United States assume effectively the mantle of global power; the political and economic unification of Europe as an alternative frame of British interests was at best a gamble and the Organization for European Economic Cooperation, which embraced some sixteen countries, had little prospect of providing the matrix of it. Britain, moreover, was not the "running dog" of American policy in those years that the Left has often alleged. Britain took issue with the United States not only on Far Eastern questions but also on relations with the Soviet Union, witness the attempt of Churchill in 1952, back in office again, to make the Administration take seriously the Soviet offer of renewed negotiations on a German peace treaty.

VII

The process of mutual adjustment to the expansion of American power moved for several reasons much more unevenly throughout the Eisenhower Administration than during its predecessor or successor Administrations. It was not merely a question of personalities, of the well-known mutual antipathy of Eden and Dulles. Eisenhower was an Anglophile, and there were thirteen Anglo-American "summits" during his eight years in office as compared with three in the eight years after Potsdam.

One reason was the yawning disparity in military strength that emerged as American military expenditure quintupled after the Korean War while British rearmament was necessarily much more circumscribed. Moreover, with the development of the B-52, and the building of Strategic Air Command bases in North Africa, Saudi Arabia and Okinawa, Britain's utility to the United States as Airstrip One diminished. A second reason was a growing conflict of view as the European Coal and Steel Community showed that the idea of European unification held promise. Britain was ready to play a role analogous to the United States in encouraging this from the outside, but in Washington it was increasingly felt that Britain herself should participate in the process, that Britain was a European power not a global one. The fact that perhaps the major diplomatic triumph of Anthony Eden's career was in rescuing the possibility of German participation in NATO after the collapse of the European Defense Community in 1954, by negotiating the Western European Union, mitigated but did not eliminate this conflict of perspective.

A third reason was Dulles' growing preoccupation with Asia and the Far East, the area where the two governments had seldom viewed the threat to international order or the means of fortifying it through the same lenses. One charge against Britain was that she acquiesced in the negotiation of SEATO, an organization in which she did not really have confidence; but the role of Australian diplomacy in urging membership on Britain, and London's sense that it provided compensation for Britain's earlier exclusion from ANZUS, must be taken into account. Fourth, there was the growing sense in Washington that Britain was losing her validity as a coalition partner by reason of the crumbling not so much of the Commonwealth as of the still large colonial empire and the British position in the Middle East. As early as May 1953 Dulles confided to himself in a note written after his first official tour of the area:

> British position rapidly deteriorating, probably to the point of non-repair. Generally in the area, India and Jordan being partial exceptions, we find an intense distrust and dislike for the British. The days when the Middle East used to relax under the presence of British protection are gone. . . . We must convince the Arab states that the U.S. operates on a policy of its own with regard to this problem [colonialism].[18]

Whether Dulles was right or wrong is less important than

the fact that he undoubtedly reflected a growing American conviction that British imperial control and influence no longer provided a usable instrument for the containment of Soviet power. Paradoxically it was a British attempt to reassert her imperial role, at Suez, that provoked the most open and resonant Anglo-American clash of the postwar years. Yet one can now see that Suez was not a considered development of British policy. It was a spasmodic reaction to one of history's mistimings; imperial influence was actually declining in advance of America's realization of what was happening and of what the full implications were for American policy. Britain reacted at the end of what Eden and his close colleagues thought was a series of American haverings over her responsibilities in the Middle East. Britain thereby accomplished—at considerable embarrassment and pain to itself—an eventual clarification of the American role in this area. In that sense Suez was not all loss, which may explain why it left so slight a permanent scar on the Anglo-American relationship.

Vis-à-vis Russia, by the 1950s there was another significant shift of roles between Britain and America. Whereas in the immediate postwar period it was Britain that had the clearer and stronger sense of the Soviet threat, by the 1950s British weight was being thrown more and more in the direction of restraint and negotiation. British opinion had never shared in the hysterical anti-communism of right-wing American thinking but, more than this, the less moralistic code of British policymaking left Prime Ministers freer than Presidents to advocate open dealings with the mammon of unrighteousness. And no doubt it was a help to Churchill, in pressing for summit negotiations—as he did tirelessly from 1951 to 1955— that his anti-communist credentials stretched back to 1917.

Yet beneath the surface of this growing divergence of official preoccupations and positions, a contrary process was at work. Despite the international damage done by McCarthyism, Englishmen and Americans were growing increasingly attracted to each other's company. This went far beyond official relationships, intelligence or military liaison, for the alienation of the prewar years had given place to a host of new interactions, among journalists, academics and businessmen. What Geoffrey Crowther accomplished with the American Survey of *The Economist* in making American politics and policy comprehensible to serious Englishmen, radio and television did for a wider audience. The fear or distaste for mass society which had been one of the earlier causes of anti-Americanism began to erode as the pattern of British life and habits changed. Though Britain was still the second most powerful state in the West and was so regarded in the mid-1950s by informed opinion not only in Britain but in France and Germany,[19] all but a small minority on the Left and Right of British politics had accepted her secondary status and the reality of American leadership. The process, however, was an asymmetrical one; with certain honorable exceptions, American press coverage of Britain has been more superficial than the converse.

In my view, it was this roseate transnational relationship, rather than the fact that Harold Macmillan had an American mother or had been a wartime friend of Eisenhower's, which accounted for the rapidity with which Anglo-American good relations were restored after the debacle of Suez, despite the gross incompetence of British and French planning or the failure of Anglo-American communication that it had demonstrated. There were other factors at work as well: the declining health and influence of John Foster Dulles; the continuing importance of mutual information about developments in the far reaches of the world; the restoration, after a decade of estrangement, of a confidential relationship on nuclear energy and atomic weapons.

VIII

It was on these foundations that the second "era of good feelings" or special relationship (a phrase rarely used by British politicians and by only two American Presidents who did not believe in it, namely Lyndon Johnson and Richard Nixon) was constructed. But it was different in character from the first, even though the personal friendship between Macmillan and Kennedy may have been as intimate as that between Bevin and Acheson. For one thing the differential in military power had widened even further by the early 1960s. Britain had a military budget that was one-tenth that of the United States' and had only about one-seventh as many men under arms. For another, the diplomatic and political significance of the other European powers had markedly increased and they were climbing the ladder of economic growth with strides, where Britain was only plodding upward.

But above all, Macmillan's conception of the Anglo-American connection, espoused though it might be among his colleagues and officials, was based upon a central fallacy. Years earlier, when he was the British representative in Algiers during the war, he had said to Richard Crossman:

We are the Greeks in this American Empire. You will find the Americans much as the Greeks found the Romans—great big, vulgar, bustling people, more vigorous than we are and also more idle, with more unspoilt virtues but also more corrupt. We must run [this headquarters] as the Greek slaves ran the operations of the Emperor Claudius.[20]

This Greek-Roman analogy continued to inform his approach to Washington. It assumed that Britain had no Roman role to play even if on a greatly narrowed stage. But more than that, it overlooked the fact that Americans had, 20 years after the assumption of a central role in world politics, acquired the ability to be Greeks to their own Romans by mobilizing the vast intellectual resources of their continental state.

Not just in terms of brute economic and military power, but of the development of the natural and social sciences, America had become the mother and Britain the daughter society. The RAND corporation, the think tanks, the Harvard-MIT arms control seminar and a host of other devices had brought intellectuals into the center of American policymaking. Though Britain had, and has, an excellent public service, no serious attempt was made to harness the universities to the needs of British policymaking. And Macmillan's concept also overlooked the fact that the wartime generation of officials and politicians who knew each other's cast of thought was beginning to disappear from public life.

The consequence was a process of British self-delusion just at a time when stock-taking of the country's position in the world was most required. In some small degree it may have retarded British recognition of the significance for Britain of the European Economic Community (EEC). More importantly, it fostered the illusion that Britain could have the best of both nuclear worlds—an "independent deterrent" and, at the same time, a much greater say in American nuclear strategy, both on such things as targeting and on arms control, than in reality she had. The anti-Americanism thrown up by Suez in Macmillan's own party was half encouraged, half bought off by this. But in fairness, another side existed even to that rather dubious coin. Macmillan and David Ormsby-Gore deserve credit for persisting with the proposal for a nuclear test ban from 1958 onward in face of sustained hostility from Dulles and initial skepticism from the Kennedy Administration. And in the Berlin crisis of 1958–62, a real Anglo-American cooperation was sustained throughout, with British influence exerted somewhat in the direction of negotiation all along.

Nonetheless, the priority given to the nuclear relationship

with the United States was not only instrumental in hardening de Gaulle's opposition to the entry of the British Trojan horse into the EEC. It led also in 1962 to what Arthur Schlesinger christened the "Pinero drama of misunderstanding" over the Skybolt missile, which led in turn to an increasingly dependent British strategic relationship with the United States as Macmillan persuaded Kennedy to substitute the Polaris system for it.

The Nassau Agreement of 1962 and the transatlantic confusion that preceded it should have been a warning to Whitehall of the rapidity with which the Anglo-American relationship was changing. Macmillan himself perceived this, I think, despite the affection which Kennedy felt for him and the value he found in the older man as a sounding board for his own decisions and ideas, including moments of swift action and great stress such as the Cuban missile crisis. But his departure from office in 1963 a month before Kennedy's assassination was followed by a period not just of British but of mutual delusion.

On the one hand the British general election of 1964 brought back to office a Labour government most of whose leading members, Harold Wilson, George Brown, Anthony Crosland, Denis Healey, Roy Jenkins, were profound admirers not only of Kennedy and his Administration's effort to move toward détente with the Soviet Union, but of the older concept of "Atlantic Community." They had backed Robert McNamara's attempt to introduce an element of flexibility into NATO strategy, by greater emphasis on conventional forces, an attempt of which the Tory government had been skeptical; and they were prepared to place the British nuclear force at the disposal of NATO, thus allaying the American fears of a German demand for a nuclear deterrent of its own. It is arguable that Labour "moderates," at any rate, know the United States better than their opposite numbers on the

Conservative benches, and certainly have a more successful relationship with most Democratic Administrations.

But Johnson was not Kennedy, and Wilson and he certainly effected no marriage of true minds. Neither shared in the tradition, experienced or inherited, of the wartime partnership; each had his heart set on a narrow concept of the national interest.

However, on the crucial issue of Vietnam, Anglo-American divergencies had an earlier inception. Washington wanted, from the beginning, to believe that relevant aspects of the Commonwealth relationship could be made to relieve the loneliness of the American position in Southeast Asia. They believed, as few people in Britain did after the 1950s, that there was not only an analogy but a continuity between the British role in Malaysia and the American role in Vietnam.

Thus as early as February 1962 McNamara told a Senate subcommittee that "the United States strongly favored the continued deployment of British land, sea and air forces in a broad area of Asia," [21] and this same view was pressed upon the Labour government. Consequently, the latter, finding itself merely tagging along in the wake of American policy on central issues of great power relations such as the nonproliferation negotiations, continued to maintain a high level of commitments in Southeast Asia and the Persian Gulf at a time when the troubles of the British economy and the weakening position of sterling made it increasingly onerous to do so.

Lyndon Johnson did not get what he wanted, namely a British commitment, however symbolic, to the Vietnam War. The transnational relationship, the extent to which informed British opinion was becoming affected by the doubts of informed American opinion about both the wisdom of the Administration's policy or the prospects of victory, made that impossible. But, whereas Wilson found his attempts to mediate between Washington and Hanoi, notably at the time of

Kosygin's visit to London in February 1967—to move as it were into the high politics of the Vietnam War—quite abortive, at the same time Johnson brutally used the dependence of sterling on the dollar to exact Wilson's support for American policy in Vietnam, except for the bombing of the North. In the end, Wilson failed in both his objectives: to maintain the parity of sterling and to retain any leverage over American policy in Asia. Both countries suffered in the process.

By the late 1960s a new element was entering into the relationship, namely the huge growth of American investment in Europe but particularly in Britain. By 1966, the year before the second British application to join the EEC, the Prime Minister was speaking of "industrial helotry," and trying to find a basis of common ground with the Six on the protection of the European technological industries. However, it was characteristic partly of the element of mutual flattery in the Anglo-American political relationship, partly of the extent to which the United States was losing interest in the development of the Community as superpower relationships took precedence over Atlantic partnership, that when Edward Heath suggested in the 1967 Godkin Lectures at Harvard that, where British officials had always thought first what would be Washington's reactions to a proposal, they would soon think first about the reaction of Paris, Bonn or Rome, he was considered to be anti-American.

IX

The British Defence White Paper of 1969, the first year in a decade in which British defense estimates actually declined, was described by Denis Healey, the Defence Secretary, as setting "the seal on Britain's transformation from a world power to a European power." To the extent to which this was true—some of it was reversed temporarily by the Conservatives when they retained a presence "East of Suez" on coming to power in 1970—it may be said to parallel the "retreat from empire" which Robert E. Osgood and others have identified as the dominant theme of the first Nixon Administration.[22] Certainly the years that followed displayed a profound change in the objectives and techniques of American diplomacy: the bilateral negotiation of a Vietnam peace settlement (and, if by any intermediary, more by France than by Britain); the prolonged, bilateral and secret negotiations on strategic arms limitations with the Soviet Union; the unilateral "opening to China." On the British side they have witnessed entry into the EEC, the endorsement of it by a large majority in a referendum, and the gradual emergence of the Nine as a working political entente on several issues of world politics; the open dispute with Washington at the time of the Yom Kippur War; and a grumbling divergence of opinion about the proper way of confronting the developing world in the United Nations and elsewhere.

Although there was much about the Nixonian "retreat" that British opinion welcomed, most conspicuously of course the end to the long, demoralizing and diversionary attrition of the Vietnam War—although there was much about the pursuit of a "multipolar" world that was similarly acceptable, particularly the "opening" to China—yet for various reasons these were not happy years for the Anglo-American relationship. There was, running through them all, a basic distrust of the Nixonian presidency which, even when taking its inception in a non-diplomatic context, spilt over onto the diplomatic stage. There was an uneasy awareness that some of the success in moderating old enmities was achieved at the price of neglecting old friends. The Guam (or Nixon) Doctrine was felt to embody a somewhat chilling assertion of American independence. The old bipolar world had been a dangerous place, but at least the NATO alliance had fitted into it as neatly as sword into scabbard. What would take its place now that bipolarity was pronounced extinct? What, in particular, would happen to the Anglo-American relationship?

Since the Nixonian collapse, both countries seem to have been living in the ruins. Yet the main reflection of this seems to have been a mood of introspection and diminished confidence, rather than a turning-away from basic principles—the pursuit of détente, the acceptance of multipolarity, the need for preserving one's guard, the recognition of the claims of the Third World. In both countries there have been hesitancies and questionings about these policies, and particularly about whether the other fellow was taking them as seriously as oneself, but at the bottom this reflected a lack of confidence in the style and competence of leadership rather than any rejection of the principles themselves. No one has seriously proposed anything to take their place. What 1976 has to produce, by the ballot box and otherwise, is a set of leaders on both sides of the Atlantic who look as if they have the talent, determination and durability to take common action in support of common interests.

X

What does one make of this long history of intimacy, of discord and collaboration? I have no grand Toynbeean conclusion, but as someone who has been traversing the Atlantic for over 40 years, there seems a provisional balance sheet to be struck. In the years when Britain was the mother society and the more politically powerful state, its policy and position accelerated the internal development of the United States, provided it with a framework of juridical, social and intellectual reference. It speeded American civilization. Yet this retarded in many ways the development of the United States as an international power, and Britain's maritime

supremacy delayed American thought about American interests. As a result, American thinking often lacked any "middle
term"—a set of working practices halfway between crass self-
interest and "globaloney." Woodrow Wilson's Fourteen
Points, evolved out of a cosmic a priorism, with little or no
regard for the United States' immediate requirements and
imposed on a very un-American warring world, was a perfect
case in point.

In the alienated interwar years when both countries thought
they were the equal of the other, they did very little for each
other. But in the 35 years or so that the United States has been
the parent society, the nineteenth-century process has been
apparent in reverse, intensified by closer intimacy in a
shrinking world. American ideas, American capital, American
pressure have for the most part been beneficent in moderniz-
ing the internal habits of a country that has been reluctant to
face the challenges of change. But, by the same token, the fact
that Britannia has been cradled to a large extent in the lap of
Uncle Sam as far as both strategic and economic security have
been concerned, has been able to converse with him on an
intimacy that until recently no other country can accomplish,
has been encouraged to place so much more emphasis on the
dialogue with Washington than with any other capital,
delayed, not fatally I hope, Britain's adjustment of her own
perceptions to a rapidly altering situation of power and
influence.

What does this promise for the third century of the Anglo-
American relationship? To anyone who believes in the
soundness, the inevitability even, of Britain's entry into
Europe, the introduction of true multipolarity within as well as
without the Western alliance must be acceptable, even
welcome. Geography, strategy, economics—Britain's long
defiance of these as an imperial and global power should not
and could not be protracted into the changed world of today.
The time has now arrived when, as Edward Heath predicted,

a British official's first reaction to many a crisis is, "What will Bonn and Paris think?" And the categories of crisis to which this reaction is appropriate are expanding all the time.

But before we give way to the exclusive assumptions of the European zealots, let us remember two things. The decisions out of which the new Europe is emerging are made, and will continue to be made as far as the eye can see, in the shadow cast by Washington. In part this is due to the imperfect level of European unity; Europe is in the condition of the American States under the Articles of Confederation, "united" only in aspiration, not in actuality. But beyond this, and however rapidly the new Europe is forged, it is hard to envisage it as a self-sufficient power center able to cope with with challenges of the non-free world without the most intimate interdependence with the United States.

And if the making of Europe does not mean the unmaking of the Anglo-American relationship any more than of the Franco-American, Italo-American, German-American, etc., it is unrealistic not to recognize the multiple and tenacious strands out of which that relationship is woven. The old Commonwealth apart, the British and the American peoples think more alike—or at least disagree less—than anyone else. Hot lines and frank exchanges between Washington and other capitals, dictated by self-preservation and balance-of-power politics, are no substitute for shared political values in a hostile world or a common language in an increasingly lazy one. The Gulf Stream of common intercourse at every level, cultural, educational, economic, official, shows no signs of diminishing its two-way flow, however intense the cross-Channel traffic may become; and in the future, as in the past, it is unlikely to be much affected by the tempests that may ruffle the surface of the "steep Atlantick stream."

How history will handle the admitted elements of contrariety that inhere in Britain's new relationship with Europe and her old relationship with America remains dependent on a myriad of unpredictable variables. Who, in 1876, would have predicted that it would handle so well the contradictions between Manifest Destiny and the Imperial Theme? No doubt 2076 will hold many surprises; they may not all be unpleasant ones.

NOTES

1. Quoted in *Britain Through American Eyes*, ed. Henry Steele Commager, London and New York: McGraw-Hill, 1974.

2. H. C. Allen, *Great Britain and the United States*, London and New York: St. Martin's Press, 1954, p. 166.

3. "The civilian theory of negotiation is based upon the assumption that a compromise between rivalries is generally more profitable than the complete destruction of the rival." *Diplomacy*, 3rd ed., London: Oxford Univ. Press, 1963, pp. 53–54.

4. Quoted by Allen, *op. cit.*, p. 82.

5. Percy Lubbock, ed., *The Letters of Henry James*, New York: Octagon Books, 1969, Vol. I, p. 143.

6. Quoted by H. G. Nicholas, *The United States and Britain*, Chicago and London: Univ. of Chicago Press, 1975, p. 46.

7. H. G. Nicholas, *op. cit.*, p. 57.

8. See Patrick Devlin, *Too Proud to Fight: Woodrow Wilson's Neutrality*, Oxford: Oxford Univ. Press, 1974, pp. 561–62.

9. D. C. Watt, *Personalities and Policies*, London: Longmans, 1965, pp. 37–38.

10. Forrest C. Pogue, *George C. Marshall: Ordeal and Hope, 1939–1943*, New York: Viking Press, 1966, p. 264.

11. Winston Churchill, *The Second World War*, Vol. 6, *Triumph and Tragedy*, New York: Houghton Mifflin, 1953, p. 353.

12. Gaddis Smith, *American Diplomacy During the Second World War, 1941–1945*, New York and London: John Wiley & Sons, 1965, p. 155.

13. See Margaret Gowing, *Independence and Deterrence—Britain and Atomic Energy*, London and New York: St. Martin's Press, 1974, Vol. I, pp. 90–92.

14. Geoffrey Crowther, "Anglo-American Pitfalls," *Foreign Affairs*, October 1941.

15. E. Varga, "Anglo-American Rivalry and Partnership: A Marxist View," *Foreign Affairs*, July 1947.

16. Gaddis Smith, *Dean Acheson*, The American Secretaries of State Series, New York: Cooper Square Pubs., 1976, p. 145.

17. W. T. Fox, *The Super-powers—The United States, Britain, and the Soviet Union*, New York: Harcourt, Brace & Co., 1944, p. 60.

18. Dulles Papers, Princeton University Library, Princeton, New Jersey.

19. Daniel Lerner and Morton Gorden, *Euratlantica: Changing Perspectives of the European Elites*, Cambridge and London: MIT Press, 1969, p. 149.

20. Quoted by Anthony Sampson, *Macmillan: A Study in Ambiguity*, London and New York: Simon & Schuster, 1967, p. 61.

21. *The Times* (London), February 16, 1962.

22. Robert E. Osgood *et al.*, *Retreat from Empire?* Baltimore and London: John Hopkins Univ. Press, 1973.

[THREE]

The United States and the European Balance

Gordon A. Craig

In November 1782, during the peace negotiations with Great Britain, John Adams talked with one of the British commissioners about the future relationship of the American republic with the European political system. In his diary he reproduced the exchange.

"You are afraid," says Mr. Otis today, "of being made the tool of the powers of Europe." "Indeed I am," says I. "What powers?" said he. "All of them," said I. "It is obvious that all the powers of Europe will be continually

Gordon A. Craig is the J. E. Wallace Sterling Professor of Humanities in the Department of History at Stanford University, California. His most recent books include *War, Politics and Diplomacy* and *Europe Since 1815*.

maneuvering with us, to work us into their real or imaginary balances of power. They will all wish to make of us a make-weight candle, when they are weighing out their pounds. Indeed, it is not surprising, for we shall very often, if not always, be able to turn the scale. But I think it ought to be our rule not to meddle. . . ."

Adams was expressing what, in the course of the next 150 years, was to become an article of faith with many Americans, the belief that, having won its freedom from the old world, the American republic should have as little contact with it as possible. What other course was feasible, given the nature of the European system of politics? Regarded from this side of the Atlantic, it appeared to be animated by the whims of princes and the intrigues of diplomats and characterized by continual friction between its members, by an endless search for an equilibrium that was in reality neither attainable nor desired, and, intermittently, by wasting and destructive wars. It represented a perpetual menace to American liberties because its members were constantly seeking to involve the republic in their tangled affairs, and because the American statesmen were not always as deaf as they should be to their seductions. Safety, therefore, lay in complete abstention from political contact with Europe.

This conclusion, formulated more drastically in 1793 by John Quincy Adams when he wrote that, in the face of the European struggle for power, it was the duty of Americans "to remain the peaceable and silent, though sorrowful, spectators of the sanguinary scene," inspired the isolationism that came to be considered by many to be the traditional foreign policy of the United States. Yet from the very beginning of the republic's history, the belief that the American posture should be one of rigorous aloofness from European affairs was challenged by two contrary views. The first held that it was patently impossible for the United States to remain indifferent to the convolutions of European power politics without running intolerable risks to its security and that, therefore, the proper line for American statesmen to follow was one of defensive accommodation to the balance of power, adjusting their policy to its nature at any particular moment, and exploiting the opportunities that it offered for the promotion of American interests. The second held that it was ideologically undesirable for the United States to impose self-denying ordinances upon itself, since occasions were bound to arise on which it was its duty to intervene in European affairs; that it must recognize its natural affinity with other peoples struggling to be free and must be willing to support them; that it must understand that there was, indeed, a balance of ideas in the world as well as a balance of power, and that it was only by tipping the former in the direction of liberty that humanity could be freed from the evils of the latter.

II

Although their public declarations sometimes suggested the opposite, Franklin, Hamilton, Washington, and Jefferson all realized that balance-of-power politics was a game that American statesmen would have to learn to play. As a country that had to dispose of its growing agricultural surpluses in order to be able to purchase the manufactured goods it needed, the United States was dependent upon the trading agreements that it could negotiate with mercantilist states that used such agreements as political weapons. In addition, as long as Great Britain, France and Spain retained possessions in North America, it was impossible for the republic's leaders to ignore with impunity the shifting relations among those states. Despite his aversion to what he called "romantick European Continental Connections" and "whims about the balance of power," Benjamin Franklin realized that his country was caught up in the contention of the powers whether it liked it or not. Because he recognized that the United States was vulnerable to attack as long as the British government maintained armed forts along its northern and western frontiers, Franklin became the advocate of a continuation of the wartime alliance with France, and his government followed his advice.

Later on, when the government of the French Republic took advantage of its position as an ally to enlist American citizens for service in its wars and to make propaganda against the U.S. government's policy of neutrality, Hamilton and Washington effected the termination of the French connection, but not because they opposed alliances in principle or believed that the European policy of their country should be a purely negative one. Hamilton, whose instincts were akin to those of the shrewdest Realpolitiker of his time, was perfectly willing to make arrangements with European governments as long as they promised to bring tangible advantages to his country; he objected, however, to the basing of foreign policy upon sentimental affinity or gratitude or any other emotion that would, in his words, involve "sacrifices of our substantial interests, preferences inconsistent with sound policy, or complaisances incompatible with our safety."

As for Washington, in the great political testament of 1796 in which he warned his countrymen against "interweaving our destiny with that of any part of Europe" and "entangl[ing] our peace and prosperity in the toils of European Ambition, Rivalship, Interest, Humour, or Caprice," he never for a moment recommended that the United States relinquish the freedom of choice that an independent state necessarily possesses in its foreign political decisions or suggested that it forswear the use of any diplomatic expedients that might serve to support its policies or defend its interests. He declared that "the Great rule of conduct for us in regard to foreign nations" should be "in extending our commercial relations to have with them as little political connection as possible," and he added that, while the United States was building up the material strength that would reduce its present vulnerability to external pressure, "it would be unwise in us to implicate ourselves, by artificial ties, in the ordinary vicissitudes of [Europe's] politics." But he also spoke explicitly of the possible necessity of "temporary alliances for extraordinary emergencies."

Thomas Jefferson's two terms as President were filled with such emergencies, and he responded to them positively, realistically, and with considerable diplomatic adroitness, having no compunction about resorting to methods that he had reprobated, at other times, when they were employed by old-world statesmen. Indeed, he became a highly sophisticated practitioner of the politics of menace and maneuver and bluff, shrewd in his anticipation of the intrusion of imponderable factors in developing situations and in his judgment of their effects, and quick to seize upon opportunities for advancing American interests by intimations of support or opposition to the embattled powers. The great triumph of his first term, the acquisition of Louisiana, was doubtless due in some part to Napoleon's frustrations in San Domingo and to the distractions caused by the renewal of the war in Europe, but Louisiana could not have been won if Jefferson had not made the most of those circumstances, if he had not been ingenious in playing the powers off against each other, and if he had not, in the end, made it clear to Napoleon's Ministers that any French attempt to take possession at New Orleans would force the United States "to marry ourselves to the British fleet and nation."

During Jefferson's second term, the European balance offered no opportunities for American manipulation in the national interest. After Austerlitz and Trafalgar, politics were polarized in such a way as to deprive the President of any leverage in the European conflict; there was nothing that he could do for either party, short of joining it in the war, that could induce it to support American interests, and no threat that he could make that would be plausible enough to discourage it from violating American rights. In his vain struggle to protect American shipping against British interference and American crews against British impressment, Jefferson was daily confronted with palpable and distressing evidence of how seriously his country could be injured by shifts in the European equilibrium; and, if he was not goaded into declaring war upon the principal violator of American neutral rights, it was certainly in part at least because he realized that the balance of power was capable of undergoing changes that would be even more dangerous to the United States than the polarization of the years after 1805.

The President's ill-starred embargo policy was rooted, on the one hand, in a realistic appraisal of the disparity of force between Great Britain and the United States and, on the other, in the idealistic conviction that the violations were not enough to justify so serious a response as war; but he may have been influenced by an additional consideration: the suspicion that the French Empire was potentially a greater threat to American liberties than Great Britain and that, despite their present differences, Britain and the United States were tacit partners against the possibility of a domination of the Western world by Napoleon. In 1803, in a letter to an English acquaintance, Jefferson had spoken of Great Britain as "a bulwark against the torrent which has for some time been bearing down all before it," and the thought of what the destruction of that wall might mean to the United States was recurrent as the French Emperor went from triumph to triumph. Even after the United States had, through a series of mischances, drifted into war with Great Britain, the former President could write, "Surely none of us wish to see Bonaparte conquer Russia and lay thus at his feet the whole continent of Europe. This done, England would be but a breakfast. . . . No. It cannot be to our interest that all Europe be reduced to a single monarchy."

The United States was spared the necessity of confronting such a situation. Napoleon was defeated, and the Congress of Vienna redrew the map of Europe in such a way as to provide a reasonable equilibrium of force among the major powers. For most of the century that followed, the European balance assumed the desirable form that Jefferson had defined in 1812, when he wrote, "We especially ought to pray that the powers of Europe may be so poised and counterpoised among themselves that their own safety may require the presence of all their force at home, leaving the other quarters of the globe in undisturbed tranquillity." The energies of the European governments were absorbed so completely in protecting the Vienna settlement against the threats posed by nationalism and industrialism that the United States had no reason to fear external interference as it went about the job of overcoming its internal divisions, extending its dominion to the shores of California, developing the economic potential of the united land mass, and laying the basis for its emergence at the end of the century as a power of the first rank. It was doubtless frustrating for politicians like Monroe and Calhoun, who longed to demonstrate that they could exploit the differences among European governments as effectively as Jefferson had done during his first term, to discover that this was no longer necessary and that policy could now, in fact, be made by proclamation; but most American leaders accommodated themselves easily enough to the advantages of being able, as Henry Clay said, "to pursue a course exclusively American, uninfluenced by the policy of My Lord Castlereagh, Count Nesselrode, or any other of the great men of Europe." So did the American people, who came, as the years passed, to regard this freedom as a natural state of affairs and one that would continue indefinitely.

By the end of the century, however, after the complicated but flexible Bismarckian version of the balance of power had begun to transform itself into what became the fragile bipolar balance between Triple Alliance and Triple Entente, there were ominous indications that this was a fallacy. American writers like Brooks Adams and Alfred Thayer Mahan responded to the new European conditions by seeking to awaken their countrymen to an awareness that their position had changed too, that it was unreasonable to talk about American isolation while the nation had economic interests in every part of the globe or to pretend indifference to foreign developments when instability abroad would have immediate repercussions on the American economy. In his essay *America's Economic Supremacy*, Adams described Germany and Russia as destabilizing factors in the European system, on the one hand, and the Far East on the other, and he intimated that it might become America's responsibility to preserve or restore the equilibrium of those areas. Among those who had the ear of President Theodore Roosevelt, it became doctrine that a policy of active intervention to preserve existing structures was in the American interest, and Henry Cabot Lodge was forever urging the President to use his authority to extricate the other powers from the messes they became involved in.

Roosevelt did not need much persuading. As early as 1897 he had repudiated isolationism as an outmoded idea, and in the first years of the new century his intervention in the ugly Moroccan dispute and his mediation in the Russo-Japanese War were experiments with a new activism designed to strengthen the equilibrium of forces. These interventions, neither of which was entirely happy in its results, were marked by a brash self-confidence that irritated the sensibilities of those old-world diplomats who did not, like Sir Arthur Nicholson at Algeciras, find it faintly comic, and by flashes of arrogance that ill-suited a nation that had for so long stood apart from the mainstream of politics. It is difficult to decide whether the presumption or the naïveté is the more pronounced in Lodge's letter of August 21, 1905, to the President: "Japan has got all we wanted her to get and all that she really needs, and it is not our interest or that of the world generally to have Russia too completely crippled."

In the decade that followed, the mere extension of American good offices in attempts to shore up deteriorating situations no longer seemed sufficient to these self-styled realists. The former diplomat Lewis Einstein, who pointed out in a series of articles that the European balance had for almost a century protected the United States and enabled it to avoid the burden of military expenditures, wrote in 1909 that its preservation might well require more positive commitments. It was high time, he wrote, that the lie be given to "the reverence with which we regard a misinterpreted tradition. Alliances can be entangling only when they are disadvantageous. To guard against their becoming so is the duty of a wise statesmanship." Four years later, impressed by the thought that German power was threatening to subvert the balance, Einstein was wondering whether it might not be necessary for the United States to extend the protection of the Monroe Doctrine to Great Britain.

Theodore Roosevelt carried this thinking a step further. As Europe came closer to war, the former President had a conversation with the German diplomat Baron von Eckhardstein, in which Roosevelt, rather indirectly, warned against a German policy that might weaken or destroy Great Britain's role of "keeping the balance of power in Europe." If Britain were no longer able to fulfill that function, he said, "the United States would be obliged to step in, at least temporarily, to reestablish the balance . . . never mind against which country or group of countries our efforts may have to be directed. In fact, we are becoming, owing to our strength and geographical situation, more and more the balance of the whole globe."

III

In addition to those political leaders and writers who were intent upon adjusting American foreign policy to shifts in the European balance of power and to the opportunities and problems that they posed for American interests, there were others whose minds dwelt more on the balance of ideas than on the mere equilibrium of physical force. To these intellectual descendants of the eighteenth-century *philosophes* and the militant radicalism of Thomas Paine, what was usually called the balance of power was merely the physical manifestation of absolutism and militarism, political reaction and religious obscurantism, the Holy Alliance and the Carlsbad Decrees, the Prussian corporal's cane and the Russian knout, and everything else that was inimical to freedom and individual rights.

In their view, it was the duty of the American republic, which had been conceived in liberty and dedicated to its maintenance, to support revolutions against this ideological system whenever and wherever they occurred, and in the first half of the nineteenth century there were frequent demands that the government come to the aid of national and liberal movements in other lands. The Monroe Doctrine was popular because it seemed to strike a blow for freedom not only in Latin America but in Europe as well, and the Greek revolution of the same period was hailed as a defeat for absolutism and the pretensions of the Holy Alliance. When the news from the Peloponnesus reached the United States, the highly respected *North American Review* demanded that the government give formal recognition to the revolutionary regime, and innumerable public meetings called for moral, financial, and even military assistance for the rebels. The United States Ambassador in France, Albert Gallatin, went so far as to propose that two or three frigates be sent to the Aegean in order to help destroy the Turkish fleet, and such leading members of Congress as Daniel Webster and Henry Clay wanted an open declaration of sympathy with the Greek cause and the sending of a commissioner to Athens.

Similarly, the year 1830 saw excited demonstrations of support for the July revolution in several American cities, and in Washington President Jackson and members of the Cabinet had no hesitation about appearing at them. The pattern was repeated in 1848, when the tide of revolution swept over Central Europe. The American government not only recognized the Frankfurt Assembly and appointed a minister to this provisional government but also dispatched an envoy to make contact with the revolutionary forces in Hungary. The suppression of the Hungarian revolution by Russian troops caused a storm of indignation in the United States that was more passionate and of longer duration than that caused by the repetition of those tragic events a hundred years later.

The bloodletting in Hungary appeared to threaten Europe with a return to the reactionary days of the Holy Alliance, and many Americans seemed to feel that their country should be prepared to intervene in the looming ideological struggle. In October 1851, at a banquet in London in honor of the Hungarian leader Kossuth, the former U.S. Secretary of the Treasury Robert T. Walker said that, if despotism should spread over the whole of the continent and if England were drawn into the struggle against it, the United States would take part "in the last great battle for freedom." And during Kossuth's subsequent trip to the United States he was entertained with a great deal of spread-eagle oratory about how nations outgrow the principles of foreign policy appropriate to their youth and how the day had come for the United States to abandon the defensive posture of the Monroe Doctrine and to take up the fight against European reaction.

Much of this rhetorical ardor was the by-product of the election campaign of 1852, in which the Democratic Party was trying to embarrass the Whigs by making it appear that their foreign policy was both negative and untrue to the principles of the American Revolution. Thus, Senator Stephen A. Douglas, who hoped to win the Democratic nomination, made speeches about defending the cause of European liberty that he probably never meant seriously and soon disavowed. But one cannot charge the movement known as Young America with this kind of disingenuousness. A militant group whose leaders included Edward de Leon, George N. Sanders, Pierre Soulé and William H. Seward, it managed to combine superheated patriotism, expansionism, national self-determination, and democratic internationalism in its philosophy, holding that democracy was the hope of the future and that the United States must lead its forward movement, with weapons in hand if necessary. In May 1852, George N. Sanders wrote in *The Democratic Review* that, in the ultimate clash between freedom and despotism, the United States and Russia would lead the opposing armies and that the confrontation was inevitable and at hand and should be welcomed.

The support that the United States actually gave to liberal and democratic movements in other countries was, in fact, moral in nature, rather than military. When the issues were fairly posed, the government always bethought itself of John Quincy Adam's sober answer to the ideological zealots. On July 4, 1821, Adams had said of his country: "Wherever the standard of freedom or independence has been or shall be unfurled, there will her heart, her benedictions, and her prayers be. But she goes not abroad in search of monsters to destroy. She is the well-wisher to the freedom and independence of all. She is the champion and vindicator only of her own." Even so, yielding to the cold logic of this advice left many Americans with a guilty conscience and a vague feeling that they had been untrue to the best instincts of their nation. For they had no doubt that the ideological struggle was a real one and that the United States was destined to be in the van when the victory came. *The Democratic Review* expressed this faith in 1852 in an article that declared: "The old nonsense about balance of power is wholly out of date, and the doctrine of the solidarity of mankind is beginning to spread; popular sovereignty is on the point of overcoming legitimacy quickly; every day the system, which is now restricted to Europe and America, is expanding; and soon it will embrace Asia, Africa and Oceania."

This One-World vision, as the German historian Günter Moltmann has called it, which inspired the radical Democrats of the 1850s, faded rapidly in the years of sectional conflict and civil war, and it did not revive until after the European system had collapsed of its own weight in 1914, and Woodrow Wilson had embarked upon his great crusade three years later. Wilson's declared purpose was to make the world safe for democracy, and how seriously he regarded that objective can be seen in his tactics during the negotiations with Prince Max von Baden in October 1918, which made the fall of the Hohenzollern dynasty inevitable. A necessary prerequisite for the creation of the new democratic order was the destruction of the balance-of-power system, which, to Wilson as to the mid-century Democrats, had been the mainstay of all the anti-democratic forces in Europe, the plaything of kings and soldiers and diplomats, and the wellspring of popular suffering for hundreds of years.

That the elimination of the classical diplomatic system was his first order of business, Wilson made perfectly clear in his speech to the United States Senate on the essentials of peace on January 22, 1917. In his moving address, which startled the President's future associates by calling for "a peace without victory," he declared:

> there must be not a balance of power but a community of power.... I am proposing that all nations henceforth avoid entangling alliances that draw them into competitions of power, catch them in a net of intrigue and selfish

[79]

rivalry, and disturb their own efforts with influences intruded from without. There is no entangling alliance in a concert of power. When all unite to act in the same sense and with the same purpose, all act in the common interest and are free to live their own lives under a common protection.

It was characteristic of Wilson that, in demanding that the modalities of the traditional diplomatic system be scrapped, he should insist that he was speaking not for himself or for his government but for the common people, and particularly for the fighting men of the free nations. In his speech at the Guildhall in London on December 28, 1918, he said that the soldiers of the Allied armies had

> fought to do away with an older order and to establish a new one, and the center and characteristic of the old order was that venerable thing which we used to call the "balance of power"—a thing in which the balance was determined by the sword which was thrown in the one side or the other; a balance which was determined by the unstable equilibrium of competitive interests; a balance which was maintained by jealous watchfulness and an antagonism of interests which, though it was generally latent, was always deep-seated. The men who have fought in this war have been the men from free nations who were determined that that sort of thing should end now and forever.

Grateful as they were for America's aid in defeating Germany, the European governments proved to be singularly resistant to this kind of exhortation and to its ideological implications, and their opposition was not slow in manifesting itself. The ardent Wilsonian Walter Lippmann wrote worriedly to a colleague in September 1918: "It is still more tremendously necessary to teach the European mind . . . that back of all our physical display lies a purpose which strikes at the roots of the old European system." He had reason to be concerned: the pupils rejected the lesson. Clemenceau, for one, was an unabashed supporter of the balance-of-power system, convinced that history had shown it to be the most effective regulator of the relationships among nations. He was not inclined to abandon it for what he considered to be the cloudy formulations of a doctrinaire schoolmaster from a country too young to appreciate the lessons of the past. Without being as brutally frank as the French Premier, the British and the Italians were inclined to agree. Like the negotiators at Vienna a hundred years earlier, they wanted to place the enemy under restraint, to assure themselves of appropriate territorial and economic compensation for their sacrifices, and, when that was done, to formulate a body of treaties and guarantees that would enable them to maintain the new status quo post bellum.

Their determination about following this traditional procedure was so strong that, in order to win their support for the League of Nations that he hoped would be able to prevent a return to the evils of the past, Wilson felt compelled to make concessions to it and to accept compromises that vitiated the Fourteen Points and defeated his hope of attaining a peace without victory. It is unnecessary to rehearse the details of a familiar story. Wilson's struggle at Paris for a just and lasting peace was gallant but unavailing. He was able to temper the most inordinate of the territorial demands of his associates, but the discrepancies between what the Fourteen Points had promised and what the Treaty of Versailles provided were still so palpable that Wilson's critics in America had no difficulty in arguing that he had betrayed his principles, while the nature of the settlement in general made the League of Nations, which he had hoped would be the symbol and embodiment of a new international order, appear to be merely an instrument in the hands of victorious powers who intended to use it to buttress their position. Indeed, in the American debate over the Treaty, the League was attacked as a subtle conspiracy to involve the United States in the old corrupt system of secret treaties and irresponsible commitments. Membership in Wilson's creation would, in the words of ex-Senator Albert Beveridge, "entangle the American nation in a European-Asiatic balance of power."

In the presidential election of 1920, the nation made it clear that it did not desire such entanglement.

IV

Despite the completeness of his defeat, Woodrow Wilson's influence upon American attitudes toward foreign policy in the subsequent period was profound. His eloquent denunciation of balance-of-power politics were not forgotten; indeed, they served to rationalize a policy of abstention from the affairs of post-Versailles Europe, which, in the course of the 1920s revealed itself to be, in spirit and practice, a somewhat less effective version of the system that had collapsed in 1914. Many of Wilson's staunchest supporters became isolationists in the postwar years, believing as firmly as ever in the essential correctness of the late President's analysis of the faults of the international system but disillusioned about the ability of the United States to do anything to correct them. Among them was Franklin Delano Roosevelt who, as vice-presidential candidate in 1920, had fought vainly for American adherence to the League of Nations.

Despite the attempts of revisionist historians after 1945 to portray Roosevelt as a man who burned with the desire to demonstrate his virtuosity on the world stage and who maneuvered his country into another war in order to gratify that desire, the most reliable evidence indicates that his isolationism was genuine and deeply felt and that he had not entirely overcome it when the Japanese took the power of decision out of his hands. His attitude toward Europe in the 1920s and during his first two terms as President was determined by the continuing popular rejection of Wilsonianism, by his disenchantment with the League as it proved incapable of controlling militarism and maintaining the public law, and by his aversion for war. As troubles multiplied in Europe and war once more became a distinct possibility, his first instinct was to stand clear. The United States, he believed, should remain a beacon of liberty and a model of sanity for other nations, but not a participant in their affairs.

His namesake's view in 1914 that, if the European balance were subverted, the United States would be obliged to step in and set it right, Franklin Roosevelt resisted until very late. His appeal to Adolf Hitler at the height of the Sudeten crisis to seek a solution by conference was accompanied by the somewhat embarrassed addendum, "The United States has no political involvements in Europe and will assume no obligations in the conduct of the present negotiations." In a letter to William Phillips after the Munich Conference, the President speculated about the American attitude if war came and talked about "[picking] up the pieces of European civilization" and helping the European peoples "save what remains of the wreck" after the fighting had stopped. He added, "If we get the idea that the future of our form of government is threatened by a coalition of European dictators, we might wade in with everything we have to give"; but he resisted this alternative long after many of his countrymen believed that the threat had become tangible.

After war came to Europe, his efforts to redress the balance in favor of the democracies were hesitant and slow in implementation (the destroyers-bases deal was not consummated until months after his announcement at Charlottesville in June 1940 that he was extending "the material resources of the nation" to the hard-pressed British), and he gave every appearance of leaning over backward to avoid the charge of wanting to repeat Wilson's unhappy adventure.

Once the United States had become a belligerent, American policy became surprisingly, and not altogether fortunately, Wilsonian in its approach to Europe. To the exasperation of the British allies, the President and his advisers were so conscious of the part played by secret treaties in the American people's rejection of Wilson's peace that they could hardly be induced to talk about the political aspects of the war at all, let alone about the territorial adjustments that would have to be made after the enemy's defeat. British suggestions that it might be well to have firm agreements with the Russians about postwar boundaries in northern Europe and the Balkans met automatic opposition from the Department of State, where the liveliest suspicions reigned concerning British desires to revive the worst aspects of classical diplomacy to the detriment of alliance solidarity. As Cordell Hull explained to Congress after his return from the Foreign Ministers Conference in Moscow in November 1943, there would, once the Four Power Declaration drafted there had taken effect, "no longer be any need for spheres of influence, for alliances, for balance of power, or any other of the special arrangements through which, in the unhappy past, the nations strove to safeguard their security or to promote their interests."

Six months later, when Lord Halifax asked what his attitude would be toward an Anglo-Soviet agreement that would define the degree of influence to be exerted by the two powers in Greece and Romania respectively, Hull protested that this would be a dangerous departure from past policy, principles and practice. In his memoirs, the Secretary of State wrote: "I was, in fact, opposed to any division of Europe or sections of Europe into spheres of influence. I had argued this strongly at the Moscow Conference. It seemed to me that any creation of zones of influences would inevitably sow the seeds of future conflict." He was not, Hull added, "a believer in the idea of balance of power or spheres of influence as a means of keeping peace"; he had studied the question during the First World War and was "grounded to the taproots in their iniquitous consequences."

The President was more pragmatic in his tactics than the Secretary of State and more willing to make concessions to imperious necessity, but he was historian enough to remember the cost of appearing to have condoned private arrangements, and he was, in any case, inclined to the view that political discussions should be postponed as far as possible until the military victory had been won. As a result, the traditional prejudice against balance-of-power politics made the early development of an American political strategy impossible, and in the last stages of the war the Soviet government took advantage of this to press more exorbitant demands than they might otherwise have done.

There is no reason to believe that this worried Roosevelt unduly, at least not until the very last months of his life. He was confident that the Grand Alliance would overcome differences about things like boundary lines and reparations and would form the nucleus of a global security organization that would be more effective in meeting the problems of maintaining peace than the old diplomatic system had ever been. In his last speech to Congress, he bravely expressed his belief that Allied solidarity at the recently concluded Yalta Conference promised to do away, once and for all, with unilateralism, exclusive alliances, spheres of influence, and balance of power.

V

Most Americans who heard that speech would probably have repudiated with indignation any suggestion that, within five years, the United States would be playing the major role in creating a new European balance and would, for the first time in its history, be concluding what to all intents and purposes was a permanently entangling alliance. When the NATO alliance was ratified in 1949, there was, of course, no very widespread understanding that it represented a diplomatic revolution. More than a quarter of a century later, when Secretary of State Henry Kissinger told the German journalist Theo Sommer that "the greatest change in American foreign policy is this, that we are permanently involved in world politics—for America . . . an entirely new experience," he was expressing a conclusion that had been reached only gradually.

In the first years after NATO's creation, there was a reluctance to admit that any long-term commitment had been made; and this was apparent both in Republican attacks upon the defensive nature of containment and in John Foster Dulles' policy of liberation or rollback, which, for a time at least, embodied an optimism about ending the ideological war with a definitive victory that was as unalloyed as that of the Young Democrats of the 1850s. But the liberation policy came to a sorry end in the double crisis of Suez and Hungary in 1956, and the shock caused by the successful Soviet launching of *sputnik* a year later and the confidently menacing tone of Khrushchev's Berlin ultimatum in 1958 made the status quo seem to be desirable and its maintenance a sensible policy goal. This implied a permanent U.S. role in supporting the balance, since without it there was little doubt that the Soviets could take Berlin and anything else they wanted. The construction of the Berlin Wall in 1961 only emphasized this.

As a result, balance-of-power politics, regarded by John Adams and Thomas Paine as a characteristic expression of the corrupt political system from which the colonies had escaped, by Woodrow Wilson as the principal cause of war between nations, and by the isolationists of 1920 as the sinister reality behind the League of Nations, which would erode American liberty if the United States joined the world community, was soon being practiced openly by American diplomats and on an increasingly elaborate scale. "We must," Secretary of State Kissinger told a group of United States Ambassadors in London in December 1975, "balance off Soviet power around the world through a combination of political, military, and economic means. In the Far East, the People's Republic of China must be a part of our political calculations. In the Middle East ... we must pursue ... a policy relevant to regional balance." As for Europe, where the balance between NATO and the Warsaw Pact had become more stable after the resolution of the Cuban missile crisis in 1962, and where the West German treaties with Poland and the Soviet Union, the Four Power Agreement on Berlin, and the decisions reached at the European Security Conference in Helsinki had reduced the possibility of military violation of existing frontiers, it became the keystone of the new multidimensional balance-of-power system. "Western Europe," Mr. Kissinger said, "continues to be the backbone of our foreign policy."

The American people have supported this European commitment with remarkable steadfastness. At the Teheran Conference Franklin Roosevelt told Marshal Stalin that the United States did not plan to maintain a peacekeeping force in Europe after the war, a statement that doubtless pleased the Soviet leader. Almost 35 years have passed since this meeting, and our forces are still in Europe; and neither the balance-of-payments problem, nor exasperation over the not infrequent foot-dragging of some of our allies on the question of military contributions, nor the traumatizing entanglement in Southeast Asia has destroyed our willingness to keep them there. This, as *The Washington Post* said not long ago, is "a demonstration of constancy of historical dimensions." The American people seem to have reached the conclusion, after two world wars, that the United States cannot safely ignore what happens to the European balance of power.

[87]

But they have also acquired a lively awareness that the balance of power cannot be maintained by military, diplomatic and economic means alone, and that, unless the balance of ideas is in our favor, the other means are bound to fail. The recent row over the so-called Sonnenfeldt doctrine was the result of an uneasy feeling that the government was perhaps forgetting this, and that Helmut Sonnenfeldt's undifferentiated description of Eastern Europe as a natural sphere of Soviet influence—which the *Frankfurter Allgemeine Zeitung* described as "elephantine trampling on the rights and sensibilities of people living under actual or threatened Soviet domination"—could only give the impression that we had lost faith in our ideals and were attempting to maintain our position by the crudest and most ignoble kind of Realpolitik.

Similarly, the concern about whether NATO could survive Communist participation in the governments of Italy and France, which some of our European critics have ascribed to American failure to understand the evolution of the Communist parties of Western Europe and their growing independence from Moscow, is really the result of a not unreasonable suspicion that, if the democratic parties in Europe cannot hold their own against communism in the battle for men's minds, it would be idle to suppose that American assistance would do them any good. If there is a revival of isolationism in the United States, it will not be because Americans have reverted to their nineteenth-century fear of entangling alliances, but rather because they have concluded that the balance of ideas in Europe has become so unfavorable to democracy that such alliances would serve no useful purpose.

It was perhaps to forestall that possibility that, in his Alastair Buchan Memorial Lecture in London on June 25, 1976, Secretary of State Kissinger, while telling his European auditors that they had no reason to fear competition with communism, in view of the military strength and economic superiority of the Western alliance, placed less emphasis upon the balance of power than upon the balance of ideas, and reminded his allies that, "if there is an ideological competition, the power of our ideas depends only on our will to uphold them."

[FOUR]

America and East Asia

John Paton Davies

Although he had understood that the Chinese were "droll in shape and appearance," George Washington was in 1785 taken aback to learn that they were not white. For their part, the Chinese viewed Americans as a new and insignificant breed of Europeans and, like the Europeans, barbarian, intrusive, hairy and malodorous.

Two hundred years ago East Asia and the new American nation were separated not only by the world's biggest ocean but also by the wilderness of most of the North American continent. And so, while Columbus had come upon America by sailing westward, the first American ship to make its way to East Asia, in 1784, did so by sailing in the opposite

---

John Paton Davies was an American Foreign Service officer from 1931 until 1954. He served in China, the U.S.S.R., and Germany, and as a member of the Policy Planning Staff. He is the author of *Foreign and Other Affairs* and *Dragon by the Tail: American, British, Japanese and Russian Encounters with China and with One Another.*

direction, through two oceans—the Atlantic and the Indian—and past three continents—Europe, South America, and Africa.

Thus, East Asia was for Americans the most remote part of the earth, and its various civilizations the most exotic. Even some 80 years later, after the purchase of Alaska, when across the 36 miles of Bering Strait, Asia became the nearest continent to the United States, it was still true that no cultures were more alien to Americans than those of China, Japan, Korea and Southeast Asia.

And yet, it was to East Asia that the greatest outpouring of American altruism flowed. It was also the area in which Americans fought four major wars—more than anywhere else overseas. The Spanish-American, Pacific, Korean and Indochinese wars were conducted in eight East Asian countries: the Philippines, China, Burma, Japan, Korea, Vietnam, Laos and Cambodia. The United States also intervened militarily in Korea, in China, and in the Russian Far East during the Russian Revolution.

So while the people of East Asia were acquainted with manifestations of ardent American idealism, they also on occasion had brought home to them expressions of American displeasure.

In no other part of the world did the United States more persistently and actively oppose imperialism and what is regarded as attempts by others to create hegemonies. But it was in East Asia (and the Caribbean) that the United States forcibly acquired colonies. In recklessly seizing the Philippines from Spain, the United States got a colony about the size of Italy and made itself an imperial power.

Events beyond the shores of the United States, however, either had little effect on Americans or, if perceived as threatening, usually stimulated a sense of national unity. The strongest exceptions to this occurred in East Asia. One was the so-called "loss of China" which at mid-twentieth century was so exploited by politicians and publicists as to foment morbid distrust and disunity in domestic American political life. The other was the disastrous American involvement in Indochina, which created widespread rancor and cynicism deeply disrupting national cohesion.

Nearly two centuries of relations with East Asia have been a costly experience for the United States both physically and psychologically.

II

Of all of the countries of East Asia it was China that Americans found most alluring. It was the biggest and richest and it seemed to hold promise of fat profit for traders. For those who felt called to save souls, it contained an abundance of them in challengingly heathen condition.

The Chinese made no attempt to encourage Americans in these assumptions. They were above being flattered by the interest shown in them, for they deemed themselves to be the only civilized people under heaven and all others to be barbarian. The Confucian literati who administered the Chinese Empire viewed their own merchants as a contemptible lower class, and foreign trade in the tradition of the exchange of tribute from vassal states and gifts benevolently bestowed on obsequious tribute-bearers by the Son of Heaven. In this make-believe context they condescended to permit Americans—as they had allowed Europeans—to trade, but only at Canton and under restrictions resembling house arrest.

Chinese officialdom's attitude toward American and European missionaries was, in the 1830s, when the first American evangelists arrived, even less benevolent. Because the authorities at that time considered Christianity to be subversive of public morality and decorum, its propagation was punishable by strangulation. The earliest American preachers therefore prudently masqueraded as merchants and bided their time, foregoing the heavenly rewards of martyrdom.

Being newcomers to the Far East, relatively few in number, and without the ready protection of their navy, the Americans at Canton in the early nineteenth century were cautious in their relations with the Chinese authorities, who described them as becomingly "submissive." The Yankee traders left it to the British to take the initiative in pressing for more liberal treatment of foreigners. While the Americans developed their own particular trade in New England ginseng (a root fancied by the Chinese as a virility-booster), furs and Hawaiian sandalwood in exchange for tea, porcelains and silk, Yankee shrewdness and avarice drew many of them into less innocent traffic.

The British had built up a lucrative business in the export to China of Indian opium. Enterprising American traders followed in the British wake and even introduced opium brought from as far as the eastern Mediterranean. Some of the considerable profit from pushing the drug was applied to creating infrastructure for westward expansion in the United States. One of the railroads that got off to a good start on opium was the Chicago, Burlington & Quincy.

Chinese objection to the debauching influence of opium was not the sole cause of the Opium War. The flourishing drug traffic had also upset the trading balance, and this led to a drain on China's silver. The reaction of the Imperial Commissioner at Canton was to seize and, without compensation, burn the stocks of opium awaiting sale. The British retaliated with naval action initiating the First Anglo-Chinese War, better known as the Opium War.

As neutrals, American traders fared nicely during the hostilities, taking over much of the British commerce, including opium. Subsequently, they benefited from the trading concessions exacted by the British from the Chinese in the Treaty of Nanking in 1842. Two years later Caleb Cushing, the first American envoy to China, concluded with the Imperial Commissioner the Treaty of Wanghsia, which duplicated the concessions already yielded, and granted extra-territorial rights to Americans, exempting them from Chinese civil and criminal jurisdiction. Then, through most-favored-nation privileges American missionaries benefited from a French-Chinese treaty providing for toleration of Christianity.

So, in the case of Yankee businessmen, trade followed the flag—the Union Jack. And with American missionaries, the cross followed the flag—the Tricolor. It was all relatively effortless—beneficiary imperialism. And thus it continued through the nineteenth century as the Europeans "opened" China by force and the threat of force.

The importunate West (including the Americans) took for granted that its intrusions were righteous. For did they not convey the material benefits of trade and the intangible blessings of enlightenment and salvation? At the same time, out of practical considerations, the Westerners were careful to confirm by treaties the legitimacy of their intrusions.

To the obdurate Chinese, the intrusions of the West were outrageous. Trade with the West, when not corrupting or depleting, was regarded by the Court and the mandarinate as essentially frivolous: what of significance could barbarians add to the refined abundance of the Middle Kingdom? Most offensive, of course, was the persistent, insatiable encroachment, not only in commerce but also in religious proselytization. As for the treaties, they were not freely negotiated: they were imposed upon the Chinese and so came to be designated by them as "unequal treaties"—a rallying slogan for anti-foreignism well into the twentieth century.

III

Japan was something else for the Americans. Europeans in

the late eighteenth and early nineteenth centuries had not been able to establish a foothold in Japan as they had at Canton. So Americans approached that country independently, on their own.

They were not welcome. No less xenophobic than the Chinese, the Japanese rebuffed American efforts to gain acceptance. It was not until 1849 that Commodore James Glynn, with a show of naval strength, induced the Japanese to treat with an American, himself, and release shipwrecked American seamen detained by them. Four years later Commodore Matthew C. Perry and his four "black ships" arrived in Edo Bay intent on opening a nation that wanted only to be left alone.

As in the case of China, American motives toward Japan were a jumble of high-mindedness and scruples of lesser elevation. It was not unusual for Americans to speak of obligations resting upon the United States to bestow civilization, progress and Christianity upon Japan. More prosaically, the islands were thought to offer rich commercial opportunities, although not on the scale of China's. Also, American whaling and shipping interests wanted relations with Japan that would protect vessels and crews in distress on the uncharted shores of the archipelago and provide supply, particularly coaling, facilities for ships plying the western Pacific.

For a people who exulted in opening and conquering the breadth of a continent, the impulse was strong to expand American influence to the forbidding, tantalizing islands across the North Pacific. To bring Japan into the family of nations would gratify the national ego. For the naval officers who were to play a leading and prominent role in the enterprise, the opportunities for promotion and renown were stimulating.

Perry and Townsend Harris, the first American civilian representative, forced themselves upon Japan at a time of turbulent change in that country. The origins of the unrest were both foreign and domestic. The foreign causes were recurrent alien pressures for the opening of Japan. On top of these came Britain's defeat of China in the Opium War, a frightening omen of what could readily befall Japan. Then the brusque American intrusion revealed Japan's weakness, alarmed its inhabitants and confronted them with the urgent need to devise means for coping with the external threat.

The Japanese were not bound by a comprehensive world view and did not preen themselves on being the only civilized people, as did the Chinese—and the West. They had much less of the smug ethnocentrism that immobilized the Chinese in complacency. The anti-foreignism of the Japanese spurred them to learn from the source that threatened them. Soon after the Perry visitation, the authorities established an Institute for the Investigation of Barbarian Books. The Japanese interest lay, as it had from early contacts with the West, in learning what made the intruders strong, in weapons, science and technology. But Western political philosophy and religion were considered to be disruptive of public order and morality, and so were ignored.

What to do about the foreign menace was entangled with the domestic crisis, the nature of which was not fathomed by most American officials at that time. The existing feudal system, in which an overlord, the Tokugawa Shogun, exercised a qualified hegemony over a variety of local military lords, was in the final stages of decay. It had replaced in the seventeenth century a centralized imperial system derived from the example of China, but it had not extinguished the monarchy. Successive emperors and their Courts endured. They did so in reduced circumstances and were paid little attention. But they were not repudiated.

The social decomposition of the mid-nineteenth century was marked by famines and economic dislocation, impoverished peasants and villagers disrupting the cities, a decline in the Shogunate's power, and the rise of outlying clans which had not been brought thoroughly under the sway of the Tokugawa House. The sinews of power in the feudal system were the samurai, a hereditary aristocratic warrior class, by tradition fiercely loyal to their lords, whose domains they administered. Those pledged to the Tokugawa Shogun and his supporters had over the course of two settled centuries lost much of their tempered martial edge and become sedentary bureaucrats and scholars, but intellectually less fettered than the Chinese literati. In contrast, the samurai of the recalcitrant clans retained much of the rigorous militancy of old.

In the turmoil and bloodshed of the 1860s the issues were mixed. In simplified definition they were: whether to persist in the policy of seclusion and so risk foreign attack or to accept open relations with foreign countries; and whether to sustain the Tokugawa Shogunate, or to seek collaboration between the Shogunate and the Imperial House, or to unify the country under the Emperor as the atavistic embodiment of Japanese nationalism.

Forces advocating nationalistic unification of the country under the Emperor and acceptance of foreign relations won. They were led by bold and intellectually venturesome young samurai of the restive southwestern clans. These purposeful young men, embracing a loyalty above that to their feudal lords, rose against the Shogun, in confused feudal conflict forced his abdication, and in 1868 installed the Emperor as supreme authority over all Japan.

This was the Meiji Restoration, so designated because Meiji was the name given to the reign of the Emperor Mutsuhito. During the 44 years of the Meiji era Japan underwent a transformation from handicrafts to heavy industries; from exegesis of Japanese mythology and Confucian classics to exploration and selective adoption of Western knowledge; from reclusive feudalism to expansive imperialism as a world power with a sense of ordained mission. Perry's purpose of "bringing a mighty Empire into the family of nations" was amply realized but not his pious dream that this be "within the influence of our benign religion."

The extraordinary phenomenon of the Meiji Restoration set Japan apart from other East Asian countries. And it revealed traits that were again apparent in the Pacific War and the remaking of Japan after defeat in 1945. Among these characteristics were a virile, affirmative hardihood and, paradoxically, rapid adaptability to changed circumstances. Furthermore, the Japanese showed no liking for one-man dictatorship, preferring collective decision-making and leadership. Although fierce internal disputes flared, the dominant characteristic was an unsurpassed national unity.

IV

Notwithstanding the profit, pride and moral satisfaction that Americans derived from East Asian ventures, that part of the world was, for the first century of contact, essentially of peripheral interest to the great majority of them. The center of American attention, the real national interest, was in the expanding and industrializing homeland. American trade with China hovered around one percent and with Japan two percent of total American foreign commerce.

Enthusiasm for American involvement in and across the Pacific flourished during the first 80 years of relations not so much in Washington officialdom as among American representatives in East Asia. Perry was disappointed that Washington did not share his eagerness for a more active policy toward Japan and for the extraction of concessions from China. Dr. Peter Parker, a medical missionary turned United States Commissioner to China, in serving God, Hippocrates and Mammon, pressed Washington to occupy Formosa and generally get tough with the Chinese in the furtherance of American business.

Korea, claimed as a vassal state by China, was in the 1880s the scene of outstanding individual initiatives by American representatives whom Washington had let out on a long, loose tether. The ambitious Commodore Robert W. Shufeldt pridefully opened the Hermit Kingdom in 1882, negotiating a commercial treaty that implied Korean independence of China. A year later another naval officer, Ensign George C. Foulk, became involved in Korean affairs and was quickly advanced to the position of chargé d'affaires of the American legation at Seoul, where he indulged in intrigues with the Japanese and Russians against devious Chinese efforts to maintain some semblance of sovereignty over Korea. Foulk was followed by Dr. Horace N. Allen, a missionary physician who for some ten years had also busied himself in scheming with the Japanese and Russians in what he conceived to be the advancement of Korean independence. Allen's continuing endeavors as American minister to Korea, were interrupted in 1894 by the Sino-Japanese War.

Perry, Parker, Shufeldt, Foulk and Allen were among the more aggressive American representatives in East Asia, implicating the United States in their striving for national (and personal) advantage and renown. They were not the last of their type, nor necessarily the most damaging to the long-term interest of the United States.

It was in Korea that the first political jostling occurred among the four countries that were to loom so large in the second half of the twentieth century—the United States, Japan, China and Russia. American intervention in Korea, official and private, was in an area of no real importance to the United States. But that peninsula was for the three countries closest to it of vital strategic concern—a corridor for attack by Japan against China or Russia, or by either of the latter two against

Japan. None of the three was more keenly aware of this than Meiji Japan.

As imperialism is an expression, in part, of anxiety, it is not surprising that Japan moved to expel China from Korea and deny it to Russia, which was looking greedily down into the peninsula from its newly established position in Vladivostok. The Sino-Japanese War of 1894 lasted less than a year, ending in a sweeping Japanese victory that astonished the West. From it the Japanese garnered Chinese recognition of Korean independence, cession of Formosa and the Pescadores to Japan, and a substantial indemnity. Japan was now launched as a modern imperialist power.

The Japanese had been apt pupils. They had learned well the lessons of the West. They had concentrated on the creation of a strong army and navy, which they put to decisive, disciplined use. So well had the Japanese absorbed the ways of the West that they spoke of the attack on China in terms of bestowing civilization on their former paradigm and of the hostilities as a holy war. Although satisfied that they had made it, that they were now members of the imperialist club, the Japanese did not for a moment assume that their mission was now completed.

Defeat at the hands of the despised Japanese was a nasty shock for the Chinese. A scramble for concessions by the European powers following the Japanese success further jolted the Chinese. Reformist elements in China clamored for a quickening of the torpid pace of modernization. The young Kuang-hsu Emperor responded by essaying the role of Mutsuhito and Peter the Great, issuing in 1898 a series of far-reaching reform edicts. His daring move was soon undone by sluggish and reactionary officials and by the Empress Dowager, Tsu Hsi, who imprisoned him and embarked on a retrograde reign.

V

Americans reacted to Japan's victory over China with surprised admiration of the victors, flavored with self-congratulation. Having pried the Japanese onto the world scene, Americans felt pride in the accomplishment of their protégés. Some Americans also thought that the Chinese had been taught a salutary lesson which might stir them from their stagnant state.

Other and less transitory opinions, some of them contradictory, shaped American attitudes toward East Asia in the last decade of the century. The slack American economy after the 1893 depression caused many businessmen to look hungrily to the fancied market of hundreds of millions of Chinese. They were anxious lest China be taken over piecemeal by European and Japanese imperialists, and American business be excluded. So they wanted Washington to pursue a vigorous policy in Asia. Those dedicated to the Christianization of the Orient likewise sought greater American involvement in East Asia. The support for proselytization, generated in virtually all American churches, was more pervasive than the economic pressure to intervene in the Far East.

A smaller body of opinion, but with disproportionately great influence in the government, was preoccupied with the dynamics of international power relationships. Its members held in varying degrees to a belief that those of Anglo-Saxon and northern European stock were superior to others, but that the United States was threatened by the swarming lesser breeds of Asia. The stridency of these warnings, incidentally, was echoed a half century later in the alarms sounded about the menace of international communism.

The aroused ideologues of the 1890s saw the encroachments upon China not only as threatening to exclude American business but also as a power struggle which might flame into a world war. Being at once anxious and purposeful, these proponents of Manifest Destiny—men such as Alfred T. Mahan, Brooks Adams, Theodore Roosevelt and Henry Cabot Lodge—advocated positive action in East Asia to protect American interests and maintain a balance of power. They were of an imperialist bent, affected by the zest for conquest—along with greed, vainglory and anxiety—that animated European and Japanese imperialists.

A provocative American policy toward Spain in the Caribbean exploded into war with that European nation, a most reluctant adversary. These hostilities provided a far-fetched excuse for seizure of the Philippine Islands. Roosevelt and Lodge were prime instigators of this heedless adventure. In high spirits most of the country went along with the escapade and the President, William McKinley, found justification for annexing the archipelago in pledging to save the souls of the Filipinos—a mission in which the Spaniards had been engaged for 300 years.

For their part, the Filipinos displayed a more lively concern for their temporal than for their spiritual condition. They had initially labored under a misapprehension regarding American intentions. They had assumed that liberation from Spain meant independence. When the Filipinos realized that their liberators intended to take the place of the Spaniards as their rulers, they began guerrilla resistance to the Americans that lasted from 1898 to 1902.

The United States thus became a full-fledged colonial power in East Asia—but without the obstinate resolve to make sure its imperialist pretensions. The Philippines were in no sense of vital interest to the American people. Whatever the shifting sentiments for economic, religious and political involvement in East Asia, they were not, however compelling at times, constant enough to sustain indefinitely an exposed strategic commitment on the other side of the Pacific. Particularly was this so because the vulnerable salient of

Manifest Destiny lay athwart the axis of Japanese southward expansion. Even Theodore Roosevelt, with maturity, came to confess that the Philippines were our Achilles' heel.

Annexation of the Philippines and Guam was a major American blunder. Its effects persisted for decades, contributing to the mutual antagonism growing between the United States and its best customer in East Asia—Japan.

One of the motives for taking the Philippines was to use the islands as a base from which to do business with China. The mirage of China as a vast and lucrative market and field for investment had enticed Americans for more than a century, and would continue to do so. But the Philippine connection was artificial and ineffective. The main effort to maintain and develop the American foothold in China took the form of diplomatic notewriting to the contending imperialist powers.

Among those in 1898 favoring a strong policy in support of China's resistance to European and Japanese encroachments was William W. Rockhill, who had served in China and was then the principal official in the Department of State dealing with Chinese affairs. The Secretary of State, John Hay, and President McKinley were more cautious. An Englishman, Alfred Hippisley, whom Rockhill had known in China as an official of the Chinese Maritime Customs, passed through Washington on vacation and presented to his American friend a formula for equal economic treatment of all foreign businesses in China. This they developed into a proposal that Hay and McKinley thought well of and which finally blossomed into what was called the doctrine of the Open Door.

The Open Door proposal was initially put forward in notes addressed by Hay in September 1899 to the governments claiming spheres of influence in China, asking, in effect, assurances of nondiscriminatory economic treatment of other foreign business in areas under their influence. Although addressed to foreign governments, the notes were meant by Hay also to placate those Americans clamoring for a more aggressive policy in China. The governmental responses to Hay's solicitations were at best wary. This did not deter Hay from proclaiming unanimous consent to his proposal. He won, thereupon, intemperate acclaim in the United States for his statesmanship.

Hay had not consulted with the Chinese about the Open Door notes. Nor was any notice taken of the Chinese opinion that the territorial concessions to foreigners, extracted under duress, were unjust. The Chinese therefore had no reason to be particularly grateful for what Washington had done.

In 1900 Hay expanded the Open Door doctrine with an imprudent pronouncement that it was American policy to "preserve Chinese territorial and administrative entity." This histrionic commitment, impossible of attainment, was typical of the hyperbole that too often afflicts presidential and secretarial pronouncements. Nevertheless, for half a century this inflated version of the Open Door was accepted by American officials as revealed scripture to be invoked against those who would wrong China.

In sum, the United States entered the twentieth century with an imperial obligation that the American people were not determined to fulfill, with illusions that China was an area of pregnant importance to the United States, with pledges to preserve that distant land's moot entity, and with reliance on expostulation as a force in international relations.

VI

Japan had taken Formosa from the Chinese; the United States had taken the Philippines from the Spaniards—and the Filipinos. Now it was Japan's turn: to take Manchuria from the Russians—and the Chinese.

The Russians had lumbered punitively into occupation of key parts of Manchuria following the anti-foreign Boxer uprising in China. There was little doubt in any quarter that St. Petersburg was intent on rounding out its Far Eastern position by acquiring at least Manchuria.

Washington, whose intent in Manchuria was visionary—expectations of extensive economic benefits—brooded over the Russian consolidation in Manchuria. On dealing with St. Petersburg, Hay commented to President Theodore Roosevelt in 1903: "Dealing with a government with whom mendacity is a science is an extremely difficult and delicate matter." Hay also reported that the American minister to China "has the pessimism about Russia which is almost universal out there. 'What's the use? Russia is too big, too crafty, too cruel for us to fight. She will conquer in the end. Why not give up and be friendly?' "

Mahan warned of Russia's advancing into China in a gigantic pincers move, through Manchuria and Central Asia, threatening China's survival and the future of Western civilization. Only the resistance of the sea powers, including Japan, Mahan asserted, could avert this catastrophe.

Whether Japan worried about the future of Western civilization is questionable. There is no doubt that it was anxious about its own future, with a Russia on the prowl moving into Manchuria. Would Korea be next?

Inevitably, Japan struck. The Russo-Japanese War lasted a year and a half, ending in 1905 with Japan, the victor, on the verge of exhaustion, Russia distracted by its 1905 revolution, and Roosevelt acting as peacemaker.

In so doing the American President won the appreciation of neither side. The Russians resented his pro-Japanese attitude at the outset, for he did not really dissemble his initial relief that Japan was "playing our game" in grappling with Russian expansion. And in the end the Japanese became disgruntled because they felt that at the Treaty of Portsmouth Roosevelt had shortchanged them on their due as the winners.

As Korea had in 1894 been the field of contention among

those four nations which were to become dominant in East Asia during the 1970s, so Manchuria was in the Russo-Japanese War the arena of four-way interaction among Russia and Japan as the combatants, China as the involuntary, ignored and victimized host of the event, and the United States as the honest broker.

Japan's acquisition of Russia's rights in South Manchuria and acknowledgment of Tokyo's paramount interest in Korea engaged Japan's attention on the Asian continent. Tokyo's compulsion to further continental expansion was bound to be directed at China, as being more vulnerable than Russia. As for Russia, the 1905 defeat was a temporary reverse. Another revolution and the passage of 40 years, then Russia would have its revenge.

Roosevelt foresaw a Russian "wish to play a return game of bowls." In-job training as President had advanced TR's understanding of power realities from the days when, as a callow Assistant Secretary of the Navy, he had dispatched Commodore Dewey on a cruise culminating in the Battle of Manila Bay. Now that he was President, Roosevelt's major concern in East Asia was to avoid the need for defending the Philippines.

To that end, Japan should be deflected from southward, oceanic expansion. Roosevelt therefore welcomed Japan's plunge into Manchuria but worried lest it be too easy and Tokyo's interest then turn southward. His preference was that Japan and Russia long be at inconclusive loggerheads. Above all, the United States could not cross Japan in Manchuria or otherwise give it cause for hostility.

With a realism seldom encountered in his successors, TR struck deals with Japan over spheres of influence. He sent his Secretary of War, William Howard Taft, to treat in 1905 with the Japanese Prime Minister for Japanese recognition of American preeminence in the Philippines in exchange for American acceptance of Japanese predominance in Korea.

More formally, in 1908, his Secretary of State, Elihu Root, and Japanese Ambassador Takahira exchanged notes in which the two governments undertook to respect one another's possessions in the Pacific, maintain the Pacific status quo and, of course, stand by China's independence and the Open Door.

Understandably, TR felt that he had done as well as could be expected in preventing a Japanese-American clash over territorial issues. But he recognized that what remained to be done was subtler and less tractable. This was the issue of racial and cultural prejudice in the United States. And it related to the Chinese as well as the Japanese.

American attitudes toward the Chinese and Japanese fluctuated and were often ambivalent. Orientals were by legend quaint, ceremonious, sage and at times fiendish. By the accounts of early sailors, traders and missionaries, Asians were honest, industrious, steeped in sin as much as vice, and prone to outbursts of bloody violence. It was generally thought in nineteenth-century America that Asians were so different from Americans—meaning the descendants of European colonists—as to be unassimilable in American society.

The first students and officials from China and Japan to visit the United States, coming to partake of the superior wisdom of the West, were appropriately greeted with friendly, patronizing curiosity. But with the immigration of laborers in growing numbers, Americans reacted with mounting hostility, particularly in the western states. The thousands of Chinese who were brought in during the second half of the nineteenth century for unskilled work in opening the West were viewed by American labor as an economic threat—excessively hard working and impossibly frugal. The Chinese were treated abominably and from time to time were murdered, singly and collectively, both gratuitously and with impunity. Without gunboats on the Sacramento and Potomac, China discovered that protests over American barbarities were ineffectual.

By the turn of the century Americans began to look

apprehensively over their western shoulder, across the Pacific, at the Asian hordes which Mahan and less respectable theoreticians proclaimed could outbreed, overproduce, under-sell and perhaps even subjugate the United States. After Japan's defeat of Russia, anti-Japanese sentiment and behavior on the West Coast intensified. Tokyo, which had been beguiled by the widespread American support for Japan in the war, was shocked by the California racism, and so in 1906 protested to Washington.

Tokyo's protest went to the issue—racism—that Roosevelt believed to be more ominous for American-Japanese relations than that of territorial expansion. While the President, too, had expressed concern about a yellow peril, he had no patience with manifestations of racism that compromised his policy of appeasing Japan. He felt that the Japanese were too dangerous to offend. Secretary Root warned that they were proud, sensitive, ready for war and could take the Philippines, Hawaii and "probably the Pacific Coast."

The Pacific Coast whites were not much moved by Washington's entreaties for tolerance. However, in 1907 Roosevelt improvised a Gentlemen's Agreement with Tokyo for limiting Japanese immigration. But this could not for the Japanese (and other Asians) remove the insult of racial discrimination—for the United States at the same time con-tinued to welcome a flood of European immigrants.

The year 1907 was a strenuous one for Roosevelt. He sent the American battle fleet around the world to reassure the Californians, arouse national enthusiasm for a bigger navy, show off in front of the Japanese (who handled the visit with tact and hospitality), and flaunt the flag in improbable places. At the same time, the United States underwent a war scare, with rumors of numerous Japanese spies at large and Japanese preparations to attack. The talkative TR added his bit to the atmosphere of unease by wondering out loud to the German

Ambassador whether the Japanese might land on the Pacific Coast and inflict a devastating initial defeat on the defenders. The Americans would, he reassured the envoy, of course rally to triumph in the end.

Roosevelt set the Navy to work on a war plan for hostilities against Japan. Although the admirals reckoned that any crisis with Japan was well in the future, they dutifully produced a strategic Orange Plan, against Japan.

The virulent anti-Japanese manifestations in the United States caused the Japanese government and its army and navy high commands to reexamine their assumption that relations with the United States were amicable and likely to continue to be so. This assumption had proceeded primarily from a belief that possible friction over territorial expansion had been rationally disposed of by mutual agreement on spheres of influence. The understanding appeared to have been effective: Washington was not contesting Japan in Korea and Manchuria, and Tokyo had, from early in the American conquest of the Philippines when it turned down Emilio Aguinaldo's plea for help in his resistance to American rule, refrained from trespassing on that American preserve.

So imperial rivalry was not the main cause of the trans-Pacific tension. The cause was primarily American racism, as regards both discriminatory immigration and agitation regarding the yellow peril. This racism acutely offended and baffled the Japanese. The imperial army and navy revised their list of potential enemies. Russia remained as definitely the most likely foe. But, although they felt that the threat was not near, the United States was ranked number two.

At the time that Perry opened Japan, the Japanese desperately wanted to keep the Americans out of their country and feared attack by the white peril. Fifty-four years later Americans desperately wanted to keep Japanese out of their country and feared attack by a yellow peril.

In the tragic absurdity of the American experience in East Asia, the United States and Japan had in the first decade of the twentieth century swung onto collision course.

VII

President William Howard Taft and his Secretary of State, Philander C. Knox, sharply altered American East Asia policy. No longer was an expanding Japan the focus of attention. Nor were the central concerns to divert Japan's aggressions westward, to maintain agreement regarding American and Japanese spheres of influence, and studiously to avoid, as far as possible, giving offense to the Japanese.

From 1909 a palsied China was Washington's main interest in East Asia. The Taft Administration's principal concerns were to broaden American economic activities in China, to strengthen China, and to preserve "our historic policy," meaning the Open Door. Taft and Knox believed that American economic expansion should be directed so as to contribute to the reform, development and independence of China. This was part of what they infelicitously called Dollar Diplomacy. Profit and altruism would thus go hand in hand.

The President and Secretary extended this touching concept to, among other worthy projects, a proposal for neutralizing Manchuria's railways under international control, wherein American influence would press for international collaboration to the benefit of all concerned. Taft and Knox appeared to have actually supposed that this vision of sharing and "fair play" (frequently invoked by Knox) would appeal to the contending powers in Manchuria. The end result was that the British, from whom Knox had hoped for support, backed away in embarrassment and the Japanese and Russians overcame their mutual antipathy enough to agree in rebuffing the

American meddling, and then entrenched themselves more firmly in, respectively, south and north Manchuria.

Nor did Dollar Diplomacy captivate Wall Street, where the dollars for the diplomacy were to come from. It was necessary for the Administration to press American capitalism to invest in China. E. H. Harriman, who toyed with the idea of a round-the-world railway, and several reluctant New York financiers joined in an ill-starred railway loan. But in general, Wall Street was distinctly loath to become involved in China.

After four years of Dollar Diplomacy, American investments in China were slightly more than one percent of total American investments overseas, up 0.2 percent over what they had been more than a decade earlier. American exports to China declined from the Roosevelt days, and during Taft's tenure of office fluctuated around one percent of all American exports.

East Asian policy under Taft was essentially a moral endeavor. Knox spoke of the American dollar aiding suffering humanity. He declared that "it would be much better for us to stand consistently by our principles even though we fail in getting them generally adopted." Whether Americans would go to war for his policy was "academic," Knox asserted; what was important was that the United States stick to its principles without compromise. And "our historic policy," the Open Door, must be preserved, thus making a policy a dogma.

Taft and Knox were abetted, if not inspired, by two zealous young diplomats, Willard Straight, chief of the Division of Far Eastern Affairs, and Francis M. Huntington Wilson, whom Knox appointed as first assistant secretary of state. Both abominated the Japanese, their culture and their encroachments on the mainland. With compensating ardor, they championed an idealized China and argued that broad support of China was in the American national interest. Straight, a restless political romantic, envisioned in 1907 Americans

[111]

"empire shaping" China. These two virtuosos were among the more effective, alas, of the bright young men with a mission who occasionally enlivened the pin-striped ranks of American diplomacy.

Appalled by Taft's policy, Roosevelt in 1910 gave his successor the benefit of his thoughts, here summarized. It was in the vital interest of the United States "to keep the Japanese out of our country" and at the same time to retain their good will. Manchuria and Korea were of vital interest to Japan. Therefore the United States should not do anything in Manchuria that might lead Japan to feel menaced by the United States.

Alignment with China, Roosevelt continued, would be for the United States a liability because of China's military helplessness. The Open Door had been and would be an excellent thing insofar as it was maintained by general diplomatic agreement. But the history of Manchuria showed that the Open Door disappeared when a powerful nation was determined to disregard it and was willing to risk war in so doing. The United States could prevent Japan from acting as it pleased in Manchuria only if Washington was ready to go to war. And to succeed in such a war would take "a fleet as good as that of England plus an army as good as that of Germany."

But Taft did not think that Tokyo would go to war over Dollar Diplomacy in Manchuria. In this he was right, for the awkward reason that his Manchuria policy was a fiasco and it was hardly necessary for Japan to move a muscle.

Japan had adjusted to the shock of racial discrimination in the United States and drawn therefrom certain strategic conclusions. Now Taft, whom the Japanese had considered to be friendly, who had negotiated for Roosevelt a sphere-of-influence agreement with the Japanese government, was trying to undermine Japan's position in Manchuria and was generally displaying anti-Japanese and pro-Chinese attitudes. Why this change when American trade with Japan, in contrast to that with China, was growing? Why this irrational American partiality for China? The Japanese concluded that with the evident increase of American ill-will toward them they must redouble their efforts to gain strength from the continent.

VIII

Woodrow Wilson's intervention in Siberia was the first American military interference in a Communist revolution swollen into a civil war. It was not an auspicious beginning to such undertakings.

The origins of this misbegotten enterprise stemmed from Russia's withdrawal from World War I and the consequent redeployment of large bodies of German troops to the western front. The British and French pled with Wilson to renew hostilities in the East, but he believed that this would be a misapplication of American resources. Persistent Allied entreaties overcame Wilson's better judgment and the advice of his chief of staff. In July 1918 he invited Japan to join in dispatching not more than 7,000 troops each to Siberia.

Wilson's ostensible reason for sending an American expeditionary force to a civil war zone in the depths of Asia, thousands of miles from the nearest conceivable front against the Germans, was to facilitate the consolidation of two groups of Czechs, released prisoners of war, at large somewhere in Siberia. The President wanted the Czechs to "get into successful cooperation with their Slavic kinsmen and to steady any efforts at self-government or self-defense in which the Russians themselves may be willing to accept assistance." Which of the several warring factions of Slavic kinsmen Wilson had in mind is not clear. In addition to troops, he proposed sending a commission composed of merchants, agronomists, labor advisers, Red Cross representatives and

[113]

YMCA "agents." They would extend an American helping hand to the troubled Russians.

The scatterbrained performance by Wilson obviously could not satisfy the Allies. But those powerful Japanese who wished to set up a puppet regime in eastern Siberia to protect extensive Japanese economic interests there welcomed the invitation to intervene.

The unfortunate commander of the American contingent, Major General William S. Graves, was given as his directive a copy of an American aide-mémoire circulated to Allied governments in which it was emphasized that the American government could not take part in nor sanction in principle military intervention in Russia. Thus enlightened, the steadfast General Graves left for Vladivostok to intervene without intervening. One day before he arrived, the two groups of wandering Czechs met and promptly joined those of their Slavic kinsmen who were fighting their Bolshevik Slavic kinsmen. This diposed of the main reason for the general's expedition. Before long it became apparent that the Japanese had injected into Siberia a force not of 7,000 but 72,000.

For a year and a half, until the Americans were withdrawn, Graves struggled to keep his forces from becoming embroiled with the Bolsheviks, the various shades of Whites, and his allies, the Japanese. That he succeeded was in nowise due to support from the French, the British or the Department of State. To the contrary, they urged that he intervene actively against the Bolsheviks and when he demurred on the grounds of his directive, they tried to have him replaced.

Wilson's Russian intervention not only did not accomplish the farcical objective that he set for it, it did not prevent the Japanese from intervening in large numbers and remaining long after the Americans had gone. It did not and could not have affected the ultimate outcome of the Russian civil war. But it did entail real risks of serious American involvement in that war, which could not have benefited the United States in any way.

The Bolsheviks represented the American-Japanese intervention as, of course, a typical imperialist attempt to crush the just uprising of Russian workers and peasants. This was a convenient propaganda theme, not only in attracting domestic sympathy but also in supporting Communist claims for accuracy of historical interpretation.

From the strategic point of view, Lenin was much interested in the bad blood between the Americans and Japanese in Siberia. Regarding the hostility between the United States and Japan he said, "The practical task of Communist policy is to take advantage of this hostility and to incite one against the other. . . . We have already set Japan and America at loggerheads, to put it crudely, and have thereby gained an advantage."

This would have had a familiar ring to Theodore Roosevelt.

IX

In the triangular relationship of the United States, Japan and China from World War I to Pearl Harbor, Japan was, with few exceptions, the actor, China the acted upon. And the United States was the self-appointed referee who judged by subjective rules and called fouls without penalties, until just before the end of the contest. This provoked the actor into a suicidal attempt to kill the referee.

Japan's aggressiveness in this 1914–1941 period began with the seizure of the German concession, and more, in Shantung, then intervention in the Russian Revolution—in acrimonious collaboration with the United States—occupation of parts of Siberia and the Maritime Province, the conquest of Manchuria, the invasion of China, the occupation of Indochina through coercion of Vichy, and the attack on Pearl Harbor.

Americans had—and still have—difficulty in understanding the intensity and breadth of the fatal Japanese compulsion to empire and, ultimately, Co-Prosperity Sphere. By the late 1930s the Japanese were in a frame of mind that was at once exalted and desperate. The reasons for this were diverse and cumulative.

With the Meiji Restoration the Japanese concluded that their scant, shaggy, green mystic islands could no longer accommodate their growing numbers, accomplishments and ambitions. They sought living space through peaceful emigration to the United States, as Europeans were doing. But they were repulsed, with insults, because of their race. These wounds of pride, repeatedly inflicted, rankled deeply and long.

The Japanese assumed that they had as much need and right to extend their domain as Britain, France, and the Netherlands had, and surely more than the sprawling United States and Russia, each so bountifully endowed. The Americans had welcomed the first Japanese ventures in imperialism. Then the Americans had inexplicably taken the side of China. Next, the Americans and the Soviet Russians declared that imperialism was evil and that Japan must not encroach on China. The Japanese took this moralizing to be hostile—and hypocritical, considering the record of the two proctors.

Russia, the Eurasian giant, had begun as the Duchy of Muscovy and then by Slavic subjugation of Tatars, Torguts, Buryats, Kazakhs, Uzbeks, Yakuts and many other non-Russian peoples made itself an empire extending from Europe across the width of Asia. Yet this was not enough for the Russians. So they contested with Japan for China—until they Bolshevized themselves. Whereupon they denounced Japan for being imperialist, while plotting to subvert the Japanese.

As for the Americans, the land they occupied had been inhabited by red-skinned people until small bands of Europeans invaded it, were reinforced by multitudes of their kind, and then by subjugation of Mohicans, Iroquois, Cherokees, Sioux, Paiutes and many other non-Europeans—and importation of black slaves from Africa—made for themselves a white empire extending across the width of North America. Yet this was not enough for the white Americans. So they took, among other places, the Philippines.

And now in the 1930s, Russia and the United States, these two glutted powers, were telling Japan that it could not overrun a backward and bandit-ridden Manchuria and open it up with railroads and industry as Russia had done in its subjugated areas of Central Asia and Siberia, and the United States in its great Southwest, an area taken not only from Indian tribes but also from Mexico. Furthermore, why was it acceptable for the Americans to maneuver the detachment of a part of Colombia to create the state of Panama and immoral for Japan to detach Manchuria from China to create Manchukuo?

If Americans had deemed it laudable to pursue their Manifest Destiny, could the Japanese rightly be denied the same? If Britain nobly bore the white man's burden in India, was Japan not entitled to carry high the yellow man's burden in China—to perform, as the French were pleased to put it, their civilizing mission, if necessary doing so by force? If the Americans were justified in imposing a Monroe Doctrine in the Western Hemisphere and in assuming the role of patron of a Pan-American system, might not Japan do the same in East Asia and for Pan-Asianism—the Greater East Asia Co-Prosperity Sphere?

To such questions the sated power answered: "Ah, but the time for empire-building has passed. We have put that behind us, and you must, too. We are now all pledged to self-determination."

The Japanese concluded in the 1930s that the Americans were consummate hypocrites and that out of sheer malice and illogical partiality to China they were determined to deny

Japan its rightful fulfillment. They reacted to the moralistic and legalistic admonitions of the two Secretaries of State of that decade, Henry Stimson and Cordell Hull, with angry contempt. They had discovered that Washington would not follow strong language with corresponding action, even when the imperial army sank an American warship, the U.S.S. *Panay*. Americans were bluffers, Tokyo assumed, and not to be taken seriously.

Haunted by the insufficiencies of their home islands, bitterly resentful over racial discrimination by Americans, apprehensive over the ultimate intentions of the Soviet Union and the United States, infuriated by American efforts to frustrate their expansion into China, and exhilarated by fervent national pride, native dynamism, a sense of crisis and a conviction of divine destiny, the Japanese in the late 1930s were psychologically ready for the fateful plunge southward—and into war with the United States.

The war in Europe provided the final impetus for the southward advance. The German conquest of France and the Netherlands left Indochina and the Netherland East Indies temptingly exposed. Germany's assault on the Soviet Union then removed the threat on Japan's western flank, a major restraint on a southward thrust.

Washington placed gradual restrictions on the sale to Japan of petroleum and iron products, culminating in the freezing of Japanese assets. The Dutch closed down on the sale of Sumatran oil. These actions imposed a time limit on Tokyo. Deprived of its traditional sources of oil and with its reserves steadily declining, Tokyo calculated that it had until November to negotiate acceptable terms for the resumption of American and Indies oil supply. If these peaceful overtures did not succeed by late November, then Japan must irrupt southward to the oil and other strategic raw materials of Southeast Asia.

American-Japanese negotiations, muddied by misunder-

[118]

standings, failed. Tokyo would not accept Washington's position that the undefeated Japanese army in China should, in effect, withdraw and return to its pre-1931 barracks. The Japanese government took this as an insulting and wholly unacceptable ultimatum. So the war plan for Southeast Asia—in part shrewd, in part wishful thinking—was put into effect. This was done not with high hopes, but with desperate, fatalistic determination. The indomitable warrior spirit of the Japanese fighting men must overcome the material odds against Japan.

The war plan called for action to neutralize the eastern flank of the southward offensive with an attack on Pearl Harbor, which was duly executed.

X

For China, with its 400 million, its inveterate miseries, and its repetitious history of conquering and being conquered, the period of 1914–1941 was one of unique tribulation.

The Manchu Dynasty had been overthrown in 1912 by a republican revolution and the so-called republic that followed was soon fragmented by contending warlords. Fighting, disorder, banditry and multiple extortions plagued the people. In 1926 a Nationalist-Communist coalition began a war to exterminate the warlords but got only part way when in 1927 the Nationalists attempted to exterminate the Communists. They fought one another, and occasional warlords, intermittently for the rest of this period. Meanwhile, the Japanese began the subjugation of Manchuria in 1931, and six years later started a major war against China that by 1941 had wreaked havoc over large areas of that country.

The dominant development in this tortured period was the rise of Chinese nationalism, a broad new cultural and political consciousness. It grew out of the intellectual ferment created by the new generation of Chinese scholars, by radical ideas coming out of post-World War I Europe, Wilsonianism, the Russian Revolution and Japanese aggression.

The erratic Sun Yat-sen and his Kuomintang, although denied tangible power by the warlords, nevertheless regarded themselves as the custodians of the political phase of Chinese nationalism. But by 1921, with the founding of the Chinese Communist Party, they had the beginning of competition. This was converted to opportunistic KMT-CCP collaboration when Sun, having been refused aid by the United States and other Western nations, negotiated in 1923 an aid deal with a newly arrived Soviet envoy.

Because the Kremlin's objective was to further a bourgeois national revolution directed against imperialism, the infant CCP was advised by the Comintern that the KMT was to take the lead in the anti-imperialist movement. Meanwhile the KMT set out to reorganize itself along the lines of the Soviet Communist Party. And Moscow sent political and military advisers and arms to Sun's Nationalist regime at Canton.

Following Sun's death in 1925, Chiang Kai-shek seized power in the Nationalist camp and, against the counsel of his Soviet advisers to proceed more cautiously, launched a northward offensive to eliminate warlords and imperialists and unify the country. The Nationalist-Communist coalition reached Wuhan on the Yangtze in a few months and Shanghai in the spring of 1927. There Chiang turned on the Communists and liquidated several hundred of them, all he could lay hands on. He then established a Nationalist government at Nanking.

The American and other western governments had up to this time viewed Chiang and his Nationalists as dangerous Reds. Certainly, some of Chiang's 1926 rhetoric was worthy of a Comintern agitator. And some of his troops wantonly killed Americans in Nanking. But his Shanghai behavior—purge of Communists, overtures to the economic establishment and renewal of old connections with the institutionalized underworld—was reassuring. Chiang became respectable and before long was on the way to the status accorded to him after 1941 by President Franklin D. Roosevelt—one of the four superstar statesmen.

Weakened by Chiang's attacks, Communist membership declined from a claimed 58,000 in the spring of 1927 to less than 20,000 by winter. Nevertheless, small military detachments led by Mao Tse-tung, Chu Teh and others created a base area and local government in a mountainous district of Kiangsi in Central China. There, and at several smaller bases, the Communists built up their military forces to a total of about 300,000.

Chiang did not react militarily to the Japanese takeover of Manchuria. Rather, he concentrated on his internal enemy, the Communists. The Kiangsi Communists withstood repeated Nationalist offensives until 1934, when a Nationalist force of nearly a million compelled them to retreat, about 100,000 in all, on the epic Long March of some 6,000 miles. Only about 8,000, headed by Mao, arrived a year later in the barren loess hills of Shensi, in Northwest China, where they established a new base area with Yenan, a dreary little town, as their capital. Communist stragglers from other areas joined the Long March survivors, bringing in late 1936 the total Red Army strength to no more than 30,000.

During the Long March, at Tsunyi in January 1935, Mao gained control of the Politburo from the "Twenty-eight Bolsheviks," whose leaders had dominated the Party. Members of the "Twenty-eight Bolsheviks" faction had been Moscow-trained and were responsive to Comintern direction. From Tsunyi onward Mao's supremacy in the Party was not challenged.

Tsunyi was a defeat for Stalin of historic proportions. It exceeded Chiang's double-crossing him—which had been embarrassing. Trotsky had ridiculed him for being taken in by Chiang. But he could and subsequently did work with the

Generalissimo, as a counter-revolutionary, on a practical basis. Mao's ousting of Moscow's proconsuls was, however, flagrant insubordination within Party ranks. And Mao, who had previously been reprimanded by the Comintern for going his own way, would continue on an impermissibly independent course, thus challenging the infallibility of the Kremlin, its pretensions to being the only source of Communist truth and authority. For Stalin in the late 1930s, Chiang was an opponent, but Mao was an arrogator, a potential competitor.

The Generalissimo was in Sian in December 1936 spurring his forces to greater efforts against the Communists when generals, who demanded that he fight the Japanese rather than other Chinese, kidnapped him. Communist representatives intervened and in the ensuing negotiations agreement for the release of Chiang was reached under conditions that led to a Nationalist-Communist United Front against Japanese aggression.

This was enthusiastically greeted by the Chinese people, who had been critical of Chiang's passivity since the invasion of Manchuria. The Kremlin also had cause for satisfaction, for the rapprochement in China was in line with its 1935 call for united fronts against Nazi Germany and Japan. Americans applauded the appearance of unity and praised Chiang as a pious Christian leader of his people. But Chiang, Mao and their respective collaborators knew that the United Front was no more than a front behind which the struggle begun in 1927 would continue.

The upsurge of nationalism and anti-Japanese feeling engendered in China by the United Front coincided with a trend in Tokyo toward a less aggressive, even conciliatory, policy toward China. The imperial army general staff was alarmed in 1936 by the growth in size and pugnacity of Soviet forces along the Manchurian frontiers. It therefore wanted to reduce rather than augment Japanese military commitments in China.

[122]

But a minor incident between small Chinese and Japanese units near Peking on July 7, 1937, after initial settlement, flashed out of control and into a major war that was to last more than eight years, cause countless deaths and end in the prostration of both countries.

China's policy in this conflict was simple: to trade space for time, while awaiting a war between Japan and the United States, which Chiang and his entourage assumed to be inevitable. When that war occurred, China would be relieved of Japanese pressure and both partners of the United Front could then occupy themselves with preparations for a fight to the death for possession of the Chinese people.

XI

Throughout this 1914–1941 period of wars, revolutions and a worldwide economic depression, the American Secretaries of State were lawyers, and of high principles. Their professional world, whether in the practice of law, on the bench, or in national politics, had been ordered by laws and contracts reliably upheld by an elaborate structure of courts, bailiffs, sheriffs, marshals, police and, if necessary the national guard and even the army. This background was poor preparation for the anarchy of international relations. It was small wonder that the Secretaries of this period, like Hay and Knox before them, inclined to legalistic interpretations and solutions and the enunciation of universal principles.

Charles E. Hughes was on solid ground, however, in negotiating the Washington Conference treaties on naval limitation and insular possessions in the Pacific, because the texts rested on substantial agreement among the signatories. These 1922 treaties marked a genuine American-Japanese détente lasting until Congress passed in 1924 Japanese exclusion legislation. The Nine Power Treaty was another matter. It was meant by Hughes to enshrine in international law the American obsession with verbal defense of China. It was not built on solid underlying agreement and so, for the Americans, was an exercise in self-deception.

The unilateral pronouncement of nonrecognition was another legalistic device of dubious worth. When in 1915 Japan presented its Twenty-one Demands to China, William Jennings Bryan declared that the United States would not recognize any agreement infringing American treaty rights, Chinese sovereignty or the Open Door. Stimson made the same hollow response to Japan's conquest of Manchuria, buttressing his case with invocation of the Nine Power Treaty and his predecessor's Kellogg Pact outlawing war, an emanation of legal ectoplasm. Cordell Hull, a Wilsonian moralist, conducted American foreign policy on the proclaimed basis of a catalogue of Utopian platitudes.

The legalistic-moralistic cast of mind was but one factor influencing the formulation of policy. Isolationism, the Great Depression, and pacifism were others. So was the influence of Pearl Buck (Chinese are like lovable characters out of the Old Testament), *Time* and *Life*, missionaries and pro-Chinese propagandists.

All of this added up to a national attitude of increasing sympathy for China and dislike of Japan as the villain, but a determination not to become involved in their conflict. At the same time, because of Washington's stern verbal support of China, Americans thought of themselves as champions of China, even as American companies supplied Japan with oil and scrap metal for its war against China. As Americans became aware of this and called for embargoes, they compensated for a subconscious sense of guilt by inflating the supposed virtues of the Chinese to heroic proportions. The preposterous overrating of the Chinese was bound to, and did, in the mid-1940s end in disillusion—also unbalanced.

XII

Franklin D. Roosevelt and Cordell Hull did not view war as a continuation of politics by other methods. War aims were one thing: absolute, non-negotiable, and charged with righteous wrath—"total victory," "unconditional surrender," extirpation of militarism, destruction of "philosophies . . . based on conquest," and no "compromise between good and evil." Postwar aims were in a separate category: conditional, negotiable, but also charged with perfectionism—"building human freedom and Christian morality," great power solidarity, collective security, creation of a united nations organization so that "the rule of law cannot be successfully challenged."

Japan's attack on British and Dutch possessions in East Asia and Hitler's foolish declaration of war on the United States linked the wars in Asia and Europe. As Japan's attack on the United States was secondary to its main objective, Southeast Asia, so Washington's reaction in the Pacific was second in priority to the prosecution of war against Germany. The strategically sound decision to concentrate first on Europe was not widely welcomed in the United States because the public wanted the quickest revenge for Pearl Harbor.

The Casablanca demand for unconditional surrender, inspired and enunciated by Roosevelt, eliminated the possibility of negotiated capitulations of Japan and Germany, thus ensuring the prolongation of the war and the creation of power vacuums in East Asia and Central Europe. A fortnight before the announcement, the Joint Chiefs of Staff had been advised of the President's intention to demand unconditional surrender, but did not even study the implications of this crucial act.

Later in 1943, at Cairo, Roosevelt and Churchill, with FDR in the lead, as usual in matters affecting China, proclaimed that

[125]

Japan would be stripped of its outlying possessions. Manchuria and Formosa would be "restored" to China. This was done largely to mollify a disgruntled Chiang. There appears to have been no thought that it might have been prudent to delay until a peace conference the disposition of at least Formosa.

As the American sea and air offensives drove the Japanese back close to their home islands, some American officials began to have second thoughts about the wisdom of unconditional surrender. Should not the Japanese people be reassured that after surrender they might have an orderly life and keep their revered institution of the Emperor? After all, only the Emperor could order the armed forces to surrender.

The President, by then Harry S Truman, refused in the spring and summer of 1945 to offer any inducement to surrender involving concessions regarding the imperial institution. Meanwhile Tokyo was sending out peace feelers to Moscow, asking for its mediation with Washington, and offering Manchukuo and Sakhalin in exchange for Soviet neutrality.

Through intercepts and from Stalin, Truman was aware of Tokyo's desire for negotiations but neither he nor Stalin responded to the overtures.

In the Potsdam Proclamation, Truman and Churchill held out some hope of a government which would be "established in accordance with the freely expressed will of the Japanese people." But nothing was said about the Emperor. The proclamation closed with the warning that if all the Japanese armed forces did not surrender unconditionally, "the alternative for Japan is prompt and utter destruction." This was on July 26, 1945. The Japanese did not surrender unconditionally.

On August 6 the United States visited prompt and utter destruction on Hiroshima. And then on Nagasaki. Tokyo broadcast on August 10 its readiness to accept the Potsdam ultimatum provided that the Emperor's prerogatives as sovereign were not prejudiced. Washington declared the next day that the Emperor's authority would be subject to the Allied Supreme Commander. As it turned out, MacArthur and Hirohito were an effective governing combination—the Shogun and the Mikado.

XIII

China, in the view of the American people, was transformed by Pearl Harbor into a gallant ally, battered but still eager to fight and lacking only American arms and guidance to smite mightily the common foe. Roosevelt, who had a willow pattern tea house impression of China derived from family lore about ancestors in the old China trade, initially shared the popular fancy about a Chinese passion to fight Japanese. Later, disillusioned, he nevertheless believed it essential to "keep China in the war." China's greater importance in Roosevelt's grand strategy was in the postwar world where China would take the place of Japan as the leading oriental power, but a friendly one collaborating with the United States, Britain and the Soviet Union to create a better world.

Pearl Harbor transformed Sino-American relations for Chiang. He had waited a long time for war between the United States (also the Soviet Union) and Japan. Now the Americans would take over the burden of fighting Japanese and he would concentrate on preparing for the inevitable postwar fight to the death against the Communists. He would, of course, stay in the war against Japan to obtain American matériel, and for the same reason even bear with disruptive American military advice and meddling—but only up to a certain point. His exaltation by FDR to the bizarre brotherhood of The Big Four gave Chiang face, as did being consulted by the busy Americans about postwar dispositions.

Postwar dispositions in China were being worked out then

in the countryside behind the Japanese lines. In the most developed part of the nation Chiang had lost the cities and lines of communication to the invaders, and the rural areas to the Communists. The Communists were growing in numerical and organizational strength, preparing for the showdown with Chiang and his Nationalists.

The likelihood of civil war following the defeat of Japan, the dynamic Communist expansion, the uncertainty of a Nationalist victory in a civil war, the incalculable costs of American intervention, and the probability that a civil war would reverse the Communist trend toward nationalism to one of dependence on the Soviet Union—all these considerations, and more, were presented by American officials in China to the State Department and the White House beginning in 1943. In August 1944, Mao indicated to an American official a desire to establish a Communist working relationship with the United States during and after the war. Washington did not react. By late 1944 the question arose among American officials whether the Communists were already predictably the victors in the oncoming civil war, and if so, whether the American government should, while continuing recognition of Chiang, begin to deal directly with the Communists as the de facto authority in the areas controlled by them and as the probable future rulers of all China.

Ambassador Patrick J. Hurley hotly opposed direct relations with the Communists. He had committed himself in a highly personal fashion to the creation of a coalition in which the Communists would submit to the supremacy of Chiang. This was where the Communists had come in, in 1927, and they did not take to the suggestion. After meeting with an emaciated Roosevelt, only a few weeks from death, Hurley declared the American policy was to support only Chiang and the Nationalists.

Although most of the career officials dealing with China favored a more flexible policy, Hurley overrode all dissent and forbade reporting to Washington anything critical of the Nationalists. He received Truman's backing for what the Ambassador represented as Roosevelt's directive. And as accepted policy, like a rut in a country road, is easier to bump along in than break out of, the American government continued to sustain Chiang on into the post-surrender period.

This meant American intervention on behalf of Chiang in the conflict between the Nationalists and Communists. American aircraft and ships lifted half a million Nationalist troops to Japanese-occupied China and Manchuria where they fanned out to fight the Communists, while American Marines in North China, allied with surrendered Japanese, obligingly held cities and railways for the Nationalists.

When Hurley resigned in high dudgeon, alleging that certain Foreign Service officers had undone his efforts to unify China peacefully, Truman dispatched General George C. Marshall to China to mediate between Chiang and Mao. This was a doomed mission: the two sides were bound to fight it out. The American involvement in China, already reduced by November 1946 when the Marines were withdrawn, was cut to nominal aid after Marshall left in January 1947 to become Secretary of State.

The Nationalists had a roughly three-to-one advantage over the Communists in troop strength. And only they had an air force, navy and arsenals. Yet by the end of 1949 the Communists had utterly routed the Nationalists. Simply stated, the explanation was, on the Nationalists' part, incompetent and corrupt leadership, degeneration of overextended fighting forces and alienation of popular support. On the part of the Communists, it was able politico-military leadership, outstanding esprit de corps and élan, and active popular support.

Roosevelt, Hull and then Truman did not recognize that China was in a profound identity crisis. China did not know who it was, and until it resolved that question through the agony of violence, it could not be a coherent factor in international life. Thus Chiang was not China, as romantically imagined by Americans, but only one of China's multiple personalities. And by 1943 it appeared that he might well be a fading one.

In these circumstances the American leaders were, at best, mistaken and the American people bamboozled into thinking that China could be a significant force in the war against Japan, that it shared American objectives and dreams of the future and that, along with Stalin's Russia, it would maintain with Britain and the United States great power solidarity in preserving peace under law.

For at least a year before intervention it had been evident that a policy of sustaining Chiang in a civil war would fail and, worse, envenom relations with the victors as it drove them into reliance on the Soviet Union. This is what happened, even though Truman withdrew from intervention relatively early in the conflict. But the damage had been done. China had, through its conquest by the Communists, found its identity, in part through enmity to the United States.

The American reaction to the Communist takeover in China was shocked perplexity. A growing group of politicians, military men and publicists asserted that, obviously, China was "lost" to the United States because treacherous elements in the American government undermined Chiang and helped the Communists win. This counterfeit revelation received surprisingly wide credence, especially after the 1950 Chinese intervention in the Korean War. It became part of a vicious larger attack on the integrity of civil servants lasting until 1955, in which Senator Joseph McCarthy was the most prominent defamer. The damage done to the conduct of American foreign policy by these assaults was long-lasting.

It was in the nature of Soviet-Japanese relations that Stalin, once he had defeated the Germans and could methodically deploy sufficient forces in Siberia and eastward, would attack Japan. Roosevelt sought assurances from Stalin that he would indeed do this. These superfluous pleas were presumably because the American Army wanted the Soviet Army to take on the formidable Japanese forces in Manchuria. MacArthur expressed a hope that the Russians would commit no less than 60 divisions.

Without consulting China, Roosevelt volunteered at Yalta to reward Stalin for doing what that sly Georgian intended to do anyway: take back "the former rights of Russia violated by the treacherous attack of Japan in 1904"—territories and railways. For the Japanese it was to be a case of one Roosevelt giveth and the other taketh away. In extenuation of FDR's cavalier treatment of other people's real property, it may be said that the terms he negotiated with Stalin were more modest than those which Stalin could have easily imposed during hostilities against Japan. On the other hand, Roosevelt had by his signature, in a sense, legalized the forthcoming Soviet acquisitions.

The Soviet Union invaded Manchuria on August 8, two days before Japan offered to surrender. It shipped the Japanese prisoners of war and anything movable of value, including factories, to Siberia. Captured light arms were left for the Chinese Communists, infiltrating from North China, to pick up as a grub stake. But during its stay in Manchuria the Soviet Army treated correctly and contemptuously with Nationalist officials as the representatives of China.

The Soviet Union emerged from its momentary war against Japan as the owner of southern Sakhalin and the Kurile chain, a welcome breach in the island blockade of the Soviet Far East. Both acquisitions were countersigned by Roosevelt at Yalta. The Soviet Army occupied northern Korea and Manchuria, the former to become a satellite, the latter a sphere of influence through rights granted at Yalta and confirmed by Chiang. The

Kremlin objective in China was to balance Chiang and the Communists against one another so as to prevent either from gaining supremacy over all China.

XIV

Surrender transformed Japan from a center of power into a power vacuum. By occupation, the United States immediately filled the vacuum on the Japanese home islands, denying a Soviet request for a zone on Hokkaido. With Japan eliminated, the United States and the Soviet Union were face to face in East Asia.

The American passion for reform found an ideal field for expression in Japan. Here were a people who had been led terribly astray. Prostrate in defeat and occupied by a conquering army, they were inescapably available.

The man who dedicated himself to this mission of conversion was SCAP, the Supreme Commander for the Allied Powers, General of the Army Douglas MacArthur. He undertook to bring about a "spiritual reformation" that would introduce democratic and Christian values into Japan. First came demilitarization, then the breakup of conglomerates, trusts and monopolies, land reform, creation of labor unions and institution of parliamentary democracy. In retrospect, the reformation was a success, in no small part because the Japanese were ready for the changes, which were often enough a logical development of trends that were incipient before the country went onto a war footing.

With the onset of the cold war and Communist gains in China, occupation policy shifted steadily from reform to rehabilitation of Japan, from that of a jailer to monitor, to instructor, to counselor, to patron, to ally. SCAP had induced the Japanese to include in their 1947 constitution renunciation of the right to resort to war and of land, sea and air forces. Less than four years later, in negotiating the peace treaty signed in 1951, John Foster Dulles recommended a Japanese army of 350,000. Prime Minister Yoshida firmly declined the invitation.

Japan has since established land, sea and air self-defense forces, currently totaling something over 200,000 volunteers. But its security against large-scale external attack still depends on American treaty guarantees. Washington's assumption of major defense responsibilities and costs has, over the quarter century, contributed greatly to Japan's extraordinary economic recovery and then expansion. Japan has exceeded MacArthur's fondest hopes—that it become the Switzerland of the Pacific.

XV

As the Chinese Communists completed their takeover of mainland China, Truman and his Secretary of State, Dean Acheson, attempted to distance the United States from the unprofitable entanglements in East Asia. The President announced in January 1950 that the United States wanted no part of the Chinese civil war and had no interest in Formosa. During the fury of the China Lobby, Acheson then publicly explained that the wise American policy toward China was to remain aloof and permit the natural force of Chinese nationalism to combat Soviet attempts to dominate China. He also paraphrased a published statement by MacArthur (and a decision of the Joint Chiefs of Staff) defining the American defensive perimeter in East Asia, which omitted the Republic of Korea and Formosa.

Thus American policy toward East Asia was perceptibly moving toward disengagement when in June 1950, Stalin's North Korean creature, Kim Il Sung, invaded South Korea. The disruptive effect was worldwide. But first, why would

Stalin—for it is inconceivable that he did not have fore-knowledge of the invasion—give his assent to, if he did not actually direct, the aggression?

The normally cautious Stalin presumably thought that this was a low-risk operation. The Americans had withdrawn their combat troops from Korea, leaving lightly armed Korean forces to whom they had denied tanks and anti-tank weapons. We know that political unrest existed in South Korea; how this was represented to Stalin by his intelligence sources we can only guess. The MacArthur and Acheson omissions of South Korea from definitions of the American defense line must have been noted. But would they have been given any more weight than the 1949–50 congressional cuts in appropriations for South Korea?

Furthermore, the campaign should be brief. The North Korean Army was far superior in experience and offensive arms to the South Korean force. It also possessed the element of surprise and should be able to overrun the South in short order in what would be represented as a civil war, liberating the southerners. It would be all over before the Americans could react.

The gain from this operation would be Soviet control of the Korean peninsula, thus denying the Americans, and an eventually revanchist Japan, lodgment on the strategic invasion corridor to the Soviet Far East and Manchuria. Additional gains might be distraction of American attention from Europe to Asia and a humiliation of the Americans. But Stalin, like other dictators, had not counted on the unpredictability of a democracy. He had blundered in Korea, but in the process had, intentionally or not, set the Americans and Chinese at loggerheads for two decades.

Truman and Acheson briskly committed the United States to the defense of the Republic of Korea. They made constructive use of the United Nations to involve other nations in repulsing aggression. And on the peninsula, South Koreans, reinforced by Americans, stemmed the enemy advance.

Concerned lest the North Korean attack be a symptom of Moscow's or Peking's intention to act aggressively elsewhere, Washington interposed the Seventh Fleet in the strait between Formosa and the mainland. To Peking this indicated that the Americans were again intervening in the internal Chinese conflict. And like Washington, Peking wondered where the next hostile move would occur.

Following a successful counteroffensive restoring the pre-invasion boundary at the 38th parallel, MacArthur advanced into North Korea. He did so in disregard of Chinese warnings. As his forces approached the Manchurian border, Chinese "volunteers" crossed en masse into Korea, converged on the dispersed American columns and drove them back into South Korea.

Communist China was now the enemy. MacArthur and many of like mind clamored to take the war to Manchuria and the rest of China. But Truman, the Joint Chiefs of Staff and Acheson held fast to keeping the war limited to Korea and a restoration of the pre-invasion situation. After MacArthur had appealed to the American people over the head of the President and Truman had relieved him of his command, the Korean War was brought under control and, in effect, to a conclusion. As a legacy, Americans and Chinese hated one another as they never had before. So perhaps Stalin did not do so badly after all.

XVI

In turning to Southeast Asia, the first thing to be said is that the American venture in an Asian empire lasted less than 50 years. Giving the Philippines back to the Filipinos in 1946 did not, however, get the United States out of Southeast Asia.

The American descent into the Southeast Asian maelstrom began in World War II. Roosevelt thought that Indochina should not be returned to France, but placed under trusteeship. He then agreed, on military grounds, to the inclusion of southern Indochina in Lord Mountbatten's theater of operations. When the Japanese surrendered, Mountbatten naturally brought in French troops to occupy Indochina.

At the same time, Ho Chi Minh formed a revolutionary nationalist regime in the North and, like Mao, sought to establish relations with the United States. Like Mao, he was snubbed. So Washington turned down another winner and went with another loser.

The French attempt to reimpose colonial rule dragged on to ignominious defeat in 1954 at Dien Bien Phu. Ho and company accepted an internationally arranged compromise: a Communist North Vietnam and a neo-mandarin South. And John Foster Dulles, then Secretary of State, managed to get the Eisenhower Administration just a little bit pregnant with Indochina. From then on, for 21 years, from 1954 to 1975, five successive Administrations thrashed about in the noxious, growing involvement. Communist victories finally facilitated a decision by Washington to terminate the grotesque intervention in Indochina.

What possessed Americans to become entangled in Indochina? One reason was the ready availability of redundant American military might anywhere in the western Pacific, and an accompanying belief in the persuasiveness of firepower as an instrument of foreign policy. Another reason was a Washington conviction, lasting some time after the Moscow-Peking split, that China and North Vietnam were integral parts of a monolithic international communism slavishly obedient to the Kremlin. Once Washington grasped the reality of the Sino-Soviet split, it feared China alone as ideologically militant and nationalistically expansive. Related to this was the domino theory, that if Hanoi, backed by Peking, were to take South Vietnam, there would be no end to it—Thailand would be next, then Singapore and so on to Tasmania and the Golden Gate. To prevent its infinite spread, communism had to be stopped wherever it appeared beyond its frontiers. A subjective reason for entanglement in Indochina was a lesson from the Truman experience with China— to "lose" a country to communism was, for the incumbent political party, to lose the American electorate.

The more important lesson from the China debacle was that, with all of its material might and know-how, the United States could not make good the organic deficiencies of leadership and collective will in a foreign country. This lesson was not applied to Indochina. A third lesson derived from China was that a Communist regime with a strongly nationalist character will resist attempts by another Communist state to encroach on its interests. What Moscow was to Peking, Peking potentially was to Hanoi. So if southward expansion by Peking was the major American concern, Hanoi was likely to be more effective in containing it than any of the regimes that bloomed in Saigon.

XVII

MacArthur's intrusion deep into North Korea not only brought China to war against the United States, it consequently pushed Peking into greater dependence on Moscow and stimulated the Soviet Union to expand its aid to China. The Kremlin continued after the war to help the Chinese build up an industrial base, but with growing misgivings. For Mao badgered the Russians to fulfill their revolutionary obligations, to intensify struggle against the Americans, even risking nuclear war.

Pointing to the sunny side of a nuclear holocaust, Mao in 1957 assured the Soviets that while half of mankind might die in such an encounter, happily imperialism would be eradicated and "the whole world would become socialist." The Russians did not accept this Chinese shortcut to a socialist world—and their being counted among the missing half of mankind, with you know who surviving. The Kremlin reckoned that the "correlation of forces" did not warrant a forward strategy and therefore held to peaceful coexistence.

Distrustful of the Chinese, Moscow increasingly held back economic and military support and Peking in return heightened its ideological abuse of the Soviet Union. By 1960 the split was open for all to see. Peking subsequently represented itself as the only center of Communist orthodoxy, invited the allegiance of the Soviet people and foreign Communist parties, and identified Soviet revisionism as an enemy ranking with American imperialism. It laid irredentist claim to half a million square miles of Soviet territory. And Chinese and Soviet troops engaged in spirited exchanges of border clashes.

Mao was multifaceted: pragmatic, shrewd, poetic and exorbitant. His attitude toward nuclear war was a manifestation of Mao's extravagance. So in domestic policy were two of his mass campaigns: the Great Leap Forward and the Cultural Revolution. Although ideologically articulated, both served Mao's purpose of attacking those domestically challenging his supremacy. He downed his challengers but gravely weakened his country.

Internal disruption and indifferent response from foreign Communists to the Chinese rallying cry added up to a frail self-reliance. This was late in the 1960s a perilous state of affairs even though the danger of an American attack out of Vietnam seemed to have subsided. There remained heavily armed and growing Soviet armies on the northern frontiers—and the object lesson of Soviet invasion of Czechoslovakia. China needed a counterbalance to the Soviet Union. Pragmatically, in 1971 Mao turned to the far enemy, the United States, to offset the near enemy, the Soviet Union.

Pragmatically, Washington accepted Peking's overture. The American government in 25 years had passed from thinking in terms of Roosevelt's version of Wilsonian community of power, to polarization of power, to monolithic power, to polycentric power, and finally to balance of power. Although older than history, balance of power is not well known to nor does it have a good name with Americans. Furthermore, Americans have not appeared to have an aptitude for playing at the balance of power, however much its manipulation by others affects us.

Power patterns act in a variety of combinations, rather like the Calder mobile tilting and gyrating as it hangs in space. Two major elements today are America and the Soviet Union. China makes it a triangle. But Japan is there too. Interaction is four ways. With the West European complex added, the interplay becomes more complicated. Then there are special patterns of power within the larger composition: the United States—the Soviet Union—Japan—China; the Soviet Union—China—Vietnam—Cambodia, and so on. Finally, consider this chain reaction: Cambodia fears its neighbor Vietnam and so turns to China; Vietnam fears its neighbor China and so turns to the Soviet Union; China fears its neighbor the Soviet Union and so turns to the United States; the Soviet Union fears its neighbor the United States but now has nowhere to turn save to self-reliance. Whereas the United States, which fears its neighbor the Soviet Union, does have within this pattern somewhere to turn—in shared fear, to China.

Whatever Washington does about balance of power, it should forthwith establish full diplomatic relations with Peking. As for the botched business of Formosa, since the regime on the island does not claim to be secessionist, the question of Formosa's future must lie between Taipei and Peking. Taipei is in a strong enough position to negotiate persuasively for the

[139]

status of a genuinely autonomous region within the People's Republic. Its mutual defense treaty with Washington is a legal anachronism and should be terminated. Washington should of course retain consular representation on Formosa.

Japan is too much taken for granted by Washington. It is by far the most important U.S. ally in East Asia, and although the unwisdom of drawing defense perimeters has been demonstrated, it is evident that Japan is definitely within that line. The United States needs high caliber, perceptive American representation in Tokyo and, asking so little for something so essential, an avoidance by any American government of gratuitous offense to the Japanese.

In the case of South Korea, so long as the United States has defense responsibilities for Japan it must regard the security of the Republic of Korea as closely related to that of Japan.

XVIII

In the final 35 years of these two centuries, American relations with East Asia culminated in three wars of extreme violence. Each spewed years of awful hate between Americans and Asians—and within American society itself.

Looking back over the past 200 years, what benefits have come to Americans from their associations across the Pacific? Riches, yes. Then, with its national heritage in North America and from Asia Minor, Europe and Africa, has American culture drawn correspondingly upon the wealth of East Asian civilizations? No, and not for reasons of quality but feelings of relevance.

Perhaps the best that has come to the United States from East Asia is not in riches, ideas or arts. Perhaps it is that which we so long resisted—Japanese and Chinese genes, as witness the roster of American Nobel laureates.

We have had the benefit of learning, or having demonstrated to us, the limits of American power and the mutability of alliances and enmities. And we may hope to have learned in China and Vietnam that in striving for intimacy with other peoples we incur responsibilities which we cannot always fulfill and which then may become destructive to ourselves and those we favor.

FIVE

The United States and the Soviet Union, 1917-1976

George F. Kennan

When, in the year 1917, Russian society was overtaken by the most tremendous and far-reaching upheaval it had ever known, American opinion-makers were poorly prepared to understand either the meaning or the implications of this event.

This was partly because there was little understanding in the United States of that day for Russian history or for the nature of the political society in which these events were taking place. Russian studies had been developed in North America only on the tiniest and most rudimentary of scales.

George F. Kennan is Professor Emeritus at the Institute for Advanced Study, Princeton. He was U.S. Ambassador to the Soviet Union, 1952, and to Yugoslavia, 1961–63, and is the author of *Soviet-American Relations, 1917–20* (2 Vols.); *Memoirs* (2 Vols.) and other works.

Knowledge of Russia rested on the tales of the occasional traveler or on the reports of press correspondents, very few of whom were qualified to see deeply into the great political and social stirrings that tormented the life of Russia in those final decades of Tsardom. The traditional antipathy of Americans for the Tsarist autocracy was understandable enough; but it was seldom balanced by any realistic examination of the nature of the possible alternatives. And in the final years before World War I, governmental and journalistic opinion in the United States had tended to be preempted by the problem of the treatment of Jews within the Russian Empire, to the detriment of the attention given to other and even deeper aspects of the slow crisis in which Russian society was then embraced.

This was the situation as of 1914. But as the First World War ran its course, and particularly in the year 1917, there came to be imposed upon this general shallowness of understanding a far more serious source of confusion: and that was America's own involvement in the war. If it be conceded that one of the most stubbornly ingrained characteristics of American democracy has been its inability to accept and experience military involvement without becoming seriously disoriented by it and without permitting it to distort judgment on other questions of policy, then it must be said that never did this weakness reveal itself more sharply and fatefully than in American outlooks on Russia during the First World War. Entering the war only a few weeks after the first of the two Russian revolutions of 1917, Americans resolutely declined, from that time on, to review Russian developments from any standpoint other than that of the war against Germany, and not of a thoughtful and objective image of that war, at that, but rather as it was perceived through the grotesquely distorting lenses of wartime propaganda and hysteria.

Thus both Russian revolutions of that fateful year were seriously misperceived. The first—the fall, that is, of Tsardom and its replacement by a regime which was liberal-democratic at least in intent—was welcomed less in its possible significance for the future of Russia than because it was seen—wholly incorrectly—as releasing forces of enthusiasm for the war effort previously suppressed by a supposedly pro-German imperial court. The second revolution, in November, which brought the Bolsheviks to power, was misunderstood by reason of the widespread belief that the Bolshevik leaders were German agents; as a result of which the new regime, not generally expected to last very long in any case, was opposed less for what it really was than out of resentment for its action of taking Russia out of the war.

It was only after the termination of hostilities against Germany that the way was cleared, in theory at least, for a view of Russian communism as a political phenomenon in its own right. But by this time a new welter of bewildering and misleading factors had entered in: such things as the passions and uncertainties of the Russian civil war; the exaggerations of propaganda on both sides; our own semi-involvement in the Allied intervention; the measures of the new Communist regime with relation to Tsarist debts and foreign property; etc. It was not, really, until the early 1920s, after the termination of the Russian civil war and the overcoming of the famine of 1921–22, that the meaning of what had occurred in Russia since 1917 began to emerge from the turmoil of events with sufficient clarity to permit the beginnings of thoughtful and reasonably informed debate in the United States over the nature of the problem which the installation of Lenin and his associates in the traditional seats of Russian power presented for American statesmanship.

II

Before going on to consider the nature of this problem and of the responses with which it met, it would be well to have a glance at one particular involvement of the United States which occurred in the confusion of those immediate post-revolutionary years and the main effect of which was to muddy the waters of mutual understanding for decades to come. This was America's part in the Allied intervention of 1918–20. Precisely because this action has so often been depicted by Soviet propagandists as an unsuccessful effort by the American government to unseat the Soviet regime, it is important to recognize its essential origins and dimensions.

The United States sent troops only to two areas of Russia: to the European north, in the neighborhood of Arkhangelsk on the White Sea, and to eastern Siberia. Both of these areas were far from the main theaters of the Russian civil war then in progress. In neither case was the decision to dispatch these troops taken gladly or—one may say—independently, in Washington. In neither case was it motivated by an intention that these forces should be employed with a view to unseating the Soviet government. In neither case would the decision have been taken except in conjunction with the World War then in progress, and for purposes related primarily to the prosecution of that war.

First—as to northern Russia. President Wilson consented to the dispatch of American forces to that region only in the face of a massive misunderstanding on his part of the situation prevailing there, only with great misgivings and skepticism as to the usefulness of the undertaking, and only when it had been insistently urged upon him by the British and French, with the support of Marshal Foch, then Supreme Allied Commander in Europe, all of whom portrayed it as a measure required by the war effort against Germany. What brought him to the decision was well described by his Secretary of

War, Newton Baker, in a letter written some years later. He had convinced the President, Baker wrote, that the decision was unwise:

> ... but he told me that he felt obliged to do it anyhow because the British and French were pressing it upon his attention so hard and he had refused so many of their requests that they were beginning to feel that he was not a good associate, much less a good ally.

The three battalions of American troops (for that is all it amounted to) were sent to Arkhangelsk, and served there, under British command. The decisions as to how and for what purposes they should be employed were British decisions, not American ones. The uses to which they were put were ones of which Wilson was ignorant at the time, ones he had never envisaged, ones of which, had he known of them, he would unquestionably have disapproved. That the units remained there after the end of the war with Germany was due to the fact that they were held there, over the winter of 1918–19, by the frozen condition of the White Sea. When the ice broke up they were removed as soon as this could be accomplished.

As for the troops that were sent to Siberia: the consent to the dispatch of these units was given only when Wilson's unwillingness to send them had been worn down by six months of pleading from the Western Allies. Their missions were restricted to the guarding of the Suchan coal mines, in the Maritime Province, and of certain sections of the Trans-Siberian railroad north of Manchuria—services, that is, that were of high importance to the lives and comfort of the inhabitants of the region, regardless of politics. The areas in question were, at the time of the dispatch of the units, thousands of miles removed from the main theaters of the Russian civil war; and the units took no part in that war. Their presence probably gave some satisfaction and comfort to the non-Bolshevik Russian forces in Siberia (although little love was lost between those forces and the Americans), and it may have had some effect in delaying the eventual extension and consolidation of Bolshevik power in the area. But this, so far as Wilson's intentions were concerned, was incidental. That they remained so long as they did, and were not withdrawn in 1919, was due rather to suspicion of the Japanese (who also had troops in the area) on the part of the Americans rather than to hostility toward the Bolsheviks.

The task of attempting to understand the permanent elements of the Soviet-American relationship will be best served if these regrettable episodes of the final weeks and immediate aftermath of the First World War be left aside, as the pathetic by-products of wartime confusion, weariness and myopia that they really were, and the focus of attention be shifted to the more enduring sources of conflict that were destined to complicate the relationship over ensuing decades.

III

The first and most fundamental of these sources of conflict was of course the ideological commitment of the Bolshevik-Communist leadership. This was something wholly new in the experience of American statesmanship. It was the manifestation of a form of hostility Americans had never previously encountered. Americans had known, of course, the phenomenon of war, as a situation defined and recognized by international law. But war was (normally) the expression of a hostility limited both in time and in intent. It was limited in time because it was coincidental with the existence of a formal state of war. It was limited in intent because the aims it was designed to serve were normally ones of a limited nature: the transfer of a province from one sovereignty to another, a change in the arrangements governing maritime commerce, the replacement of one ruler by another for dynastic reasons, etc.

But what American statesmen now saw themselves faced with, in the person of the new Russian-Communist regime, was something quite different: a governing faction, installed in the seats of power in another great country, which had not even dreamed of declaring war formally on the United States but which was nevertheless committed, by its deepest beliefs and by its very view of its place in history, to a program aimed at the overthrow of the entire political and social system traditional to American society—committed, that is, to a program calculated to inflict upon the society of the United States a damage more monstrous in the eyes of most Americans than any they might expect to suffer from even the worst of purely military defeats at the hands of the traditional sort of adversary.

This situation was destined to undergo many changes and modifications in the course of the ensuing decades. There would be times when the ideological hostility on which it was based would be soft-pedaled for reasons of tactical expediency. In general, the cutting edge of the hostility would be progressively blunted over the course of the decades by the erosion of frustration and the buffeting of contrary events; so that it would come, with the years, to assert itself more as a rhetorical exercise than as a guide to policy. Particularly with respect to the United States, where its chances for political success were singularly slender, this messianic dedication would gradually lose its bite with the passage of the years, so that Americans would ultimately come to fear it less for its possible effect upon themselves than for its effect on other peoples: its effect, that is, in alienating those peoples from that portion of the international community with which America could have a comfortable and friendly relationship and adding them to that other sector (to be greatly increased in the Third World after World War II) in which America, and all that she stood for, would be regarded only with prejudice, misunderstanding and rejection.

But these would be gradual changes. They lay, as of the early 1920s, well in the future. They were not yet generally visible or predictable. The American statesmen of that day had to take the ideological challenge at its own words, and deal with it accordingly.

It would be wrong, of course, to suppose that this sort of hostility remained one-sided, or even that it was wholly one-sided from the start. It naturally bred its own reaction on the part of many Americans; and it would be idle to pretend that this reaction was always thoughtful, reasonable, devoid of prejudice, sensitively responsive to the nature of the challenge itself. It was a reaction that would manifest itself, down through the years, in many ways, most of them unpleasant: in the anti-Red hysterias of 1919–20 and 1950–53; in the vulnerability of large sections of the American public to the sanguine urgings of the Chinese-Nationalist and "captive nations" lobbies; in the exaggerated military apprehensions and phantasmagoria of the post-World War II period. Hampering at every turn the development of a sound and effective response to the challenge which had provoked it (or provided the rationalization for it), this exaggerated reaction would constitute at all times a complication of the Soviet-American relationship in its own right. And it was not slow in making itself felt in the immediate aftermath of the Revolution. It was one with which American policymakers were obliged to contend from the start, in their efforts to design an effective response to the challenge in question.

Before proceeding to examine this response, it would be well to note that there were two features of this unprecedented relationship that were fated to constitute basic and unalterable elements of the problem it presented for American statesmanship. One was the fact that, fiery as were the assertions of intent upon the part of this ideological opponent to destroy *our* system, and heartily as this challenge was accepted by sections of our own public opinion, neither side was in a position, or ever would be in a position, to achieve total destruction of the other. Each might hope for it; each might do what little it could to abet processes that seemed to run in that direction. But neither could, by its own action, achieve it; nor did ulterior forces produce this result. The result was that each had to accept, for better or for worse, the other's existence and to start from there in the designing of policy.

This—"peaceful coexistence" if you will—was a reality of the relationship from the beginning. It did not need a Khrushchev or a Brezhnev to discover it or create it.

The other inalterable element of this problem, destined to become wholly visible and compelling only in later years but also present, in reality, from the start, was the fact that in this complicated world of ours there could be no international relationship which was one of total antagonism or total identity of interests—none which did not contain both sorts of ingredients, however uneven the mix. Just as there could be no relationship of friendship undiluted by elements of rivalry and conflict, so there could be no relationship of antagonism not complicated by elements of occasional common purpose or desiderata.

The fact that these *were,* precisely, the basic elements of the problem was not always clearly visible to all the American statemen who had to deal with it, any more than it was to all sections of American private opinion. But the fact was always there, on the visible surface or below it; and those who attempted to ignore it risked the prospect of being yanked back sooner or later, and sometimes in painful ways, to the plane of reality.

IV

It would be unfair to search in actions of the American statesmen in the 1917–20 period for the elements of a serious and considered response to this problem. The situation was too chaotic, their oversight over events too imperfect, to expect this of them. But with the end of Allied intervention, and with the gradual grinding to a halt of civil conflict in Russia, the situation became clearer; and it is instructive to observe the emergence of a more systematic and principled response.

The first to make the attempt to design such a a response were those who were responsible for the conduct of American diplomacy at the end of the Wilson Administration.

These did not really include Wilson himself, except as the influence of his thinking from earlier days still made itself felt. He lay, at that time, ill and helpless in the White House. But it was impossible for his assistants not to take some attitude toward the problem, and this they proceeded to do. It was a purely ideological attitude, as uncompromising in its acceptance of the Bolshevik challenge as were the authors of that challenge in their creation of it. It was succinctly expressed in the note that Secretary of State Bainbridge Colby addressed to the Italian government on August 10, 1920. "It is not possible for the Government of the United States," Colby wrote:

> to recognize the present rulers of Russia as a government with which the relations common to friendly governments can be maintained. This conviction has nothing to do with any particular political or social structure which the Russian people themselves may see fit to embrace. It rests upon a wholly different set of facts.
>
> . . . upon numerous occasions the responsible spokesmen of this Power . . . have declared that it is their understanding that the very existence of Bolshevism in Russia, the maintenance of their own rule, depends, and

must continue to depend, upon the occurrence of revolutions in all other great civilized nations, including the United States, which will overthrow and destroy their governments and set up Bolshevist rule in their stead. . . . We cannot recognize, hold official relations with, or give friendly reception to the agents of a government which is determined and bound to conspire against our institutions.

The essential features of this response are easily observed. It accepted the first of the elements of the problem noted above: the existence of the Soviet state and the impossibility, for the United States, of doing anything to change that situation, beyond the refusal to accord formal diplomatic recognition. It revealed no awareness of the second element: namely the existence of a limited area of common interest; indeed, its authors would have been skeptical of the thesis that such an area existed, or could exist. Nothing of this nature was visible to them.

This declaration was, of course, one of the swan songs of the Democratic Administration of that day. That Administration shortly was to be replaced by the first of the successive Republican Administrations of Harding, Coolidge and Hoover.

The Republicans accepted the reasoning of the Colby note, as far as it went; but to the motivation of the policy of nonrecognition they added one more feature not present in Mr. Colby's pronouncement. This was a reference to the failure of the Soviet government to recognize any obligation in principle to assume the foreign debts of previous Russian regimes or to reimburse foreigners for property previously owned by them in Russia and now nationalized by the Soviet authorities. In the view of these Republican statesmen, the Soviet government, in order to regularize its relations with the United States, would not only have to cease its advocacy of revolution in the United States and its ill-concealed support for elements working to that end, but would have to assume the financial obligations incurred by previous Russian regimes to the U.S. government and to American nationals.

On this, the relationship rested for 13 years. Individual American businessmen were not prevented from traveling in Russia and trading with the Soviet foreign trade monopoly, at their own risk. Herbert Hoover, emerging with halos of glory from his leadership of the American relief effort in Europe at the end of the war, was not prevented from organizing and conducting in Russia, in 1921–22, as a private undertaking, the magnificent work of the American Relief Administration, which saved several million people from starvation and may well, for all anyone can tell, have saved the Soviet regime itself from utter failure and collapse. But the American government itself was officially blind to a regime whose attitude and behavior it found unacceptable as a basis for formal relations.

The Soviet government, for its part, was quite aware, over the years in question, of the complexity of its relations with the Western countries, and of its need for certain forms of collaboration with them even in the face of ideological hostility. It did not, however, find itself too adversely affected by the American stance. What it wanted from the Western powers was trade, recognition, and credits. Trade it got, without difficulty, from all of them, including even the United States. Recognition it received, mostly in the years 1924–25, from all the leading European powers. Commercial credit, too, it succeeded in obtaining from some of them, notably the Germans, within the relatively narrow limits prescribed by circumstances. All these benefits were achieved without paying the price the U.S. government was demanding: which was the suppression of the Comintern and the sort of activity its existence implied, as well as major concessions in the field of debts and claims. Thus the incentive on the part of the Soviet leaders to meet these American demands became weaker with the passage of the years. They wanted American recognition and financial help; but they were not prepared to pay, and did not need to pay, the price the Republican Administrations of 1921–33 were demanding.

V

Franklin Roosevelt's assumption of the presidency, in 1933, marked, of course, a fundamental turning point in the relationship. To him, the old question of debts and claims seemed, in itself, unimportant, likewise the issue of propaganda. He recognized that these issues engaged the feelings and interests of important segments of American opinion, and thus presented domestic political problems he would have to meet; but he could not have cared less about them from his own concept of America's external interests.

On the other hand he was, in contrast to his Republican predecessors, very conscious indeed of the existence of at least one area of common interest with the Soviet Union: with relation, namely, to the threat of Japanese penetration onto the mainland of Asia. This was shortly to be supplemented by similar feelings on his part with relation to Hitler's obvious intention to win for Germany a dominant position on the European continent.

Franklin Roosevelt was contemptuous from the start of the reasoning of the State Department and of the upper-class Eastern establishment which had for so long inspired Republican policy toward Russia. He was much influenced by Mr. William C. Bullitt, the brilliant and charming dilettante who, as a very young man, had been sent to Russia in 1919, during the Peace Conference, by Lloyd George and Colonel House, had returned convinced that it *was* possible to deal with Lenin and his associates and disgusted with the Allied leaders for declining to do so. FDR, persuaded as he was of his own great powers of ingratiation and persuasiveness, readily lent his ear to Mr. Bullitt's suggestions that the Soviet leaders, being human, would now be responsive to a more friendly and conciliatory approach, and that, having even more to fear than did the Americans from a Japanese penetration into Manchuria (not to mention an expansion of Nazi power into Eastern Europe) they could easily be made into an asset from the standpoint of possible resistance to these developments. And the result, of course, was the reestablishment of diplomatic relations between the two countries in the autumn of 1933.

It was characteristic of FDR that the preliminary Soviet-American agreements (the so-called Roosevelt-Litvinov letters), on the basis of which the establishment of diplomatic relations was arranged, were ones designed, in his own eyes, not at all to assure to the United States any real advantage in the forthcoming official relationship, but rather to meet the prejudices and disarm the criticisms of groups within the American political community whose opposition to recognition was to be expected. Such of the wording of the Litvinov letters as appeared to assure a cessation of subversive propaganda and activity with relation to the United States, and a settlement of the questions of debts and claims, was thus much too vague and full of loopholes to satisfy anyone really wishing to see these issues resolved; and in this sense it could be charged, and was, that Roosevelt's acceptance of it constituted a direct misleading of the American public. But there is no reason to suppose that FDR doubted that desirable results could be obtained in the end, by one means or another, regardless of the precision of the language of the understandings. For real gains in the Soviet-American relationship the President was inclined to rely not on written documents but on the power of his own charismatic personality.

The result, for anyone who knew anything about Russia, was predictable. The issues of debts and claims were never resolved; it remained for the passage of time to drain them of most of their meaning. The propaganda and the support for subversion did not cease. Trade, instead of increasing, declined. The Soviet authorities, recognition having now been obtained, the Japanese threat having for the moment slightly abated, and it having become clear that in any case the Americans were not going to fight the Japanese for their benefit, now lost interest either in making good on the concessions they had semi-promised or in making new ones. The new American Embassy in Moscow, founded initially with exuberant optimism under the auspices of Mr. Bullitt as the first Ambassador, soon fell victim to the age-old Russian aversion to dealing with the resident-diplomat (regarded as too *avisé*, too guarded and skeptical, too patient and too little susceptible to being rushed into hasty agreements) and its preference for dealing directly with the foreign statesman, innocent of any close personal knowledge of Russian realities.

So Mr. Bullitt, not surprisingly, left in disgust after a year or so of frustration, to join at a later date the ranks of the Soviet Union's most bitter critics and opponents on the Washington scene. His successor, Mr. Joseph E. Davies, a man to whom for various reasons the appearances of good relations were more important than their reality, made a valiant attempt, if not a very plausible one, to maintain those appearances. But he, too, soon gave up the struggle, and retired from the Russian scene in 1938. The American Embassy was left, thereafter, to share for years to come the dim semi-existence customarily led by the Moscow diplomatic corps, isolated, guarded, seen but not heard, useful—in this case—primarily as a school for young Russian-speaking diplomats, obliged to contemplate and to study the Russian scene while they pondered the reasons for their own isolation.

The years immediately following the resumption of Soviet-American relations were, of course, the years of the purges. With the millions that perished in those fearful agonies, there perished also—there could not help but perish—the magical afterglow of the hope and idealism of the Lenin period. By the end of the 1930s not even the greatest enthusiast could ignore the dread hand of terror, denunciation, and moral corruption that had gripped Russian society. Only the most wishful and uninstructed of foreign sympathizers, outraged by the phenomenon of European fascism and inclined to give the benefit of the doubt to anything that even appeared to oppose it, could retain the illusion that here was a superior and more humane civilization.

But such sympathizers did, of course, exist in the United States. They were encouraged by what seemed to them to be the implications of the economic crisis that had now overtaken their own "capitalist" country. They encouraged, and helped to preserve, in Franklin Roosevelt and certain of those around him a somewhat battered but undefeated partiality for the Soviet regime: a readiness to dismiss the tales of horror and injustice of the purges as just some more of the anti-Soviet propaganda that had been pouring out from reactionary circles ever since the Revolution, and a readiness to continue to believe in the essential progressiveness of the Soviet "experiment," all the more acceptable, seemingly, by way of contrast to the European fascism and Japanese militarism just then advancing upon the world scene.

The Nazi-Soviet Non-Aggression Pact of 1939 was of course a great blow to people who held these views. Together with the ensuing Russian attack on Finland and taking over of the Baltic states, this unexpected development was enough to suppress down to the year 1941 the latent pro-Sovietism just described. But it was not the mortal blow. The inclinations in question survived, below the surface, into the eventful year of 1941. And when in June of that year Russia herself was invaded by Hitler, it was as if the unhappy events of 1939–40 had never occurred: Robert Sherwood's moving play of the suffering of the Finns under the Russian attack was soon revised with the replacement of the Finns by the Greeks, and the Russians by the Germans. A new era, once again dominated by the fact of America's being at war, was beginning to dawn in the history of Soviet-American relations.

VI

Never, surely, has the congenital subjectivity of the American perception of the outside world been more strikingly illustrated than in the change of attitude toward Russia that followed Pearl Harbor and the ensuing German declaration of war on the United States, in December 1941. Gone, as if by magic, were most of the memories and impressions of the past. Forgotten, now, were the Russian purges, along with the reflection that the men now running Russia's war effort and diplomacy were the same who had once conducted those bloody persecutions. Forgotten, too, were the cruelties only recently perpetrated by Beria's police establishment upon the innocent populations of Eastern Poland and the Baltic states. Forgotten was the fact that Russia's involvement in the war was neither the doing nor the preference of her own rulers: that, on the contrary, they had made desperate efforts to remain aloof from it, and would, had this been possible, have witnessed without a quiver of regret further Western reverses in the war, provided only that the contest was sufficiently bloody and prolonged to exhaust Germany's war-making potential along with that of its Western opponents. Ignored, in large measure, was the fact that the demands which Stalin was making on his Western allies, even as early as the end of 1941, were substantially the same as those he had placed before Hitler as the price for Russia's initial neutrality. In place of all this there emerged, and was systematically cultivated in Washington, the image of a great Soviet people, animated by the same noble impulses of humane indignation and yearning for a future free of all tyranny by which Americans conceived themselves and their allies to be animated, fighting with inspiring heroism and grandeur against an opponent in whose repulsive political personality all the evil of an imperfect world seemed to be concentrated.

The image was, of course, not wholly wrong. The heroism was there. So was the grandeur of the effort. That the Western powers owed their military victory to that effort, in the sense that without it their victory could never have been achieved, was undeniable. It was also true that a great proportion of the Soviet people conceived themselves to be fighting for the defense of their homeland—an aim with which Americans could at least sympathize even if the homeland was not theirs.

But what was important, of course, in the given circumstances, was not what the mass of the Soviet people conceived themselves to be fighting for but what their rulers perceived as the uses they wished to make of victory; and this, as the past had shown, was a different thing.

Weighty reasons were offered for the idealization of the Soviet ally, and the encouragement of belief in the possibilities of postwar collaboration with it, that inspired so much of Franklin Roosevelt's wartime policy. Without a belief on the part of the public that Russians and Americans were fighting for the same thing it would have been impossible, it was said, to maintain American enthusiasm for the war effort and the readiness to give aid to Russia in the pursuit of that effort. Without American aid, without American moral support, without expressions of American confidence in Russia, Stalin might have been tempted, it was argued, to make a compromise peace with the Nazis, permitting Hitler to concentrate his entire great force against the West.

There was much in these arguments. The weakest part of them was perhaps that which most appealed to the American military establishment, now the center of American policymaking: the fear of a complete Russian collapse or (as the tide turned) of a separate Russian-German peace. Stalin, of course, would have loved the latter, though not until the Germans had been expelled from at least the pre-1939 territory of the Soviet Union; and once things had gone that far, and the Germans had begun to crumble, then his own appetite was stimulated to a point where he saw no need to stop. But that fear of such a development, coupled with a sense of humiliation over their own inability (until 1944) to pick up a larger share of the military load, haunted the American military leadership throughout the war and inclined them to give moral and material support to their Soviet opposite numbers in every possible way, is clear.

Behind this whole argument, however, there lay a deeper question: and that is whether it ever pays to mislead American opinion, to be less than honest with it, even in the interests of what is perceived by the political leadership as a worthy cause. It is characteristic of wartime psychology that the end tends to be seen as justifying the means. But when the means include the manipulation of opinion by the creation and propagation of unreal images, there is always a price to be paid at a later date; for the distortions thus engendered have some day to be straightened out again.

And so it was in the years after 1945. It must be said in defense of FDR and his associates that they probably never fully realized (although they came closest to it in the days just preceding the President's death) the extent to which they *were* actually misleading American opinion on this point. Amid the stresses of a great war effort it is particularly easy for the wish to play father to the thought. Stalin, too, encouraged, in his own delicate and cautious way, the propagation of this myth: soft-pedaling, while the war was in progress, certain forms of criticism of the Western Allies, and making adroit use of those idealistic semantic generalities which can mean all things to all people.

But the fact remains, however extenuating the circumstances, not only was the unreal dream of an intimate and happy postwar collaboration with Russia extensively peddled to large portions of the American public during the war, but they were encouraged to believe that without its successful realization there could be no peaceful and happy future at all.

The events of the final weeks of the war and of the immediate post-hostilities period rapidly demolished this dream. Event after event: the behavior of the Soviet forces in the half of Europe they overran; the growing evidence that the Soviet authorities had no intention of permitting the free play of democratic forces in the countries of that great region; their cynical reluctance to collaborate in the restoration of economic life and stability in areas they did not control; the continued secretiveness and inscrutability of Soviet policymaking and political action; the failure to enter upon any extensive demobilization of the Soviet armed forces; the narrow, suspicious and yet greedy behavior of Soviet representatives in the new international organizations—all these things fell heavily upon a public in no way prepared for them; nor was there any Franklin Roosevelt, now, with his talent for the leadership of opinion, to make the transition in company with those whom he had, wittingly or otherwise, misled—to ease them out of the wartime euphoria he had once eased them into.

The results were not unnatural. Unrequited love now turned too easily into unreasonable hatred. To people taught to assume that in Russian-American postwar collaboration lay the only assurance of future peace, the absence of that collaboration, in the light of a conflict of aims becoming daily more visible, inevitably conduced to visions of war. To people unsettled by the recent experience of being at war, the real personality of Russia, in all its vast complexity, was often lost to view; and in its place, assuming in many respects the aspect of the late-departed Hitler, there emerged one of those great and forbidding apparitions to the credence in which mass opinion is so easily swayed: a monster devoid of all humanity and of all rationality of motive, at once the embodiment and the caricature of evil, devoid of internal conflicts and problems of its own, intent only on bringing senseless destruction to the lives and hopes of others.

Neither of these reactions—neither the exorbitant wartime hopes nor the angry postwar disillusionment—were shared by all sections of American opinion; and where they were shared, not all experienced them in like degree. There were those who labored, with moderate success, to correct them. Alone the effect of these aberrations might not have been deep or enduring. But they happened to fall in, most fatefully, with the emergence of a new pattern of fears and misunderstandings— this time of a military nature.

The failure of the Soviet government to carry out any extensive demobilization in the post-hostilities period has already been mentioned. Here again, taken outside the context of ulterior circumstances, this might not have been unduly alarming. For centuries it had been the custom of Russian rulers to maintain in being, even in time of peace, ground forces larger than anyone else could see the necessity for. The reasons for this must be assumed to have been primarily of a domestic political and social nature. But this time the circumstances—and along with the circumstances, the reactions— were different in a number of respects.

In the first place, in contrast to the situation of earlier decades and centuries, the Russian armed forces now had an area of deployment in the very heart of Europe, with secure lines of support and communication behind them. In the past, it had been possible to employ their great numerical strength in Western Europe only after first overcoming both the geographic and the military impediments of the territory that lay between Russia's traditional western borders and the industrial heartland of the European continent. Now, a Soviet offensive, if one wished to launch one, could be started from within 60 miles of Hamburg or 100 miles of the Rhine. To military planners, trained to give greater weight to capabilities than to intentions, this could not fail to be disturbing. And not to military planners alone. The peoples of Western Europe, all of whose memories, with one or two exceptions, included the overrunning of their homelands by foreign troops at one time or another, and usually within the past century, suffered from *la manie d'invasion* and found it difficult to believe that the Russians, having already overrun so many countries since 1944, should not wish to overrun more.

Secondly, Western strategists, inclined anyway, for reasons of professional prudence and others, to a chronic overrating of the adversary's capabilities, now found themselves confronting no longer the traditional primitive and slow-moving Russian ground forces, defensively strong on their own ground but not well fitted for offensive purposes against a strong Western opponent, but rather, modern, mechanized units with equipment little inferior, sometimes not inferior at all, to that of the Western armies themselves. The result, of course, was increased anxiety.

But overshadowing both of these factors, as a source for the militarization of American thinking about the problem of relations with Russia, was of course the development by the Russians of a nuclear capability, visible from 1949 onward.

The writer of these lines knows no reason to suppose that the Soviet leadership of Stalin's day ever allotted to the nuclear weapon anything resembling a primary role in its political-strategic concepts. There is no reason to doubt that Stalin saw this weapon as he himself described it: as something with which one frightened people with weak nerves. Not only was he aware from the start of its potentially suicidal quality, but he will be sure to have recognized, as one in whose eyes wars were no good unless they served some political purpose, that for such purposes the nuclear weapon was ill suited: it was too primitive, too blindly destructive, too indiscriminate, too prone to destroy the useful with the useless.

[163]

Merciless as he could be, and little as his purposes may have coincided with ours, Stalin was entirely rational in his external policies; war, for him, was not just a glorified sporting event, with no aim other than military victory; he had no interest in slaughtering people indiscriminately, just for the sake of slaughtering them; he pursued well-conceived, finite purposes related to his own security and ambitions. The nuclear weapon could destroy people; it could not occupy territory, police it, or organize it politically. He sanctioned its development, yes— because others were doing so, because he did not want to be without it, because he was well aware of the importance of the shadows it could cast over international events by the mere fact of its inclusion in a country's overt national arsenal.

But it was not to this weapon that he looked for the satisfaction of his aspirations on the international plane. Indeed, in view of the physical dangers the weapon presented, and the confusion which its existence threw over certain cherished Marxist concepts as to the way the world was supposed to work, he probably would have been quite happy to see it removed entirely from national arsenals, including his own, if this could be done without the acceptance of awkward forms of international inspection. And if his successors were eventually forced into a somewhat different view of the uses of the weapon, as they probably were, it was surely the Western powers, committed from the start to the first use of the weapon in any major encounter, whether or not it was used against them, that did the forcing.

Little of this was perceived, however, on the Western side— and on the American side in particular. Once again, the interest in capabilities triumphed over any evidence concerning intentions. The recognition that the Russians had the weapon, and the necessary carriers, served as sufficient basis for the assumption that they had a desire to use it and would, if not deterred, do so.

In part, this was the product of the actual discipline of

peacetime military planning. The planner has to assume an adversary. In the case at hand, the Russians, being the strongest and the most rhetorically hostile, were the obvious candidates. The adversary must then be credited with the evilest of intentions. No need to ask *why* he should be moved to take certain hostile actions, or whether he would be likely to take them. That he has the capability of taking them suffices. The mere fact that they would be damaging to one's own side is regarded as adequate motive for their execution. In this way not only is there created, for planning purposes, the image of the totally inhuman and totally malevolent adversary, but this image is reconjured daily, week after week, month after month, year after year, until it takes on every feature of flesh and blood and becomes the daily companion of those who cultivate it, so that any attempt on anyone's part to deny its reality appears as an act of treason or frivolity. Thus the planner's dummy of the Soviet political personality took the place of the real thing as the image on which a great deal of American policy, and of American military effort, came to be based.

Nor does this exhaust the list of those forces which, in the aftermath of World War II, impelled large portions of influential American opinion about Russia into a new, highly militaristic, and only partially realistic mold. The fall of China to its own Communists, a development that was by no means wholly agreeable to the Soviet leadership, came soon to be regarded as the work of Moscow, implemented (was there ever an odder flight of the imagination?) not directly but through the agency of naïve or disloyal Americans. Out of this, and out of the related discovery that there was political mileage to be made by whipping up suspicions of fellow citizens, there emerged the phenomenon known as McCarthyism, the unquestioned premise of which was the existence of a diabolically clever Russian-Communist enemy, consumed with deadly hostility and concerned only with our undoing. And not long thereafter came the misreading by the official Washington establishment of the nature and significance of the Korean War—a misreading by virtue of which an operation inspired overwhelmingly by local considerations related to the situation in the Manchurian-Korean area, and one from which the Soviet government studiously kept its own forces aloof, came to be regarded and discussed in Washington as, in effect, an attack by the Soviet Red Army across international borders, and as only the first move in a sort of Hitlerian "grand design" for military world conquest.

It was out of such ingredients that there emerged, in the late 1940s and early 1950s, those attitudes in American opinion that came to be associated with the term "cold war." These were never to dominate all of American opinion. Many people, while generally prepared to give a polite show of outward credence to the image of the Soviet adversary just described, remained aware of the scantiness of their own information and were prepared, by and large, to reserve judgment. In their extreme form the fixations in question remained the property of a small but strongly committed right-wing minority, the electoral weakness of which was repeatedly demonstrated, and of the military budgeteers and nuclear strategists, who had little electoral significance at all.

Nevertheless, the image of the Soviet Union as primarily a military challenge was now widely accepted. And for reasons that warrant more scholarly investigation than they have received, the resulting fixations acquired a curiously hypnotic power over the professional political community. A certain show of bristling vigilance in the face of a supposed external danger seems to have an indispensable place in the American political personality; and for this, in the early 1950s, with Hitler now out of the way, the exaggerated image of the menacing Kremlin, thirsting and plotting for world domination, came in handy. There was, in any case, not a single Administration in Washington, from that of Harry Truman on down, which, when confronted with the charge of being "soft on communism," however meaningless the phrase or weak the evidence, would not run for cover and take protective action.

These observations should not be misunderstood. The reality that deserved recognition in place of this exaggerated image was never its opposite. There were indeed, throughout this period, as there always had been before, threatening elements of both Soviet rhetoric and Soviet behavior. That behavior remained marked at all times, in one degree or another, by features—disrespect for the truth; claims to infallibility; excessive secrecy; excessive armaments; ruthless domination of satellite peoples; and repressive policies at home—that were bound to arouse distaste and resentment in American opinion, and thus to feed and sustain the distorted image of Soviet Russia we have just had occasion to note. It is not too much to say, in fact, that if the Soviet leaders did not want to live with this image, they could have done a great deal more than they actually did to disarm it; a few obviously specious peace congresses and the ritualistic repetition of professions of devotion to the cause of "peace" (as though peace were some sort of abstraction) were never enough.

Most serious of all, as distortions of understandings from the Soviet side—particularly serious because massively and deliberately cultivated—were the dense clouds of anti-American propaganda put out, day after day, month after month, and year after year, in the postwar period by a Soviet propaganda machine that had never been inhibited by any very serious concern for objective and observable truth, and was now more reckless than ever in its disregard for it. The extremes to which this effort was carried, particularly in those final months of Stalin's life that coincided with the high point of the Korean War, were such as to be scarcely conceivable except to those who experienced them at first hand. Here, the United States was portrayed, of course, as the most imperialist, militaristic

[167]

and generally vicious of all aggressors. And this affected the climate of relations at both ends; for on the one hand, the very extremism of these attacks confirmed Americans in their view of the sinister duplicity of Soviet policy (why, it was asked, should a government that was really of peaceful intent have such need for the lie in the statement of its case?); while on the other hand, those Soviet leaders and officials who had a part in the making of policy, despite the cynicism with which they launched this propaganda, could not help being affected by it themselves, and were influenced accordingly in their interpretation of American behavior.

Against this background of mutual misunderstanding, the course of Soviet-American relations in the immediate postwar years, and to some extent down into the Khrushchev era, was determined by a series of spontaneous misinterpretations and misread signals which would have been comical had it not been so dangerous. The Marshall Plan, the preparations for the setting up of a West German government, and the first moves toward the establishment of NATO, were taken in Moscow as the beginnings of a campaign to deprive the Soviet Union of the fruits of its victory over Germany. The Soviet crackdown on Czechoslovakia and the mounting of the Berlin blockade, both essentially defensive (and partially predictable) reactions to these Western moves, were then similarly misread on the Western side. Shortly thereafter there came the crisis of the Korean War, where the Soviet attempt to employ a satellite military force in civil combat to its own advantage, by way of reaction to the American decision to establish a permanent military presence in Japan, was read in Washington as the beginning of the final Soviet push for world conquest; whereas the active American military response, provoked by this Soviet move, appeared in Moscow (and not entirely without reason) as a threat to the Soviet position in both Manchuria and in eastern Siberia.

And so it went, less intensively, to be sure, after Stalin's death, but nonetheless tragically and unnecessarily, into the respective misinterpretations of such later events as the bringing of the Germans into NATO, the launching of the first Sputnik, the decision to introduce nuclear weapons into the continental components of NATO, the second and prolonged Berlin crisis provoked by Khrushchev in the late fifties and early sixties, and finally the Cuban missile crisis. Each misreading set the stage for the next one. And with each of them, the grip of military rivalry on the minds of policymakers on both sides was tightened and made more final.

VII

One of the most fateful effects of this preoccupation with the military aspects of the relationship was to dull in a great many Americans, including many legislators, opinion-makers and policymakers, the sensitivity to real and significant changes occurring in Soviet society and leadership. Most fateful of all was their effect in obscuring the significance of Stalin's death. The changes that followed on that event were of course gradual ones, and ones of degree. In part, they were the objects of deliberate efforts at concealment on the part of the new leadership. All this, admittedly, made them not always easy of recognition. But they were important. They greatly deserved American attention. And they were not indiscernible to trained and attentive eyes, of which the American government had a number, if it had cared to use them.

The Khrushchev era, and particularly the years from 1955 to 1960, presented what was unquestionably the most favorable situation that had existed since the 1920s for an improvement of relations with Russia and for a tempering of what was by this time rapidly becoming a dangerous, expensive, and generally undesirable competition in the development of armed forces and weapons systems.

Khrushchev certainly had his failings—among them, his boasting, his crudeness, his occasional brutalities, his preoccupation with Soviet prestige and his ebullient efforts to ensure it—most of these were the failings of a man who was outstandingly a peasant *parvenu*, not born to the habit or expectation of great power and with a tendency to overdo in the exercise of it. But he was intensely human, even in relations with the ideological opponent. One could talk with him—talk, so far as he was concerned, to the very limits of one's physical stamina (his own appeared to be unlimited).

The primitive and naïve nature of Khrushchev's faith in Marxist-Leninist principles as he understood them was, strange as this may seem, an advantage; for it caused him to wish, even in confrontation with the capitalist visitor, to convince, to convert, and—to this end—to communicate. This, from the standpoint of efforts to reach a better understanding, was far better than the crafty cynicism of a Stalin. To which must be added the recollection that Khrushchev's secret speech, at the Twentieth Congress of the Party in 1956, dealt to the extreme Stalinist tendencies in the Party and in the world communist movement a blow from which they were never fully to recover.

The Khrushchev period, too, was of course not lacking in serious crises. In addition to the Berlin crisis mentioned above, there was, above all, the Hungarian rebellion of 1956. It should not be taken as an apology for the Soviet action at that time if one points out that this action was neither correctly understood nor usefully reacted to on the American side. The misunderstanding arose (as it was again to do in the face of the Czechoslovak crisis of 1968) from the apparent inability of a great many Americans to understand that the Soviet hegemony over Eastern Europe, established by a force of arms in the final phases of the war and tacitly accepted by this country, was a seriously intended arrangement that the Soviet leadership proposed to maintain, if necessary, by the same means with which they had acquired it.

As for the American reaction: the resort to armed force by the Western powers was never a feasible alternative; the conflict could not have been limited; and even Hungary was not worth a nuclear war. Where the United States might usefully have acted was by an offer to make certain modifications in its military posture in Western Europe if the Soviet government would let things in Hungary take their course. But the preoccupation of the American Secretary of State at that moment with the deplorable happenings of the Suez crisis, together with the already firm commitment of the United States and the other NATO members against anything resembling a disengagement in Europe, made such an offer impossible.

The situation remained, therefore, essentially unchanged. In certain relatively powerless sectors of the American government, establishment people continued to explore, patiently and with insight, the possible channels of approach to a less dangerous and more hopeful state of affairs. But in other and more powerful echelons, other people continued to carry on with the concepts born of the Korean War, as though Stalin had never died, as though no changes had occurred, as though the problem were still, and solely, the achievement of superiority in preparation for a future military encounter accepted as inevitable, rather than the avoidance of a disastrous encounter for which there was no logical reason at all and which no one could expect to win. The interests of the gathering of military intelligence continued to be given precedence over the possibilities for diplomatic communication. And who does not remember the result? The almost predictable accident occurred. The U-2 plane was brought crashing to the ground in the center of Russia, carrying with it the prestige of Khrushchev, discrediting him in the eyes of his own colleagues, shattering his ascendancy over the Soviet military establishment, hastening the end of a career already seriously jeopardized by other factors.

VIII

Four years were still to elapse before Khrushchev's final fall—years marked by President Kennedy's rather unsuccessful effort to establish a personal relationship with Khrushchev, and by the further complication of the Cuban missile crisis. Whether the unwise effort to put missiles in Cuba was something forced upon Khrushchev by his own colleagues, or whether it was a last desperate gamble on his part with a view to restoring his waning authority, seems still to be uncertain; but that it completed the destruction of his career is not. And from 1965 on, with LBJ now in the White House by his own right and with Khrushchev removed from the scene, a new period opened in Soviet-American relations.

The omens, at the outset of Mr. Johnson's incumbency, were not, by and large, wholly unfavorable. The shock of the recent unpleasantnesses still weighed, to be sure, upon the atmosphere of relations. But even the fall of Khrushchev had not canceled out many of the favorable changes in Soviet conditions against which Soviet-American relations had to proceed; modest improvements, and gradual ones, to be sure, but not without their significance. The terror had been mitigated. The independence of the secret police had been greatly curtailed. There had been some relaxation of the restrictions on association of Russians with foreigners. There was a greater willingness on the part of the authorities to permit many forms of participation by Soviet citizens in international life, culturally and in the sports. These changes were, to be sure, only partially recognized in Washington. Many people, as the future would show, remained quite blind to them. But LBJ and his Secretary of State, Dean Rusk, were not wholly oblivious to them, nor did they fail to try to take some advantage of them. The result was that certain gains were made, in the 1966–68 period which, if one had been able to build further on them, might well have developed into the sort of thing that later, in the early 1970s, came to be known as "détente." (The word was in fact even then in use.) Agreements were reached on the opening up of direct airline communications, on the establishment of consular representation in cities other than the respective capitals, and (in very modest measure) on certain fishing problems. New arrangements for cultural exchange were agreed upon, and the first soundings were taken for what were later to be the SALT talks and the collaboration in space exploration and research.

These beginnings soon fell victim, however, to two developments: first, the Soviet action in Czechoslovakia in 1968; secondly, and of much greater importance, the American involvement in Vietnam. It was not until the first could be forgotten, and the second brought into process of liquidation in the early 1970s, that prospects again opened up for further progress along the lines pioneered by Messrs. Johnson and Rusk some four to six years earlier.

IX

The positive results of the phase of Soviet-American relations that came to be known (somewhat misleadingly) as the Nixon-Kissinger détente are too recent to require extensive recapitulation. These results were compressed, for the most part, into an extraordinarily short period, but one full of activity: from the time of the Kissinger visit to China in the summer of 1971 to the Brezhnev visit to the United States in June 1973. The individual bilateral agreements arrived at in the course of the various negotiations and high-level visits were too numerous to be listed here. They covered some 15 to 20 subjects, sometimes overlapping, and sometimes representing successive stages in the treatment of a single subject. Not all of them were of great political importance; a number of them represented beginnings, rather than the full-fledged achievement of wholly open, fruitful and secure arrangements; but they represented steps forward. The most important of them was, without question, the SALT agreement signed by Messrs. Nixon and Brezhnev on the occasion of the former's visit to Moscow in May 1972.

These were all bilateral Soviet-American agreements. They were flanked, of course, in their early stages, by the achievements of what came to be called Chancellor Willy Brandt's "Ostpolitik." (Again, this was a poor term—as though this were the first German government, or the last, ever to have a policy toward the East.) There were also the highly confusing and largely meaningless negotiations that were to lead, eventually to the Helsinki agreements—multilateral negotiations in which the Americans took only an unenthusiastic and secondary part. But by and large, the Nixon-Kissinger détente was a movement of a positive nature in bilateral Soviet-American relations, observed even with some uncertainty and misgiving by America's European allies.

From the Soviet standpoint this effort of policy was stimulated and made possible by two changes in the international situation that marked the early 1970s: the liquidation of America's Vietnam involvement and the Nixon visit to Peking, followed by the establishment of a de facto American-Chinese official relationship. At the American end it was of course simultaneously the presence in positions of authority in Washington of two men: Richard Nixon, then at the height of his power and prestige, bringing to the White House a reputation as a cold-war hard-liner which gave him a certain margin of immunity from right-wing attack as he moved to improve relations with Russia; and Henry Kissinger, who brought to the operation a measure of imagination, boldness of approach, and sophistication of understanding without which it would have been difficult of achievement.

Both sides saw in this effort toward the improvement and enrichment of the relationship a chance for reducing the dangers of unlimited rivalry and proliferation in the field of nuclear weaponry; and both, be it said to their credit, were aware of the immense, almost mandatory, importance of progress in this direction. In addition to this, the Soviet side saw reinforcement for itself in its relations with Communist China, and a measure of assurance against too intimate or exclusive an association between that power and the United States. The American side was astute enough to realize that the various rigidities that marked the cold war, both as a state of mind in America and as a condition of American-Soviet relations, were not conducive to American interests in other areas of the world. In addition to this it is evident that Mr. Nixon was not wholly indifferent to the domestic political fruits to be derived from the drama of successive summit meetings.

These recognitions, however, also roughly defined and delimited the aims and the scope of détente. Beyond them, it was not possible to go. The Soviet leaders were determined that the development should not affect the intactness of the dictatorship at home; nor was it to hinder them from continuing to adopt, with relation to the problems of third countries, a rhetorical and political stance of principled revolutionary Marxism, designed to protect them from charges by the Chinese Communists that they were betraying the cause of Leninism-Marxism. There is no evidence that they ever attempted to conceal from their Western opposite numbers the nature or the seriousness of these reservations.

Whether, in their actions affecting the 1973 Middle Eastern war and—somewhat later—Angola, the Soviet authorities did not violate at least the spirit of the earlier understandings with Messrs. Nixon and Kissinger is a question that surpasses the limits of this examination. But some people on the American side certainly thought that this was the case; and the impression was used to justify the very clear changes that did occur in American policy.

The pressures against détente had never been absent in Washington, even at the height of its development; they had only been repressed by the momentary prestige and authority of the White House. As the power of the Nixon presidency disintegrated in 1973 and 1974, the anti-détente forces moved again to the battle lines, and with great effectiveness. This was, to some extent, only to be expected; for the overdramatization of the earlier contacts and negotiations had bred false hopes and concepts of what could be achieved; and a certain disillusionment was inevitable. The signs of this reaction were already apparent in late 1973. Efforts to save the situation by another (and very misconceived) Nixon visit to Moscow, in June 1974, were unavailing. Some limited further progress was made, to be sure, in the field of cultural exchanges. But by this time, resistance in the Pentagon and elsewhere to any further concessions of consequence in the SALT talks, as well as to any acts of self-restraint in the development of American weapons programs, was too strong to be overcome, particularly by a desperate and harassed Nixon, or even by a bewildered Gerald Ford, by no means personally unresponsive to hard-line pressures.

The Jackson-Vanik Amendment, and the subsequent demise of the trade pact, dealt a bitter blow to any hopes for retaining the very considerable momentum that had been obtained in the development of Soviet-American relations. The very modest and tentative results of the Vladivostok meeting led only to new protests and attacks from anti-détente forces that now had the bit in their teeth and were not to be gainsaid. By the beginning of 1975, although the various cultural agreements reached under the heading of détente were still in effect and were being, so far as can be judged from the public reports, punctiliously observed by both sides, the prospects for further success in the SALT talks had been heavily damaged, and along with them the political atmosphere in which, alone, further progress could be made in the improvement of the Soviet-American relationship generally.

What followed—the wrangling over the language of the Helsinki agreements, the conflict over Angola, even the most recent spate of expressions of alarm in Washington over the pace of development of the Soviet armed forces—these were in the main the products rather than the causes of the limited deterioration of the Soviet-American relationship which the period since mid-1973 has witnessed.

X

It would be idle to pretend, as the year 1976 runs its course, that the prospects for the future of Soviet-American relations are anything less than problematical. Formidable impediments continue to lie across the path of any efforts at improvement. The Soviet authorities will no doubt continue to adhere to internal practices of a repressive nature that will continue to offend large sections of American opinion. They will continue to guard what they regard as their right or their duty to subject the United States to periodic rhetorical denunciation and to give to anti-American political factions in third countries forms of support that Americans will find unreconcilable with a desire for good relations with this country. They will, rather because they are Russians than because they are Communists, continue to cultivate and maintain armed forces on a scale far greater than any visible threat to their security would seem to warrant. They will continue what they will describe as efforts to achieve parity with the United States in naval and long-range nuclear capabilities; and others will continue to be in doubt as to whether these are not really efforts to achieve a decisive, and irrevocable, superiority. They will continue to hide all their undertakings behind a wholly unnecessary degree of secrecy—a secrecy which invites exaggerated fears on the other side and enhances the very dangers to which it is supposed to be responsive. None of this will be helpful to the development of the relationship.

On the other hand, the Soviet leadership has, and will continue to have, a high degree of awareness of the dangers of a continued nuclear competition. Along with all its exaggerated military efforts, it does not want, and will not want, a world war. It has a keen realization of the suicidal nature of any nuclear war; and it has too many internal problems to allow it to wish to assume inordinate risks. It is now governed, furthermore, by a relatively old, habit-worn and weary bureaucracy, which is going to have to give over in the relatively near future. Waiting in the wings is a new generation of officials who, insofar as one is able to judge them at all, would appear to be no less tough than their elders, no less capable, and certainly no less nationalistic, but more pragmatic, less confined by ideological rigidities, less inhibited in association and converse with foreigners. To which must be added that curious streak of friendly and sometimes even admiring interest in the United States—a mixture of curiosity, eagerness for peaceful rivalry, and sometimes even real liking—that runs through the Soviet population and has never failed to be noted by observant American students of Russian life.

All these factors lend assurance that, given an American policy reasonably adjusted to these contradictions of the official Russian personality and conscious of the immensity of what is at stake in the future of the relationship, there need be no greater danger of apocalyptic disaster arising out of that relationship than there has been in the past—and the United

States, after all, has contrived to live in the same world with this regime for over half a century without finding it necessary to resort to arms against it in order to protect American interests. Possibly there could even be a further successful effort to improve things.

But if this is to occur, American statesmanship will have to overcome some of the traits that have handicapped it in the past in dealing with this most unusual, most dangerous, and most serious of all the problems of foreign policy it has ever had to face. It will have to overcome that subjectivity that caused Americans to be strongly pro-Soviet at the height of the Stalin era and equally anti-Soviet in the days of Khrushchev, and to acquire a greater steadiness and realism of vision before the phenomenon of Soviet power. It will have to make greater progress than it has made to date in controlling the compulsions of the military-industrial complex and in addressing itself seriously to the diminution, whether by agreement or by unilateral restraint or both, of the scope and intensity of the weapons race.

American politicians will have to learn to resist the urge to exploit, as a target for rhetorical demonstrations of belligerent vigilance, the image of a formidable external rival in world affairs. And American diplomacy will have to overcome, in greater measure than it has done to date, those problems of privacy of decision and long-term consistency of behavior which, as Tocqueville once pointed out, were bound to burden American democracy when the country rose to the stature of a great power. In all of this, American statesmanship will need the support of a press and communications media more serious, and less inclined to oversimplify and dramatize in their coverage of American foreign policy, than what we have known in the recent past.

It is not impossible for American government and society to make these advances. To do so, they have only to match the best examples of American statesmanship in the past, but then to give to their achievements, this time, a more enduring commitment and a deeper general understanding than was the case at other high moments of American performance.

There is not, however, infinite time for the achievement of these results. Certain of the trends of international life at this moment for which the United States bears a very special responsibility, notably the steady expansion and proliferation of nuclear weaponry and the preposterous development of the export of arms from major industrial countries, are ones which it is impossible to project much farther into the future without inviting catastrophes too apocalyptic to contemplate. The greatest mistake American policymakers could make, as the country moves into the years of a new Administration, would be to assume that time is not running out on all of us, themselves included.

[SIX]

The United States and Latin America: Ending the Hegemonic Presumption

Abraham F. Lowenthal

Like the last streak of lightning in a summer storm, the Chile Report of the Senate Select Committee on Intelligence illuminates the contours of recent relations between the United States and Latin America, even as that landscape is changing. With impressive detail and understated force, the Report not only documents what the United States did in Chile from 1963 through 1973; it also illustrates the

Abraham F. Lowenthal, formerly Director of Studies for the Council on Foreign Relations, now heads the Latin American program at the Woodrow Wilson International Center for Scholars. He has written *The Dominican Intervention* and other works.

hegemonic presumption upon which this country has long based its policies toward Latin America and the Caribbean.

But the days of unchallenged U.S. control of the Western Hemisphere are numbered, if not already past. U.S. relations with Latin America are consequently being transformed. The historic "special relationship" between the United States and Latin America is coming to an end—in fact if not yet in rhetoric. A new U.S. approach toward hemispheric relations is required.

II

The Senate's Chile Report shows that the U.S. government engaged for over a decade in a massive, systematic, and sustained covert campaign against the Chilean Left. The Report removes from further controversy these key facts about U.S. involvement in Chilean politics:

1. The United States spent about $3 million during the 1964 election campaign in Chile, mostly on behalf of Eduardo Frei's Christian Democratic campaign; an equivalent level of spending in a U.S. election would be over $75 million, much more than was used to finance Richard Nixon's lavishly funded 1972 election.

2. The United States spent some $8 million on covert intervention in Chilean politics from 1970 through 1973. Among the items financed were political activities among workers, students, women's groups, professional organizations, and other civic associations; propaganda; planted "news" stories and editorials in Chilean newspapers and magazines; and even the inspiration and subsequent diffusion of articles on Chile by CIA-subsidized "journalists" from other countries.

3. The United States also employed various economic pressures—first to try to prevent the election of Salvador Allende, Chile's Marxist leader, and then to abort his

presidency. Although the CIA formally rejected the suggestion of the U.S. corporation ITT that the company might contribute up to $1 million to combat Allende, the Agency did suggest an alternate recipient of anti-Allende financing.

4. President Nixon, his adviser for National Security Affairs Henry Kissinger, the Director of the Central Intelligence Agency, and the Attorney General adopted a highly secret plan, not revealed even to the U.S. Embassy in Santiago, to stimulate a military coup in order to prevent Allende's ever coming to power after the 1970 popular election.

5. After that coup attempt failed (not without costing the life of René Schneider, Chile's Army Chief of Staff), the U.S. government expressed its hostility to Allende's brand of socialism in many other ways: by cutting off access to international loans and credits and stimulating local capital flight; by feeding misinformation to Chilean military officers to foster fear of supposed Cuban subversive activities; and by financing opposition movements, even from the terrorist Right.[1]

What the U.S. government did in and to Chile during the 1960s and early 1970s was not unique in U.S-Latin American relations, although it was in some ways anachronistic, a residue of programs set in motion early in the 1960s, at the height of the cold war and of the Alliance for Progress. The covert intervention in Chile was probably unprecedented in scope, style and duration, perhaps because the circumstances were so special; no other socialist revolutionary movement has come close to triumph in South America, much less been elected to office.

But though the degree of clandestine U.S. intervention against Allende may have been exceptional, particularly as late as the 1970s, none of the specific activities undertaken in Chile was unprecedented. On the contrary, what the U.S. government did in Chile climaxed an extended era of U.S. interventions in Latin America.

In Argentina in 1945, the United States published a "Blue Book" lambasting Juan Peron's incumbent regime in a vain (and counterproductive) attempt to aid Peron's political opponents.

In Guatemala in 1954, the CIA successfully orchestrated an invasion to oust the Left-leaning Arbenz regime, and the U.S. Ambassador led the effort to establish a successor government.

In Bolivia during the 1950s and 1960s, the United States retained several cabinet officials on the CIA payroll, provided budget support for over one-third of the national government's expenditures and flooded the country with technical assistance advisers. U.S. influence on Bolivian public policy was vast, if not always effective; one key adviser later recalled that "a much needed reform in the real property tax system . . . and an effective income tax . . . went by the board solely because there was no one who had the time, the fluency in Spanish, and the persuasiveness to put the measure across." [2]

At the Bay of Pigs in 1961, the U.S. Navy convoyed a U.S.-trained and U.S.-supplied anti-Castro army to ignominious defeat, thus culminating (although not concluding) extensive U.S. attempts to oust Fidel Castro's regime. Propaganda, economic pressures, sabotage, covert support for counterrevolutionary groups, even attempts to assassinate Cuba's leaders—all punctuated this hostile campaign.

In Guyana (British Guiana) in the early 1960s, the U.S. government used its penetration of the trade union movement as well as other instruments of covert intervention to thwart Cheddi Jagan's nationalist movement.

In Brazil in 1964, so obvious was U.S. enthusiasm about João Goulart's overthrow that the U.S. government sent official congratulations to the ensuing military government almost before it could be installed. Even prior to that, intense American concern about Brazil's political course led the United States to influence local decision-making in Brazil's northeast, at the expense of that region's prospects for development.[3]

In Santo Domingo in 1965, over 22,000 U.S. Marines and paratroops landed to forestall what Washington perceived as a possible communist takeover. The "request" for U.S. forces, drafted in English with help from a U.S. attaché, came to the U.S. Embassy from a hastily assembled Dominican junta that had itself been set up with American participation.[4] And U.S. officials had been meddling frantically in Dominican affairs for years, before the 1965 military intervention, as John Bartlow Martin's memoir *Overtaken By Events* so fully reveals.

Even in Ecuador—far from the United States and of little obvious economic or strategic importance—more than half the members of the Communist Party's Central Committee in the mid-1960s were CIA agents or informers, according to Philip Agee's account, *Inside the Company*.

This is not the time or place to judge all these cold-war episodes. Many of them, perhaps all, seemed justified when they occurred because of the threats U.S. policymakers perceived to this country's "national security." Understanding themselves to be locked in a worldwide and all-out contest with the Soviet Union, U.S. officials undertook intervention in Latin America not for its own sake, nor for economic exploitation, but for what they regarded as defensive reasons. But one important point is clear: all these interventionist activities flowed from America's hegemonic presumption—the belief in this country that the entire hemisphere was a rightful sphere of U.S. influence. That belief led U.S. officials to regard as unacceptable the emergence of any anti-American political group in any Latin America country. And over-whelming U.S. power made it possible for this country to involve itself deeply in internal politics throughout the Americas in order to ensure that any group which challenged U.S. domination did not come to power, or did not last.

III

The hegemonic presumption of the United States in the Western Hemisphere emerged gradually over many decades, asserting itself first in the Caribbean and only later throughout the Americas. During the first few decades of this nation's independent existence the United States seemed mostly indifferent toward Spanish and Portuguese America. Goods sent from the United States to Latin America in 1796 accounted for only three percent of total U.S. exports. This country's political interest in the region was hardly greater than its commercial involvement. The U.S. delegates to the first Pan American Congress, convened in Panama exactly 150 years ago by Simón Bolívar, never arrived. John Quincy Adams, one of the earliest architects of U.S. foreign policy, argued against those who urged more active U.S. involvement in the Latin American struggles for independence; he emphasized that "there is no community of interest between North and South America. There is no basis for an American system." Even the Monroe Doctrine of 1823, often interpreted as a major U.S. initiative toward the hemisphere, may be better understood as a convenient endorsement of British policy, explainable largely in terms of domestic American electoral politics.[5]

Beginning in the mid-nineteenth century, however, the burgeoning United States of America became a nation of continental scope and industrial prowess imbued with grand notions of Manifest Destiny. From that period on, close relations with Latin America and the Caribbean have invariably been an important part of this country's international stance. The United States has made its presence strongly felt in the Americas: economically, politically, militarily, socially and culturally. Sometimes the impact of the United States has been benign, supportive and protective; often it has been stifling or even exploitative. But never in the past hundred

[186]

years has the North American presence in hemispheric life been insignificant.

The nature of inter-American relations has changed from time to time, mostly reflecting shifts in the wider international position of the United States. Latin America's relationship to this country has been like that of the circus mirror that heightens and exaggerates. Tendencies of U.S. policy that are subordinate in other parts of the world have been enlarged and given free rein in Latin America, often in disturbing ways. "Gunboat diplomacy" and "dollar diplomacy" both found their fullest expression in the Western Hemisphere early in the twentieth century. The unwillingness of the United States to tolerate ideological deviance has been most clearly exemplified in the conduct of hemispheric affairs.

The more noble of North American impulses have also been magnified in the context of U.S.-Latin American relations. The U.S. desire to spread democracy's gospel has been most strongly reflected in the doctrines and practice of Western Hemisphere relations. So have the U.S. aims, often genuine and deeply felt, to promote economic betterment and to champion equality of opportunity.

For many decades, U.S. relations with the other countries of the hemisphere accounted for most of this nation's international involvement. Of the 50 times the United States sent troops outside North America during the nineteenth century, for example, 43 instances were in Latin America and the Caribbean. More than half of all U.S. foreign investment at the end of World War I was within this hemisphere. Sixty percent of all U.S. diplomatic personnel stationed abroad in the 1920s were assigned in Latin America and the Caribbean. At the height of this country's "isolationism" in the 1920s, active U.S. involvement in the Americas continued uninterrupted.

From the mid-nineteenth century to the 1930s, U.S. interest focused on Mexico, Central America and the Caribbean. This was the first region to feel the projection of exploding North American power. Washington's expansionist impulse swept across the border with Mexico, incorporating Texas into the United States. Santo Domingo came within one Senator's vote of being annexed by the United States in 1870. Cuba, freed of Spanish rule in 1898, was subjected by 1903 to the Platt Amendment, granting the United States the right to intervene. Panama was forced at its inception to concede to the United States the right to "act as if it were sovereign" within part of Panamanian territory. Puerto Rico was taken over outright.

Financial and commercial interests in the Caribbean were perhaps the main concerns of U.S. foreign policy from the late nineteenth century until World War I. The highest priority of U.S. policy was the preemptive aim to exclude competing influences from this border region. Within the 25 years beginning in 1898, U.S. soldiers landed in Cuba, Puerto Rico, the Dominican Republic, Haiti, Nicaragua, Honduras, Panama, and even Mexico. Most of these countries became virtual U.S. protectorates. When the United States was not ruling directly, it was forming juntas, training constabularies, collecting taxes and customs, reforming education, or revising laws. American motives were sometimes generous, but U.S. programs were often naïve in the extreme, and respect for local sovereignty or sensibilities was rarely a constraint.

When the U.S. troops departed—as they did from everywhere but Puerto Rico and Guantanamo by 1934—they left behind countries deeply penetrated by the United States and very sensitive to U.S. influence. In the Dominican Republic, the U.S. dollar remained the official currency for years after the U.S. occupation; in Panama, the dollar still circulates as freely as the country's own paper money.

Until the eve of World War II, the "Latin American policy" of the United States mainly dealt with Mexico, Central America and the Caribbean. Every time in this century that American troops have been sent to Latin

America, they have gone to the circum-Caribbean region. Well over half the total U.S. investment in Latin America in 1929 was concentrated in these nearby countries, especially in Cuba and Mexico. To take another kind of measure, of the 40 articles *Foreign Affairs* had published on hemisphere relations by 1943, 31 primarily discussed Mexico, Central America or the Caribbean; only one article was devoted to Brazil.

It was not until the 1930s that the United States began to extend considerable attention to South America as well. Although its most specific meaning and application was in the Caribbean, the "Good Neighbor Policy" proclaimed by President Franklin D. Roosevelt in his 1933 Inaugural was conceived and announced as a hemisphere-wide policy. The rhetoric of Pan-Americanism, previously purveyed by the United States largely for commercial reasons, now gained new currency as Latin American desires to constrain U.S. interventionism dovetailed with U.S. aims to secure cordial hemispheric relations in a time of political and economic troubles. President Roosevelt convened an inter-American conference in Buenos Aires in 1936, Secretary of State Hull devoted considerable effort to solidifying neighborly ties, and Ambassador Josephus Daniels invested his formidable energies to secure an amicable resolution of the dispute arising from Mexico's expropriation of U.S. oil companies.

Beneath the level of rhetoric, international conferences, and negotiations, the U.S. War Department was busy by 1940 building airstrips and other military installations in most countries. The FBI was just as busy establishing a major intelligence network. By the time the United States entered World War II, this country was more fully ensconced throughout Latin America (except in Argentina) than ever before.

The foreign policies and military measures taken by most countries of the region during World War II were closely coordinated with the war-making efforts of the United States.

All the Latin American states formally entered the war on the Allied side, and Brazil even sent an entire division to fight in Italy. Strategic materials from Latin America contributed importantly to the U.S. campaign. Latin America supplied the United States with all of its quinine and balsa wood; 56 percent of its tin; 43 percent of its crude rubber; 83 percent of this country's copper imports, and 76.7 percent of its imported vanadium. Regional trade patterns came to concentrate increasingly on commerce with the United States.

After the war—with Germany and Japan defeated, England, France and Russia severely weakened, and the U.S. economy booming—Washington's influence throughout Latin America (as elsewhere) grew to unprecedented dimensions. Economically, Latin America moved increasingly into the U.S. orbit. The share of Latin American exports destined for the United States, which had climbed steadily from about 12 percent in 1910, spurted to 45 percent by 1958. The share of U.S. imports coming from Latin America reached a historic high of some 37 percent in 1950, more than half again what it had been before World War II. U.S. investment in Latin America quintupled in the 25 years after World War II, seeking out new opportunities in manufacturing and in services to complement the earlier involvement in natural resource extraction. American investment gained predominance in practically every country in the region.

Politically, the two decades immediately following World War II marked the zenith of U.S. power in the Americas. An Inter-American System was created, institutionalizing North American paramountcy. The Rio Treaty of 1947 (the Inter-American Treaty of Reciprocal Assistance) formalized close political and security relations in the hemisphere. The Organization of American States (OAS), with headquarters in Washington, was established in 1948 as a regional institution authorized to impose and enforce collective sanctions and to act as a forum of first instance for disputes arising within the

Americas. A network of inter-American military institutions—schools, defense councils, training programs, and the like—provided a means to ensure continuing U.S. influence in that sphere through devices ranging from standardized weapons and procedures to personal influence. A host of bilateral and multilateral modes of providing foreign aid channeled U.S. technical, educational and economic advice. The Inter-American Development Bank was created in 1959 to channel U.S. and other resources to Latin America, with Washington retaining predominant influence over the use of its funds, and even an effective veto on soft loans.

In their relations with the rest of the world, the countries of Latin America and the Caribbean looked to the United States for leadership. Whether for their own motives or because of Washington's pressures (and usually for both reasons) they almost uniformly supported this country's major foreign policy initiatives: in establishing the United Nations and its accompanying postwar international institutions; in opposing presumed Soviet expansionist aims; in backing Israel's creation; in extending assistance for Europe's reconstruction; and in "uniting for peace" to oppose North Korea's invasion in 1950.

The predominant U.S. concern with the cold war was largely (and rather unquestioningly) adopted by the nations of Latin America and the Caribbean as their own. An OAS resolution adopted at Caracas in 1954 barred international communism from this hemisphere, for instance. During this cold-war period, less than half the members of the OAS even maintained diplomatic relations with the Soviet Union. No country of the region, except Cuba, had any international relationship remotely comparable in significance to its ties to Washington.

President John F. Kennedy's proclamation of the Alliance for Progress in 1961—itself primarily a response to the Cuban revolution and its challenge to U.S. hegemony—heralded the apogee of North American involvement in hemisphere affairs.

For a brief moment, Washington appeared to care deeply about the whole region: to be concerned about its economic growth, its social and political development, and its internal security. The number of U.S. government personnel assigned to Latin America jumped, crowding the suburbs of Latin American capitals with embassy officers and "spooks," technicians from the Agency for International Development, cultural and military advisers—and dotting the countrysides with Peace Corps volunteers. Predictably, inter-American institutions blossomed as U.S. concerns with the region intensified. The staff and budget of the OAS quintupled after 1961, and the programs of the Inter-American Development Bank expanded at a similar pace.

The U.S. government engaged itself deeply in the domestic affairs of countries as diverse as Venezuela and Chile, Peru and Brazil, Bolivia and Panama, Cuba and the Dominican Republic, Guatemala and Honduras. U.S. pressures forced elections to be held, and sometimes determined the results. U.S. influence caused civic action programs to be started, planning boards to be established, and currencies to be devalued. U.S. troops were used only in Santo Domingo in 1965, but the United States also influenced Latin American politics by granting or withholding diplomatic recognition or "aid"; by providing technical assistance and advice; by training military and police units and supplying them with sundry types of equipment; and by all the techniques illustrated in the Chilean and Cuban cases.

By 1965, when the Dominican invasion dramatically reversed this country's prolonged adherence to its pledge to forswear unilateral military intervention, the United States had convincingly asserted its sphere of influence throughout the whole Western Hemisphere. In September of that year, the U.S. House of Representatives provided perhaps the clearest official statement ever that this country has a right to shape political choices throughout the Caribbean, Central and

South America. In what amounted to an after-the-fact defense of the Dominican intervention, the House declared that even the threat of intervention by "the subversive forces known as international communism" would justify the United States resorting to armed force, in the "exercise of individual self-defense." This underlying and widely accepted North American attitude—that the U.S. government has a right to remove from hemispheric political life whatever forces it deems threatening—conditioned the Nixon-Kissinger response to Salvador Allende's election in Chile.

Although Washington's hegemonic presumption has been most clearly demonstrated by overt and covert intervention in the name of national security, its influence has by no means been limited to the strategic sphere. The hegemonic presumption helps account for other striking aspects of recent inter-American relations: the intensely active U.S. pressure for reform during the Alliance for Progress years; Washington's efforts in the 1960s to force Latin American regimes to respect democratic procedures, accompanied by covert U.S. measures to influence their results; the attempts by the U.S. Congress to determine what kinds of military equipment Latin American nations could purchase; and the extraordinary lengths to which the U.S. government has been willing to go to aid specific U.S. corporations in their clashes with Latin American hosts.[6]

IV

Trends in Latin America and elsewhere are, however, quickly eroding the bases for this country's hegemonic presumption which only ten years ago seemed beyond serious challenge.

Cuba's success in institutionalizing a revolutionary socialist regime allied with the Soviet Union provides the most dramatic daily reminder that U.S. hegemony has waned.

Having survived countless U.S. efforts to unseat him and having outlasted five American Presidents already, Fidel Castro has shown that "geographical determinism" can be reversed. His Soviet patrons have brought units of their Navy into the Caribbean each of the past several years, ending a 70-year period in which unfriendly fleets were excluded from the American Mediterranean.

The decline of U.S. domination in the security realm is not limited to the extreme case of Cuba. The almost total Latin American dependence on U.S. arms during the period from World War II until 1965 has given way to a remarkable diversification of weapons sources. From 1968 through 1972, 87 percent of Latin America's arms purchases came from countries other than the United States. All six Latin American countries with supersonic jets fly French Mirages. Peru's flirtation with the Soviet Union, moreover, has led to the first significant military training program undertaken by an extra-hemispheric power in South America since World War II.

In economic terms, the degree of U.S. dominance in the hemisphere has declined sharply as Latin American nations have diversified their production and their commerce. Whereas Latin America as a whole sent almost half its exports to the United States in 1950, the regional figure now stands at 32 percent. The share of Latin America's imports coming from the United States has dropped from 57 percent to 37 percent in 25 years and is still declining. Japan has multiplied exports to Latin America tenfold since 1960, and other nations of Eastern and Western Europe are also significantly expanding their trade with the region. Peru, for example, now exports almost exactly as much to the communist countries and to the European Community as it does to the United States.

Although direct U.S. investment in Latin America continues to be very substantial, its nature is changing (mainly from resource extraction to manufacturing and service) and its relative significance for Latin America's development is declining as other nations begin to invest more heavily in the region. In 1964 the United States supplied almost half of the total of Brazil's foreign investment; by now the U.S. share is less than 30 percent. In 1973, new Japanese investment in Brazil exceeded that of the United States for the first time; and since 1973 investors from the oil-rich Arab countries have been attracted to Brazil as well. Across the entire region, the share of private gross capital flow coming from the Eurocurrency market has climbed to over 75 percent.

Nationalizations, compensated or not, have since 1960 removed all U.S. direct investment from Cuba, most from Peru, a good deal from Chile, and much from other countries, including the entire Venezuelan petroleum industry, taken over by Caracas with hardly a hitch on January 1, 1976. The U.S. firms continuing to do business in Latin America are finding their styles cramped and their incomes shaved by host governments that are increasingly able to bargain effectively for more advantageous terms. Strict new rules for foreign investment are being implemented in countries as different as Peru, Jamaica, Brazil and Guyana. Gaining strength from regional cooperation, the members of the Andean Common Market have been fairly successful, at least until recent setbacks, in establishing new modes of foreign investment.

In general, the weak and dependent governments of Latin America that used to look to Washington for leadership are being replaced by ever more self-confident regimes, eager to exert their influence in international affairs. All over Latin America, the state has been strengthened enormously in recent years. Cuba's socialist experiment provides the most extreme example, of course, but even in Brazil, government expenditures now account for 37 percent of the gross national product, compared with 17 percent in 1950, and the Brazilian state now plays a significant entrepreneurial role in the dynamic intermediate and capital goods sectors. In Peru, the state's share of total national investment climbed from 13 percent in 1965 to over 50 percent by 1973. In Venezuela—once a capitalist bastion—state enterprises now run the petroleum, petrochemical, and iron sectors.

Latin American governments tax more, spend more, regulate more, prohibit more, and control more than regimes in the region have ever done before. They have access to a rapidly expanding resource base. Brazil's economic miracle—industrial exports have multiplied 20-fold since 1964 and GNP has climbed at 10 percent a year for almost a decade—has been most impressive. But all over the region, Latin America's economies have done well: 5.1 percent growth per year in the 1950s, 5.6 percent in the 1960s, and over 6 percent in the 1970s. However unequally distributed Latin America's growth may be, it has significantly expanded the region's power.

Many of those who actually run the strengthened Latin American states reject U.S. dominance. Traditional elites favorably disposed toward the United States are being replaced by technocrats—civilian and military—often of a nationalistic bent. These new leaders, many of them well-trained (often in U.S. graduate schools), tend to identify their interests independently of, and even through confrontation with, the United States.

Within the United Nations and elsewhere, the Latin American countries are finding their own way. Mexico's and· Brazil's votes on the U.N. resolution identifying Zionism as "racism," Brazil's early recognition of the Soviet-backed Popular Movement for the Liberation of Angola (MPLA), and the many Latin American votes favoring Angola's admission to the General Assembly demonstrate this fact. On many issues—fishing zones, nuclear proliferation, debt management, buffer stocks, special drawing rights, and others—the Latin American nations differ among themselves, but few nations any longer start automatically with a U.S. position or U.S. premises. The eventual influence of the various Latin

American countries on the struggle to create a viable "new international economic order" is not yet clear, but they will surely act independently of Washington's dictates. Latin Americans have taken the lead in founding and strengthening the United Nations Conference on Trade and Development (UNCTAD), establishing cartels, promoting indexing, devising fade-out formulas, and elaborating codes of corporate conduct; their pursuit of these objectives is not likely to cease now that Third World efforts are beginning to pay off.

Nor are the political activities and interests of the Latin American countries beyond the Western Hemisphere any longer easily inhibited by the United States. Venezuela's role as a founding member of the Organization of Petroleum Exporting Countries (OPEC); Mexico's initiative in promoting the Charter of Economic Rights and Duties of States; Peru's close relations with the Soviet Union; Brazil's nuclear arrangement with Germany; Cuba's intervention in Angola— all illustrate the new capacity of Latin American nations to play important parts on the global stage regardless of Washington's script. Latin American states are participating actively not only in UNCTAD (where, as in other U.N. negotiations, they are part of the Third World "Group of 77"), but in the Conference on International Economic Cooperation, in the Conference of Non-Aligned Nations, and in various cartels and commodity arrangements.

Ever since the Consensus of Viña del Mar statement presented to President Nixon in 1969, the Latin American nations have increasingly organized themselves to exert pressure on the United States: against the import surcharge in 1971, against the anti-OPEC provisions of the 1974 Trade Act, against the continued OAS embargo of Cuba, in solidarity with Panama's struggle to assert its sovereignty in the Canal Zone, and in favor of a proposed OAS charter reform intended primarily to hamstring the United States.

Bilaterally, too, the countries of Latin America are facing up to the Colossus of the North. Brazil, although still in many ways allied with the United States, has begun to clash with Washington on a wide variety of increasingly important matters, including fishing rights, population policy, export subsidies, commodity agreements, and nuclear power. Peru, only a few years ago dependent on the U.S. Embassy for reliable information regarding foreign private investment within the country's own borders, now bargains hard with American and other transnational firms. Panama, a country with no significant natural resource beyond its location, has mobilized regional and even extra-regional support to challenge perpetual U.S. control of the Canal. Colombia ended its bilateral aid accord with the United States because it resented the "aid" relationship, and when Washington criticized Cuba's Angolan involvement, Colombia's President publicly rebuked the United States for its own extra-hemispheric military interventions. Cuba itself, of course, once so overwhelmed by the United States that it was described as "no more independent than Long Island," has fundamentally overturned its relationship with this country.

V

The response of the U.S. government under Secretary of State Henry Kissinger to the quickly changing facts of hemispheric and international life has been doggedly to reassert the "special relationship" and the sense of "hemispheric community" which are said to exist between the United States and Latin America.

Both concepts have a venerable tradition in inter-American discourse. The "Western Hemisphere Idea"—that the countries of the region have a special relation toward one another that sets them apart from the rest of the world—has been a familiar theme since before the Monroe Doctrine.[7] The notion goes beyond the obvious assertion that nations linked by geography are likely to have some common interests. It maintains that the nations of South America share among themselves so much history, so many values, so many cultural traits as to ensure hemispheric amity and the pursuit of regional approaches to common problems. "Pan-Americanism" has been a powerful idea, accepted not just by orators on ceremonial occasions but by the architects of numerous regional economic, military, cultural and political institutions.

The idea of an inter-American "community," of a natural harmony between the United States and Latin America, has also influenced U.S. rhetoric and policy toward the region throughout this country's independent history. From John Quincy Adams and Simón Bolívar on, there have always been doubters of the presumed mutuality of interest between the Americas, North and South. But the dominant view, from Henry Clay to Henry Kissinger, has been to emphasize—or simply to assume—shared or compatible interests.

The closely related concepts of "special relationship" and "inter-American community" have often been advanced as the framework for articulating U.S. policy toward Latin America and the Caribbean. The key speeches outlining John F. Kennedy's Alliance for Progress and Richard Nixon's Mature Partnership were laced with these doctrines. So was Nelson Rockefeller's 1969 Report, *The Quality of Life in the Americas*. Rockefeller called for reinvigorating the "special relationship" through a series of new regional mechanisms and by reorganizing the U.S. government to deal with Western Hemisphere affairs as a Cabinet-level concern.

Although many of Rockefeller's specific recommendations were rejected or ignored, his vision of U.S.-Latin American relations continues to be accepted by many in the United States, apparently including Secretary Kissinger. When sharply unfavorable international trends helped the Secretary late in 1973 to discover Latin America anew and to seek support there for U.S. initiatives, the message Kissinger carried with him to Tlatelolco in Mexico was that the United States was prepared for a "New Dialogue" with Latin America on the basis of hemispheric "community."

Aside from feeling that a unilaterally proclaimed dialogue—like a unilaterally proclaimed alliance—is inherently problematical, the Latin American Foreign Ministers welcomed Secretary Kissinger's sudden interest in hemispheric problems. One after another, however, they resisted the language of "community," because they felt it obscured, intentionally or not, the unresolved issues between the United States and Latin America; all references to "community" were purged from the communiqué closing the Conference. Thus educated, Secretary Kissinger dropped the phrase but not the concept. As recently as February of 1976, speaking in Caracas on the occasion of his second formal visit as Secretary to Latin America, Mr. Kissinger referred no less than 11 times in nine pages to the "special relationship." And reporting to Congress on his return, the Secretary promised further efforts to "perfect the undeniable community which exists in this part of the world."

Latin American leaders from many countries and from various places on the political spectrum are coming to reject the idea of a special and exclusive relationship between their countries and the United States. Previous notions of Pan-American harmony are being replaced all over the continent by perceptions of conflict. Inter-American organizations long overwhelmed by the United States—the OAS (for which the United States pays two-thirds of the budget) being the prime example—are being allowed to atrophy. New intra-Latin American regional and subregional institutions excluding the United States, such as the Latin American Economic System (SELA) and the Andean Common Market, are gaining stature, if not yet proven strength. Most important, many leaders in Latin America and the Caribbean think that their nations' interests may often be closer to those of developing countries outside the hemisphere than to those of the United States. Few Latin Americans still assume that their countries' interests and Washington's are inevitably the same; on the contrary, many think that the United States will oppose their concerns, as well as those of the rest of the developing world. Few Latin American leaders now expect U.S.-Latin American relations to be overwhelmingly friendly; most anticipate tensions, if not hostility.

In part, this changed Latin American expectation is due to the role the United States has played as a bulwark of the established international economic and political order. In part, the new Latin American approach to the United States and to inter-American relations simply reflects increased assertiveness flowing from enhanced power. But it also reflects an objective change—the transformation of Latin American economies from inward-turned import substitution to outward-oriented export promotion. Most Latin American countries (except for some of the smallest) are no longer mainly interested in obtaining bilateral concessional assistance from the United States; now they care primarily about securing universal trading rules which will facilitate improved access to the industrial world's markets.

As Latin America's economies change, and as the region's stake in global rules and arrangements increases, hostility may deepen between the countries of Latin America and the Caribbean (and less-developed countries generally), and those of the industrial North, including the United States. The "new international economic order" will be the rubric. Commodities, tariffs, countervailing duties, debt management, special drawing rights, technology transfer, the conservation and management of resources, the terms on which capital and labor migrate, the making and management of international rules and institutions will be some of the specific issues. The name of the game, however, will be redistribution: of resources, of income, of status and of power. The challenge for U.S. policy in the Western Hemisphere for years to come will be to protect essential U.S. interests in an era when real conflict, not unchallenged hegemony, should be presumed.

VI

If hegemony is no longer a fact and the "special relationship" is not an appropriate guide for policy, how should Washington approach its relations with the countries of Latin America and the Caribbean? Surely we should base our approach on a thoughtful assessment of our nation's interests and how these relate to those of the other countries in the hemisphere, rather than simply on inherited doctrines or on unexamined habits of thought. But what are our interests, and what should be the aims of our hemispheric relations?

The first step toward an improved Latin American policy would be to realize that for most purposes we probably should not have a distinct Latin American policy at all. The main problems the United States will face in the Western Hemisphere over the next decade are not regional but global questions: making more fair and secure the terms of exchange between producers and consumers of primary products; expanding food and energy production and improving their distribution; using and conserving world resources (of the earth, space and the oceans) efficiently and equitably; curbing the diversion of funds for military purposes; limiting pollution and dealing with its consequences; improving the welfare of individuals and communities; protecting fundamental human rights; trying to end state and antistate terrorism in all its forms; assisting the victims of natural disasters and avoiding man-made catastrophes; and building more effective structures of global decision-making. The United States could better its relations with Latin America most by focusing seriously, and in a sustained way, on these critical issues.

In taking up these questions, the United States will find that its relations with Latin America and the Caribbean assume renewed importance. As the most powerful and prosperous part of the Third World, Latin America will significantly influence how the international economic order evolves. As major exporters of both primary products and manufactured goods, Latin American countries will greatly affect the future of world trade. As an area with considerable potential to expand agricultural production, Latin America will play a central role in dealing with world food problems. As a region with advanced technological capacity, Latin America will help determine whether or not nuclear technology spreads, and whether industrial pollution worsens. With many of the world's major fishing countries, Latin America will significantly affect the law and future use of the seas. As an arena where long-dormant interstate conflicts have recently been rekindled, Latin America will provide key tests of the prospects for curbing arms races. As a region with long-standing doctrines regarding respect for human rights but one now suffering from a plague of brutal repression, Latin America's evolution will importantly affect the future of human rights and their institutionalized protection or suppression.

The primary aim of U.S. policy toward the countries of Latin America and the Caribbean should be to secure their active cooperation in dealing with this broad global agenda. Their cooperation should not be sought, nor will it be extended, because of special regional ties or bonds of traditional friendship. It should be sought, and may well be granted, because the countries of Latin America have very much to gain from, and a good deal to contribute to, solving these global problems. Mutually profitable economic and cultural exchanges between the United States and Latin America would be aspects of working together on the issues of greatest concern.

In dealing with its global agenda, special sensitivity by the United States to the impact of its actions and inactions on its closest neighbors makes good sense; special regional policies for universal problems do not. On some specific problems— reporting on human rights violations, for instance, or perhaps for cultural exchanges—regional institutions may still have a place; on most issues Latin American countries should be dealt with on the basis of their interests, not their location.

While we should no longer assume that common interests automatically bind the United States and Latin America, we need not accept total hemispheric conflict as inevitable. The challenge for U.S. policy in the Americas is to nurture common interests where they exist or are latent, to help resolve intra-hemispheric tensions when conciliation is feasible, and to mitigate the effects of conflict when clashes occur. We should not be surprised or alarmed by recurrent or even deepening frictions in U.S.-Latin American relations: over tariffs and subsidies, debts and remittances, investments and nationalizations, exchange controls, technology transfer, immigration and other issues. We should neither ignore these frictions nor try to suppress them, but should rather build and fortify structures which anticipate and help resolve conflicts. New formulas should thus be sought to reconcile the interests of importers and exporters, producers and consumers, borrowers and lenders.

Spelling out in detail how the United States should try to gain help from Latin America and the Caribbean for dealing with global concerns would require another essay, but five key principles may be advanced:

1. In the United States we should free ourselves—in rhetoric, attitude and practice—of the legacy of interven-

tionism and paternalism. We should discipline ourselves to respect the sovereignty of all Latin American countries, regardless of their size or ideology.

Putting this principle into practice means (among other things) renouncing overt and covert intervention, abandoning coercive or discriminatory procedures, reaching an agreement with Panama which treats that country as a juridical equal, and making mutual respect the basis of our approach toward Cuba and every other country in the region—and toward Puerto Rico as well.

2. In dealing with Latin America, we should concern ourselves with the shared problems of economic security and of improving individual and collective welfare, and should focus less on security questions in the narrowly defined military sense.

Putting this principle into practice means accepting the fact that the days of absolute military security in the hemisphere are long and irrevocably gone, and understanding the truth that the greatest threat other countries of the region have perceived has often been from the United States. It means realizing that nations other than Cuba, particularly in the Caribbean, may choose socialist means of production and organization without implying any threat to this country. It also means accepting as natural that the nations of Latin America and the Caribbean will develop various links both among themselves and to nations outside the hemisphere. We ought to concentrate not on trying to limit the ties Latin American countries have outside the hemisphere, but on encouraging the states of Latin America to generate support from across the world for attempts to solve global problems.

3. We should resolve to help make the Americas safe for diversity. Though we should not try to impose on any nation our own ideological or economic preferences, we should make clear our own values—our commitments to freedom, to

democracy, to justice and equity, to individual dignity. And we should avoid associating ourselves closely with those who violate standards we regard as fundamental.

Putting this principle into practice means refraining from interference in the domestic affairs of other nations, while retaining a legitimate concern for the protection of universally recognized rights. More specifically, it means understanding that while we have no right to "destabilize," we do have an obligation not to aid those who torture and repress, and to assist the victims of repression whether they are victims of the Left or of the Right. And it means facing up to the fact that U.S. influence—still considerable though no longer over-whelming—has too often been used to support those who trample on rights we consider essential.

4. We should recognize that our relations with the countries of Latin America and the Caribbean are not all similar or of equal priority.

In practice this means analyzing how the interests and objectives of the various states of Latin America and the Caribbean differ among themselves, and how they relate to our own interests. The main unifying feature in recent Latin American history has been shared resistance to U.S. hegemony; as our predominance ebbs, intra-regional and subregional differences may well emerge. The United States ought to devote special priority to improving its understanding of and relations with three sets of countries: those where U.S. economic interests are concentrated (primarily Brazil and Mexico); those likely to exert particular influence in interna-tional forums (primarily Brazil and Venezuela, but also Cuba, for different reasons); and those most closely tied to the United States by patterns of trade and migration (particularly Mexico and the island territories of the Caribbean). As the era of U.S. hegemony throughout the Americas draws to a close, particular thought should be devoted to how the United States might best relate to the Caribbean territories, so many of which appear as satellites in search of an orbit.[8]

5. Finally, we should recognize that the end of U.S. hegemony implies that we cannot expect to achieve all of our goals in the region.

The United States is by far the strongest country in the Western Hemisphere, the only truly great power, and it will remain so for many years to come. We need not fear that our influence will be minimal or our main aims usually thwarted. But we must accept the fact that international and regional changes will limit our capacity to have our way.

One key fact which reduced influence will highlight is that priorities will conflict in the hemisphere. Devising sensible procedures for resolving investment disputes may run counter, at least in the short term, to the perceived interests of particular U.S. corporations. Insisting on the protection of essential human rights may tend to threaten the political stability our corporations expect abroad. The expansion of Latin American exports may involve increasing sectoral unemployment in our country, to which we will have to respond either by restricting imports or by providing effective adjustment assistance to displaced companies and workers. Our desire to deal effectively with the critical danger of nuclear proliferation may bring us into direct conflict with the understandable national ambitions of several Latin American states.

To fashion sound policies, the United States will face difficult choices in a hemisphere in which it is still very powerful but no longer unquestionably in charge. Recognizing that the Western Hemisphere is no longer our "sphere of influence" will therefore be painful, but no other basis for policy toward Latin America will be possible in this country's third century.

NOTES

1. See *Covert Action in Chile, 1963–1973*, Staff Report of the Select Committee to Study Governmental Operations with Respect to Intelligence Activities, U.S. Senate, 94th Cong., 1st Sess., December 18, 1975.

2. See George J. Eder, *Inflation and Development in Latin America: A History of Inflation and Stability in Bolivia*, Ann Arbor: University of Michigan Press, 1968, p. 163.

3. See Riordan Roett. *The Politics of Foreign Aid in Northwest Brazil*, Nashville, Tenn.: Vanderbilt University Press, 1972, and Joseph Page, *The Revolution That Never Was: Northeast Brazil, 1955–1964*, New York: Grossman, 1972.

4. For details, see Abraham F. Lowenthal, *The Dominican Intervention*, Cambridge, Mass.: Harvard University Press, 1972.

5. See Ernest R. May, *The Making of the Monroe Doctrine*, Cambridge, Mass.: Harvard University Press, 1975.

6. The classic, almost pathological, case of Peru's dispute with the International Petroleum Company (IPC) nicely illustrates this final point: over the course of several years Washington repeatedly punished or threatened to punish Peru's government in order to force a settlement acceptable to IPC. The end result, ironically, was to help bring to power a nationalist military regime which expropriated the IPC within weeks of taking office.

7. See Arthur P. Whitaker, *The Western Hemisphere Idea: Its Rise and Decline*, Ithaca, N.Y.: Cornell Univ. Press, 1954.

8. See also my article, "Toward A New Caribbean Policy," *SAIS Review*, Fall 1974, pp. 5–19.

[SEVEN]

U.S. Foreign Economic Policy, 1776-1976

Charles P. Kindleberger

It is tempting to view the evolution of U.S. foreign economic policy from 1776 to 1976 as one from isolationism to participation to leadership of the world economic system, a process now starting to show signs of reversal. In terms of the theory of private and public goods, this country for some 170 years looked after its private national interest, then spent a quarter of a century playing a leadership role, pursuing at the same time what it conceived as the public international interest, before exhausting itself and perhaps turning back exclusively to its own affairs.[1] Or, in Albert Hirschman's brilliant model of relations within social groupings, the country has moved from "exit" to "loyalty" to "voice"—first a

---

Charles P. Kindleberger is Professor of Economics Emeritus at the Massachusetts Institute of Technology. He is the author of *International Economics; Economic Growth in France and Britain; The World in Depression, 1929-39* and other works.

participatory voice and then the voice of command—and may be again heading for the exit.[2]

But such themes would be too simple. The country is not a unified actor with a single set of purposes, but an amalgam of shifting interests which engage customarily in ambiguous compromises. Economic foreign policy may be global or may make distinctions among regions (North America, Europe, Latin America, Asia, Australasia and most recently Africa); among functions (trade, money, capital and aid transfers, migration, not to mention foreign growth and integration). At any one time there are complex trade-offs among various national and international interests rather than any one dominating the others. There is likely to be a high positive correlation among policies regarding different aspects of the country's economic relations with the rest of the world; nonetheless, there is no escape from detailed description and analysis.

Our interest attaches principally to the recent past. I propose first to sketch the period to World War I rapidly. Thereafter follow sections dealing separately with the 1920s, the Depression, the years following World War II through the 1960s, and then from about 1968 to the present. A brief section concludes with reflections on the prospects now facing both the United States and the world.

II

The American Revolution represented not so much a withdrawal from European and especially British life as an insistence on relating to Europe on different terms from those decreed by British decision. The Navigation Acts which determined where and how colonial shipping could be used, taxation from Whitehall, impressment of colonials as sailors in the British Navy—all were economic as well as political issues in which colonial interests were threatened by imperious decisions at a distance. The isolationism of Washington's Farewell Address (1796) and the Monroe Doctrine (1823) came later, with a revulsion against the Napoleonic Wars over more than 20 years—wars that incidentally enabled the struggling nation first to win its military independence and second to conduct its economic affairs independently.

But the nation had little in the way of a unified national interest. The Constitution of 1789 prohibited export taxation, deliberately foreclosing the possibility that central government could hurt the interests of an exporting state through taxing its output sold abroad. The idea originated not from the free trade of Adam Smith's *Wealth of Nations* of 1776 but in earlier Physiocratic doctrine, which Smith also embraced. "Laissez-faire, laissez-passer" was a French agricultural doctrine to free food for exports, as opposed to the doctrine of supply which would keep it at home for domestic consumption. The latter echoes today in embargoes on steel scrap, peeler logs, soybeans, wheat and the like.

In the absence of export taxes, federal revenues came largely from duties on imports. The Continental Congress levied a tariff of five percent "for revenue only" across the board. Debate followed almost immediately. Madison and Jefferson, from Virginia, wanted low tariffs to expand export trade through buying imports freely. Massachusetts and Pennsylvania sought protection for manufacturing. The tariff of 1789 was a moderate compromise, with five percent duties in general except for rates ranging up to 15 percent on a limited list of manufactures. Alexander Hamilton's well-known "Report on Manufactures" of 1792 did not affect the course of events.[3]

More significant was the Embargo of December 1807, precipitated by British impressment of American seamen. That Embargo, the Non-Intercourse Act of 1809, and war with England in 1812 produced substantial change in the course of economic development. War is the ultimate protective tariff. Embargo and war stimulated the cotton and woolen textile mills of New England and the iron foundries of Pennsylvania. With the restoration of peace, the tariff question became acute. It was a matter not of procreating infant industries, but of preventing infanticide. Agriculture was preoccupied with supplying Europe with grain, cotton and tobacco after the Congress of Vienna, and did not immediately resist; it began to do so after the fall of European agricultural prices, and the passage of the Corn Laws in Britain in 1819. Tariffs were raised further in 1824, but after the "tariff of abominations" of 1828 reaction set in. Early in the 1830s some duties were lowered, and in 1833 the Compromise Tariff produced a more general reduction. That this was followed by the depression of 1837—a result of the expansion of bank credit by the Second Bank of the United States—and led to the Whig, later Republican, view that tariff reductions spell depression.

In this period—and indeed until the last 40 years—the tariff was a domestic issue only. Higher duties in 1842 and reductions in 1846 and 1857 were unrelated to the free-trade movement under way in Europe. Led by Britain, which rationalized tariffs in the 1820s and 1830s before dismantling the Corn Laws and the Navigation Acts in the 1840s and freeing the export of machinery, the Continent moved to tariff reduction on a reciprocal basis during the boom of the 1850s, but especially after the Anglo-French (Cobden-Chevalier) Treaty of 1860. British leadership in the movement was important, as was the ideological character of certain free-trade forces under the influence of the economic doctrines of Smith, Ricardo and Mill.

Canada was sharply affected by the repeal of the Corn Laws and the Navigation Acts, and some Montrealers contemplated annexation to the United States. A less far-reaching remedy was found in reciprocal trade in natural products in a treaty of

1854. The special economic status of Canada, between the United States and Britain and having particular relations with each, remained an issue for the rest of the period.

While the United States was largely absorbed in its own affairs, many of those affairs, or those of constituent parts of the country, involved foreign economic questions. The Louisiana Purchase of 1803—financed by a loan issued in Amsterdam—riveted the attention of the Middle West briefly on Europe, from which it turned again on a heightened basis to exploration, Indians, land settlement. New York merchants and financiers, New England shipbuilders and traders, Southern planters, canal-builders and railroaders all had eyes on European markets. In transportation, the United States pioneered in fitting steam engines to ships: in the liner, or scheduled vessel that sailed each Saturday whether it had a full cargo or not, and in clipper ships. Cotton-growing in the South exploded in the 1820s and 1830s, and moved rapidly inward from the sea islands and the coastal belt to the Gulf states and across the Mississippi. New York bankers established branches in Liverpool (later moved to London) to finance the movement of staples eastward and of a wide variety of goods westward. The First Bank of the United States sold shares abroad, and the Second Bank borrowed in London on bullion.

With the rise of shipping came an upsurge of immigration, initially from Britain and Scandinavia, and after the disastrous crop failure of 1846, in a flood from Ireland and Germany. (An American myth holds that the Germans who flowed to these shores after 1848 were moved by conscience in revolt against monarchical repression and military conscription. The Carl Schurzes among the migrants, however, numbered several hundred out of hundreds of thousands.) Industrialization in Britain, Germany and Scandinavia after mid-century slowed down the flow of overcrowded peasants from these sources.

In the 1880s, however, there developed an entirely new economic interaction between the United States and Europe. Up to that time the farms of the New World had furnished largely exotic foods and materials not produced on a large scale in Europe—cotton, tobacco and sugar. But after the Civil War, the opening up of the Northwest Territories, with 40 acres and a mule for war veterans, made possible dramatic increases in grain production, while newly constructed railroads and iron-clad, steam-powered, screw-propeller ships became available to move the grain to Europe. Along with similarly stimulated supplies from Canada, Australia, Argentina and the Ukraine, the new flow led to a drastic fall in the price of wheat in Europe, and uprooted a vast army of peasants and landless workers in Southern and Southeastern Europe—who poured into the steerage holds of ships bound for Ellis Island and New York.

Limitation of immigration of "undesirables," including the ill, convicts, and Oriental "slave labor," had been undertaken in the United States in 1862 and 1875. In 1885 an attempt was made to stem the flow from Europe through a ban on contract labor. There was, however, no stopping the flood of workers who came individually and without work, looking for a new chance. The strong tradition of the United States as a place of asylum for the oppressed of Europe prevented the passage of any effective legislation to limit immigration, such as by a requirement of ability to read and write English.

Moreover, immigration from Europe met a critical need in the American growth process. In Europe, economic growth to a considerable extent was achieved through what is called the [Sir Arthur] Lewis model of "growth with unlimited supplies of labor," hardly distinguishable from the Marxian "reserve army of the unemployed." Unlimited supplies of labor off the farm held down wages, raised profits, led to reinvestment of profits and sustained growth. In the United States, early growth came from unlimited supplies of land which furnished a good livelihood to independent farmers. When manufacturing began to flourish—mainly because of the spillover of demand from affluent agriculture and only partly as a response to protectionist tariff policies—the massive infusion of labor sustained the process.

A high land-labor ratio from the beginning meant high wages, and high wages in turn predisposed American manufacturers to labor-saving invention. Eli Whitney responded with the cotton gin, which made possible the expansion of the cotton crop and of British and New England cotton-textile industries. He further perfected interchangeable parts. The Colt revolver, the McCormick reaper, the Singer sewing machine, and the typewriter were among the labor-saving devices which poured forth from Yankee ingenuity. They quickly led to manufactured exports and subsequently to subsidiary factories abroad. The roots of the multinational corporation in manufacturing, usually thought of as a product of the jet aircraft and transatlantic telephone 100 years later, stretch back virtually to the middle of the nineteenth century. The Colt revolver and the McCormick reaper scored successes at the Crystal Palace Exhibition of 1851 and the Paris Exposition of 1855.

Finance had gone abroad as a handmaiden of trade long before manufacturing. Industry and the states of the republic had borrowed in foreign financial centers since the 1820s, and had chalked up a substantial record of default and failure. The role of the federal government in these matters was small until the 1840s, when the first borrowing of consequence since the Revolution was undertaken to finance war with Mexico. Peabody, Seligman, Morgan, Drexel, and other less illustrious names gradually shifted their overseas operations from trade to investment banking more generally.

In monetary affairs, the United States sought to adhere to bimetallism, and then to the gold standard, although its finances seemed chaotic in the view from European centers, as speculative excess led to boom and bust, mania and panic, especially in 1836, 1857, 1872, 1893 and 1907, which sent shock waves reverberating back to Liverpool, London, Paris, Amsterdam and Hamburg. It was necessary to suspend specie payments and to issue greenbacks during the Civil War, resulting in depreciation of the Union dollar—though to nothing like the extent of Confederate money or the Continental currencies. After the war, the question was merely one of when to resume specie payments, and how. Resumption was achieved in 1879. An important change had been made in 1873, when the flood of silver from Nevada after 1869 depressed its price. A continuous preoccupation since the Coinage Act of 1792 had been to get the ratio of silver to gold right, so as to thwart Gresham's Law that overvalued money drives undervalued out of circulation. Up to the 1830s, when the United States ratio was 15 of silver to 1 of gold to the general European ratio of 15.5 to 1, the country gained silver and lost gold. In 1834 and 1837 the ratio was changed to 16 to 1. By 1872, however, 16 to 1 was too high a value for silver, and bimetallism was then abandoned in favor of gold, to the distress of Populists for the rest of the century.

Tariff policy at this time was dominated by fiscal considerations. When the Treasury was pinched, as in 1862 during the Civil War, tariffs were raised; when revenue was ample, as in 1872, lowered. But by 1890, as a result of depression, the McKinley tariff raised rates, especially on wool and sugar, only to have the act of 1894 under President Cleveland partly reverse the result, largely on the basis of trust-busting and opposition to monopoly. Action against trusts, however, stopped at the water's edge. No action was taken against the collaboration of large American firms with one another or with foreign firms in foreign markets, except insofar as they conspired to restrain competition in the U.S. market.

By the turn of the century, the United States was beginning

to move away from an isolationist parochialism to a role in world society. As early as 1853-54, Commodore Perry had opened up Japan to American and European shipping and trade. When the Berlin Conference of 1885 among the European powers accelerated the pace of imperialistic acquisition, the United States became restive. In 1898 the explosion of the *Maine* in Havana harbor provided an excuse for a war against Spain in which Cuba, among others, obtained its independence, but Puerto Rico and the Philippines became United States protectorates. In the chaos which followed liberation, American investors (trusts?) acquired major properties in Cuba, especially the Isle of Pines, in an episode which recalls the carpetbagging in the South during the Reconstruction after the Civil War.[4] Fearful of being left behind by European powers, the United States sought an open door in China. The beginnings of foreign aid may be found in U.S. use of its share of the indemnity required of China after the Boxer uprising of 1900 for charitable work in China.

The sharp depression of 1907 raised questions about the efficacy of the national banking system established in 1863. No longer completely self-sufficient, the country established the Aldrich Commission which reviewed banking legislation in other countries to study how to improve banking organization. Senator Aldrich also gave his name to the Payne-Aldrich Tariff of 1909 which raised tariffs to their highest point in the history of the country before World War I. Democratic victory in 1912 with the election of President Wilson brought the passage of both the Federal Reserve Act and the sharply reduced Underwood Tariff of 1913. The Payne-Aldrich Act was said to favor trusts, and to have produced depression in 1910.

Up to 1914, dominant economic issues were argued in terms of domestic interests in a world taken as given, which U.S. action did little to affect, rather than in terms of economic

[217]

theory or foreign relations. The British-dominated international economic system served American interests well. The
country could afford to be loyal to that system, despite the
claims of Southwestern farmers and Western miners that it
depressed prices. Gold in California in 1848, silver in Nevada
in 1869, the expansion of wheat acreage in the 1870s, and the
bubbles followed by bursts throughout the century from 1815
to 1914 affected the system in ways we chose to ignore. That
was the business of someone else—perhaps in London. America did what it did. Feedback to other nations was ignored.

III

World War I changed the entire position of the United
States in the world economy. According to economic analysis
a country progresses through a series of stages: young debtor,
mature debtor, young creditor and mature creditor. The
United States went from the first to the fourth in three years,
from 1914 to 1917. Assembly-line methods devised by Henry
Ford just prior to the war were expanded to produce
equipment and munitions for the Allied powers of Europe and
for the United States itself. Based on the Federal Reserve
System, the financial apparatus of the country grew in parallel.
J. P. Morgan & Co. financed British and French private
borrowing in the United States, and served as fiscal agent in
supporting the pound and franc in foreign-exchange markets.
In the end, the U.S. government itself undertook to finance
Allied borrowing in dollars, especially those for consumption
and reconstruction in 1918 and 1919.

Revisionist historians maintain that the entry of the United
States into World War I was a continuation of the imperialist
policies of the turn of the century, and of the expansion of
American trusts into overseas markets needed to sustain the
rate of profit at home. These policies are thought to have been

motivated by the Eastern establishment's desire, conscious or unconscious, to take over world economic domination from the City of London and other European economic power centers. The U.S. government is said early to have sought the expansion of overseas banking in order to push the use of the dollar in world trade and finance.[5] The theory suffers a logical flaw. Aggressive economic designs would have been more readily achieved by staying aloof from the battle, remaining "too proud to fight." The simpler and naïve purpose of "saving the world for democracy"—a non-economic motive—better fits the facts and the logic.

Saving the world was one thing; keeping it saved was something else. President Wilson had plans for remaining involved in European and world affairs. They were not widely shared. The United States refused to ratify the Treaty of Versailles, to accept reparations, or to join the League of Nations with its Economic and Financial Department to worry about world economic questions. It did, however, join the International Labour Organisation, established at Geneva in response to a proposal of the French trade unionist, Albert Thomas, and did cooperate with the League on a wide number of issues. General commitment to participate in the world political and economic system was withheld.

The war interrupted a wave of immigration which had reached, on a gross basis, one million persons in 1913. In 1917 an Immigration Act was passed after long debate, and over the veto of President Wilson, providing that immigration be based on quotas conforming to national origins of the existing population. This restricted immigration from Southern and Southeastern Europe in favor of the Northern and Western sections. In 1921 and 1924, overall quotas were reduced. The action is generally ascribed to trade-union desire to limit the workforce and preserve wage gains achieved during the war. More fundamentally, the motivation was socio-political rather than economic, reflecting widespread concern that it would be difficult socially to absorb the vast numbers of would-be immigrants backed up in the countries of supply.

The most serious economic issues arising from the war dealt with reparations and war debts. Having been strengthened economically rather than hurt by war, the country refused to accept reparations, but insisted on being repaid by its Allies for war and postwar loans. It further maintained that war debts and reparations were unrelated, contrary to French and British positions, the latter expressed in the Balfour Note of August 1922. Not until the Hoover moratorium of June 1931 was the connection acknowledged; and even after reparations had been buried at Lausanne in July 1932, Hoover in 1932 and Roosevelt in 1933 continued to try to collect war debts.

The United States played a role in reparations, however, through private individuals. When the Versailles arrangements broke down after the German inflation and after the occupation of the Ruhr by Belgian and French troops, Charles G. Dawes served in 1923-24 as chairman of a commission to write a new plan. The conventional wisdom has held that Dawes was simply American window-dressing for a staff plan drawn up by British civil servants, but this is now known to be oversimplification. One British aim in the Dawes Plan was that the revised Reichsbank should hold foreign exchange, that is, pounds sterling, among its reserves. On U.S. insistence the Dawes Plan specified that Reichsbank reserves be held in gold—an echo of a controversy between France and the United States forty-plus years later but with the U.S. role reversed.[6]

By 1930, when Owen D. Young served in a similar capacity on a revised reparation scheme, U.S. involvement in European financial questions was complete. While much of the attention of government was focused on domestic problems—the Florida land boom, the rise of the automobile industry, and the decline in agriculture—Eastern finance was being drawn into world affairs. The Dawes Plan provided for

[220]

issuance of a loan for Germany. The New York *tranche* (or slice) was oversubscribed 11 times and gave a sharp stimulus to foreign lending generally. The Agent-General for Reparations, established under the Plan, was S. Parker Gilbert, formerly of J. P. Morgan & Co.

During the 1920s, moreover, Benjamin Strong, the President of the Federal Reserve Bank of New York, was often called upon to arbitrate the central-bank quarrels of Europe, largely between Montagu Norman of the Bank of England and Emile Moreau of the Bank of France. Strong had a leading role in urging the return of the pound to par in April 1925. Then, within two years, he faced a dilemma, whether to lower interest rates in New York to assist the British with outflows of capital, or to raise them to slow down the boom in business and in security prices. He chose the former, and from March 1928 the stock market soared.

Economists call it a "dilemma position" when monetary policy is pulled in one direction by external and in another by internal requirements. For a long time, Strong's choice of aid to Britain's maintenance of the gold standard over curbing the speculative excesses of the stock market was regarded as a bad one. More recently, "monetarist" economic historians such as the Nobel-laureate Milton Friedman have shifted the debate, arguing that, while Strong was wrong in favoring foreign over domestic considerations, he should have ignored the stock market and focused on a steady expansion of the money supply.[7] I am no more moved by this revisionism than by the political brand. Money supply was growing, and in fact declined very little up to March 1931. To the economic revisionists, it was not growing fast enough, a subtle argument but unconvincing.[8]

In Wilson's Fourteen Points, only the third had dealt with economic questions, and called for "removal, so far as possible, of all economic barriers and the establishment of an equality of trade conditions among all nations consenting to the peace and associating with its maintenance." It evoked little response, either at home or abroad. The United States in Harding's Administration took action in the Fordney-McCumber Tariff of 1922 to nurture its new crop of wartime infant industries. Tariffs were similarly raised all over the world.

The League of Nations undertook to reverse the trend in a series of conventions, many of them technical, for lifting trade from the chaos into which it had fallen during the war and the period of postwar monetary disturbance. In 1927 a World Economic Conference, with the United States as observer, met in Geneva and adopted a series of resolutions for lowering tariffs and opening up trade channels. No action was taken under it. Instead, Herbert Hoover, campaigning for the presidency in 1928, promised to do something for agriculture to alleviate its plight under the pressure of falling prices, which had begun in 1925. That something was to be what Josef Schumpeter called "the Republican household remedy": increased tariffs. In due course, this commitment ended up as the Hawley-Smoot Tariff of June 1930.

On tariff matters, disaggregated economic interests and recommended policies diverged for ideological reasons, or what is perhaps better explained as cultural lag. The North and Middle West, interested in manufacturing, favored Republican high tariffs; the South, with a traditional stake in the export of cotton, was Democratic and opposed to protection. (Middle Western agriculture was ambivalent: interested in exports of grain and lard, but worried about farm imports from Canada and Australia.) But the economic base underlying these positions was changing. In the Middle West, manufacturing had risen through mass production to an export position, which would benefit from freer trade; in the South, especially North and South Carolina and Georgia, the cotton-textile industry, moving in from New England in the 1920s and 1930s, gave many states a greater interest in cotton textiles than in cotton production. Not until after World War

II did the South begin to qualify its doctrinaire espousal of free trade; and a Senator such as Robert Taft from Cincinnati, a city exporting machine tools to the world, never altered his inherited protectionist views in the economic interests of his constituents. Detroit in the 1920s was rising to a position like Manchester in Britain during the first half of the nineteenth century. It was slow in drawing policy consequences.

IV

To Herbert Hoover, the Depression which started in 1929 was the fault of Europe, and there was little that the United States could or should do internationally to remedy it. The Hawley-Smoot Tariff of 1930 was a domestic measure, undertaken to relieve agriculture. If the movement to raise tariffs spread beyond farm products to manufactures, and if tariff rates were raised to unconscionable levels, as 34 protesting nations abroad contended, Hoover nevertheless regarded it as a private U.S. matter. He did not answer widespread criticism that creditor nations should not raise tariffs on the ground that this prevents debtors from paying interest and amortization—an oversimplified and dubious doctrine, as it happens. (Tariffs under stable conditions raise income which spills over into further imports, to change for the most part the structure rather than the total quantity of imports.) Mostly, however, he failed to see the Hawley-Smoot Tariff as the major action in setting off a retaliatory tariff war of the beggar-thy-neighbor sort. World trade shrank in a declining spiral, as the quantities and prices of traded commodities continuously fell.

The impact of the Depression in the United States ricocheted abroad in other ways. The United States stopped buying as much abroad and also stopped lending, thus cutting down on available foreign exchange in two ways. In British

[223]

lending of the nineteenth century, foreign and domestic investment alternated: when the periphery lost receipts from exports, it was able to borrow. This was not a matter of policy, but of the action of market forces. In the United States lending policy was minimal. The Department of State had asked Wall Street to notify it of impending bond issues so that it could indicate if there were foreign-policy objections to particular loans. And the Johnson Act of 1930 stipulated that borrowers in countries in default on war debts could not have access to American capital markets, but this manifestation of congressional irritation on war debts should not have had any effect on major borrowers in Germany, the Dominions and Latin America that owed no war debts. Nevertheless, there was nothing that President Hoover could do to stimulate lending. It picked up in the second quarter of 1930 and then mysteriously collapsed.

In 1931, Hoover acceded belatedly to the suggestion for a moratorium on war debts and reparations; failed to take vigorous action to stop the financial runs on Austria, Germany and Britain, partly because of the necessity of agreeing with France; and ignored the strongly deflationary impact of the appreciation of the dollar—flowing from the depreciation of the pound sterling—on U.S. farm prices, banks in agricultural areas, and ultimately on banks more generally. Mr. Hoover had an enviable record in international affairs as mining engineer and as administrator of food relief for Belgium immediately after the war. His vision of interrelations among world economies under stress, however, was a limited one, and contrasted sharply with the broader view espoused by such Eastern establishment spirits as Dwight Morrow, a Morgan partner.[9]

Foreign economic policy suffered in 1932-33, when Hoover was unable to govern and Roosevelt refused—after the election but before his inauguration—to make decisions before he bore responsibility. With the Inauguration and the Bank Holiday, the "Hundred Days" involved a hectic series of decisions, largely on domestic programs—the Agricultural Adjustment Act, National Recovery Act, Thomas Amendment, and the like. Within the Roosevelt Administration an intense struggle took place between the Middle Western views of advisers like Moley and Tugwell, and the Eastern-Southern retinue of Norman Davis, James Warburg and Cordell Hull. The former dominated, and problems like the clash between agricultural imports and measures to raise domestic prices, or the World Economic Conference (scheduled for 1932 and postponed to 1933), were put to one side.

The dollar was allowed to depreciate, and when the World Economic Conference finally met in June 1933, President Roosevelt torpedoed it by refusing to accept an agreement worked out by the experts in which Britain would stabilize the pound, Germany would renounce foreign-exchange control adopted in the summer of 1931, France would give up import quotas undertaken because of the ineffectuality of tariffs in keeping out foreign grain, and the United States would stabilize the dollar. The conference broke up in early July after concluding only a small agreement sought by Senator Pitman of Nevada for the silver interests. Its consequence was to divide the world economy further. The Gold Bloc of Continental Europe—France, Belgium, the Netherlands and Switzerland—drew together, as did the sterling area of most of the British Commonwealth and a few countries closely allied to Britain in trade. At the center of the sterling area was the preferential trade system of the Commonwealth worked out at Ottawa in August 1932.

Under Roosevelt, however, the inward-looking phase of American policy did not last long. At the end of 1933 he and Secretary of the Treasury Morgenthau had lost interest in daily changes in the gold price and were exploring a stabilization agreement with the British. Failing this, in February 1934 they fixed the dollar in terms of gold anyhow, at $35 an ounce.

In the same month Roosevelt gave Cordell Hull—the Secretary of State with a fanatical preoccupation with free trade—the green light to introduce a bill to lower tariffs on a bilateral basis. (Under the unconditional most-favored-nation clause the country had adopted in the 1920s, reductions negotiated with one country would be extended to others.) This was signed into law in June 1934. Within the half-decade to 1939, 20 agreements were concluded, the first with Cuba in August 1934, the most important with Britain in November 1938 and two with Canada, in November 1934 and November 1938.

An awakening interest in foreign policies, both political and economic, also led the United States to normalize relationships with the Soviet Union, from which recognition had been withheld since the Revolution of 1917 on the ground that successor governments are required to assume the debts of their predecessors, which the Soviet government had been unwilling to do. Trade relations with the Soviet Union, which had been minimal to this time, expanded somewhat with the establishment of Soviet official buying agencies in the United States, but the development was not substantial.

To the South, Roosevelt initiated a Good Neighbor Policy, without, at that time, much in the way of specific content. It was, however, a significant change both from the Monroe Doctrine, which had been directed mainly against European intervention, and from the imperialism of the turn of the century—the imperious use of the Marines to collect debt service from Nicaragua and Haiti, and unquestioning support for such companies as United Fruit and Mexican Eagle in their operations in the area.

Of multilateral and more general import was the Tripartite

Monetary Agreement entered into on September 26, 1936. The occasion was the collapse of the Gold Bloc, and especially of the French franc. The agreement provided a convenient cover under which the franc rate would be adjusted as part of an international exercise to provide exchange-rate stability. The engagement was limited: each country undertook to hold currency of the others without conversion to gold only for 24 hours. Symbolically, however, it marked an initiative by the United States in stabilizing the world economy. A separate similar exercise was undertaken in the spring of 1937, when the country refrained from changing the price of gold under pressure of the "Gold Scare" in which foreign private citizens and even a few central banks sold gold for dollars against the prospect of a reduction in the gold price. At some inconvenience, but no real cost, the U.S. Treasury held to the $35-an-ounce price, buying all gold that was offered to it and sterilizing it by raising reserve requirements and open-market operations.

Exactly what forces produced the change in American economic policy in 1933 and 1934 from isolation to involvement is not self-evident. Elements contributing to the shift included recovery from the depths of the Depression that had focused attention on domestic concerns, perhaps a shift of the President's interests from the Populist position adopted during the campaign and especially during the first exciting days in office to his more comfortable views as an Eastern establishment figure; growing preoccupation with the threat to world peace posed by dictators in Europe and the Far East, with a natural extension of interest from foreign policy to foreign economic policy; and, as already noted, familiarity and boredom with the esoteric games of changing the gold price to alter the exchange rate to raise U.S. commodity and share prices—especially after July 1933, when the technique ceased working. The circumstances and the personality of the

President played a large part. More fundamental reasons would argue that the inward-turning of 1928 to 1933 was a deviation from trend, to which 1934 marked a return.

A European effort to regularize the international economy through agreement was initiated in 1937, leading to the preparation of a report under the direction of Paul Van Zeeland, former Prime Minister of Belgium. Appearing in 1938, the report was ignored under the stress of recession in the United States, which had struck in September 1937, and of rapidly expanding rearmament in a Europe threatened with war.

Foreign economic policy records two episodes associated with the rising threat of war. In 1935 Italy launched an unprovoked attack on Ethiopia, and the League of Nations somewhat diffidently called for sanctions on the delivery of oil to Italy. Though not a member of the League, the United States nonetheless supported the campaign and urged American oil companies to stop selling oil to Italy. The large companies complied with the request; unfortunately a rapid increase in Italian oil prices induced the entry of a host of single-ship operators who escaped control and delivered to Italy at Eritrean ports more gasoline than it had previously imported.

And, in 1938, the United States took another economic-warfare action of its own in cutting off the export of scrap iron and steel to Japan, foreshadowing a cutoff of oil in the summer of 1941, which helped precipitate the decision of Japanese military leaders to make war on this country.

As war began in Europe in 1939, President Roosevelt honored more in the breach than in the observance the Neutrality Act of 1939, passed by the Congress in an effort to keep this country uninvolved; got around the Johnson Act of 1930 by interpreting it to apply only to private lending in the United States, and not to government advances to foreign borrowers; and finally, after the tide of battle had turned against Britain in 1940, and well before the United States had entered the war, enacted Lend-Lease in February 1941 as a way to transfer resources to its Allies without piling up the kind of recount of war debts that had occurred after World War I. A special feature of Lend-Lease was the Hyde Park Agreement of December 1941 with Canada, under which supplies and components needed by Canada for incorporation in matériel produced for Britain would be lend-leased to Britain, but delivered to Canada. This had the effect of keeping Canada off the books as a recipient of U.S. assistance. Before U.S. entry into the war, the United States and Canada established a Joint Economic Committee of the two countries to expedite cooperation in mobilization and in planning postwar reconstruction. When the United States did enter, joint boards were established with Britain in a number of economic areas, parallel to the military arrangements, and especially in procurement, shipping and food.

As one condition of qualifying to receive assistance, the Lend-Lease agreement required that the recipient promise to cooperate with the United States in the design and construction of a liberal postwar world economic system. In the summer of 1941, President Roosevelt and Prime Minister Churchill met aboard a warship off Newfoundland. In addition to strategic planning of military operations, they drafted an Atlantic Charter that laid down broad principles for the establishment of a liberal economic system after the war.

V

In the Department of State, Leo Pasvolsky was assigned the task of preparing postwar plans for U.S. policy for the world economy. No government agency waited for such plans to emerge. The Treasury moved ahead with monetary reconstruction. In 1943 the Agriculture Department organized a

[229]

Hot Springs meeting on food. From the Department of State came a design for world trade. The United Nations was to be assigned a watching brief over world economic policies generally, but with operating responsibilities assigned to specialized agencies.

These responsibilities are indicated by the substantives used in the titles of the major world organizations. First in functional order was the United Nations *Relief* and *Rehabilitation* Agency (UNRRA). Relief was the provision of foodstuffs to hungry allies after the war. Rehabilitation consisted of restocking. The Bretton Woods bank was the International Bank for *Reconstruction* and *Development* (IBRD), beginning with the reconstruction of war damage, and going on to the development of countries which had not begun industrialization. The International *Monetary* Fund (IMF) would deal with exchange rates, balances of payments and the financial side. An International *Trade* Organization (ITO) was to lower restrictions and set rules for commerce. The world order would be pieced out with lesser specialized agencies in health, meteorology, aviation and the like. While these institutions were being brought into being, the United States enlarged by $3 billion the lending capacity of the Export-Import Bank, established in 1934 primarily to assist exports and employment. Of this, $1 billion was initially set aside for a loan to the Soviet Union, pending settlement of Lend-Lease and other wartime financial arrangements. The loan failed to materialize for reasons that have never been made clear but that undoubtedly reflected the influence in that first Truman year of such men as James Byrnes and Leo Crowley.

As the country least hurt by war, the United States took a major role in contributing to UNRRA, stocking it in large part with surplus army provisions. A first *tranche* of $2.75 billion was to be followed by a second equal amount in August 1945. A number of countries raised objections. Canada chose to give its aid directly to Britain. Britain refused to join unless the feeding of Austria and Italy were shifted from military aid (in which its share was 50 percent) to UNRRA (in which it was 8 percent). The U.S.S.R. insisted that while it was a donor, to the extent of 2 percent, and hence not entitled to receive aid, the Ukraine and Byelorussia should be recipients. With one vote in 17, the United States reluctantly agreed to take over the Canadian 6 percent, thereby increasing the U.S. total from 72 to 78 percent, and to add recipients, thus diluting the aid provided for others. It resolved thenceforward to render aid bilaterally, rather than through multilateral organizations that lacked objective principles of aid-giving and were subject to logrolling.

The need for relief, rehabilitation and reconstruction had been seriously underestimated in the postwar period, on several scores beyond the dilution mentioned. In August 1945, on the surrender of the Japanese, Lend-Lease was stopped precipitously—a decision made by President Truman and Secretary of State Byrnes en route to the Potsdam negotiations without consulting their economic advisers. The decision was based on commitments made to the Congress in the Lend-Lease legislation process, commitments which they both, as former Senators, felt bound to honor. In his *Memoirs* Truman recognized this as a serious mistake and put most of the blame on Byrnes. In addition to this blow, price control was removed in June 1946, so that a given amount of dollars went less far. Military destruction had been overestimated, but a serious underestimation of greater significance was made of the under-maintenance of capital, using up of stocks, and wearing out of consumers' inventories of clothing and household goods. Post-UNRRA direct assistance by the United States was undertaken in the strenuous conditions of 1946, along with the use of IMF and IBRD loans for emergency consumption rather than the reconstruction and balance-of-payments purposes for which they had been established.

The British position had been alleviated temporarily by an

Anglo-American Financial Agreement which provided for a
$3.75 billion loan to enable Britain to resume convertibility of
the pound. During the early debates on postwar policy, John
H. Williams of the Federal Reserve Bank of New York and
Harvard University had opposed the IMF as a universal device
for restoring world monetary health, and argued an opposing
"key-currency" principle in which certain major monies,
around which pivoted large currency areas, would be restored
to health separately and in sequence. As often happens when
alternative courses are debated, both the IMF and the British
key-currency loans were adopted. The initial amount of the
loan was cut from $5 billion, perhaps a political necessity since
the measure ultimately passed the Senate by only one vote.
(The vote ratifying the agreement in Parliament was also
close, as the Opposition contended that the conditions of the
United States in granting the loan were too onerous.) As it
worked out, the British were unwilling or unable to negotiate
the write-down or funding of accumulated sterling balances or
to institute effective controls on the export of capital. In
consequence, the convertibility of sterling instituted in July
1947 lasted only six weeks before the bulk of the loan was
gone.

Relief for the defeated countries of Germany and Japan was
a low priority for the Allied governments but not altogether
ignored. U.S. policy toward Germany was complicated by
joint occupation with Britain, France, and especially the Soviet
Union; in Japan, where the United States was the sole
occupation power, decision-making was easier. U.S. policies
called for avoiding the connections between reparations, war
debts and foreign lending which had held after World War I.
At Potsdam the United States insisted that the four zones of
occupation be treated as a single economic unit, and that the
first charge on current German production from all zones be
commercial exports necessary to pay for imports, rather than

reparations. The point was to prevent some occupation powers from taking out reparations from current production while others were obliged to feed the population in their zones. Reparations, it was agreed, should be paid through removal of capital equipment from Germany that was in excess of the peacetime requirements of the German people.

Strong forces in the United States pushed for restrictive and repressive policies in Germany. Under a Joint Chiefs of Staff directive (JCS 1067), drawing its inspiration from the so-called Morgenthau Plan, the U.S. commander was instructed to take no steps to revive the German economy beyond those necessary to prevent such disease and unrest as might endanger the occupation forces. In July 1945, however, French, Belgian and Dutch need for coal made it necessary to try to restore German coal production for export. By fall, Poland was asking for spare parts for German machinery in Silesian coal mines. It proved impossible to reach sustainable agreements with the Soviet Union on what they could remove from Germany as war booty, restitution and reparations, and in particular the Soviet Union did acquire foodstuffs from the eastern zone of occupation while Britain and the United States were feeding their zones in the west. Gradually the zonal arrangements broke down, and so did arrangements for reparation removals. The economic importance of Germany in the revival of Europe became clear. By September 1946, the Secretary of State made a speech at Stuttgart outlining a more positive policy of German economic recovery in a European setting.

Governing and feeding Germany were further complicated in the fall of 1946 by a British government approach to the United States, stating that the country was unable to continue to pay the import bill for its populous zone of occupation including the Ruhr. A Bizonal Agreement in December 1946 provided that the two zones would be treated as a unit and that the United States would advance the bulk of the sums needed for imports. Later the French joined, with the smaller, self-sufficient zone.

Continued British economic weakness led in February 1947 to that country preparing to give up its support of Greek resistance to domestic and foreign infiltrating communist forces, and to another substitution of American for British responsibility, in the Truman Doctrine, for military aid to Greece and Turkey. Much of the assistance, especially in roads in Turkey, served a double economic and military purpose and could be said to be the beginnings of U.S. aid to economic development. Its main purpose was military.

A harsh winter in Europe in early 1947, which burst pipes, blocked transport, flooded fields and rotted seed, threatened economic breakdown throughout Western Europe. Funds made available from the United States under the British loan, UNRRA relief and post-UNRRA aid were nearing exhaustion. Political stalemate with the Soviet Union over German questions, plus economic disintegration which overwhelmed the stopgap measures applied to separate countries, produced in Washington a strong desire for a new, cooperative, enlarged effort to achieve recovery in Europe. On June 6, 1947, Secretary of State George C. Marshall gave a speech outlining a European recovery program. He proposed that Europe should prepare a program of recovery which would involve the cooperation of all the countries participating, including Germany, and that with it as a basis the United States would undertake a new coordinated program of aid.

The invitation was extended to all the countries of Europe, including the Eastern bloc and the Soviet Union. Foreign Minister Molotov met with Foreign Ministers Bevin and Bidault in Paris but refused to participate unless the United States handed over a fixed sum first and let the countries of Europe use it in their own way. Following this refusal, Czechoslovakia and Poland, which had previously accepted the invitation to participate, reversed their decisions. When the three western zones of occupation of Germany went ahead with monetary reform in their own zones and in their districts of Berlin, in June 1948 as the Marshall Plan got under way, Soviet military forces blockaded land access to Berlin, effectively dividing the country. Western links to Berlin and the Berlin economy were maintained only by airlift.

Considerable ambiguity attached to U.S. views as to what was meant by a European recovery plan. In the eyes of many, it meant the extension to Europe as a whole of French techniques of *planification* begun with the Monnet Plan of 1946. To William L. Clayton, Under Secretary of State for Economic Affairs, and Lewis W. Douglas, Ambassador to the Court of St. James, it implied return to liberal principles of free markets. The preamble to the European Recovery Act of April 1948, and Paul G. Hoffman's speech of October 31, 1949, emphasized the reproduction in Europe of a vast continental market like that of the United States. The United States applauded when in May 1950 French Foreign Minister Robert Schuman proposed a measure of functional integration in the European Coal and Steel Community. It supported a European Payments Union. At the same time, it maintained pressure for the elimination of quota restrictions, which largely discriminated against U.S. exports in the interest of economizing on dollars, and worked more broadly for the adoption of generalized rules for trading in the draft Charter of the International Trade Organization (ITO) signed at Havana in 1948.

As indicated earlier, the ITO was to be a cornerstone of a worldwide system of liberal trading, setting down procedures for lowering tariffs on a multilateral basis, providing for freedom of investment, limiting restrictive business practices, and establishing machinery for handling necessary exceptions and adjustments. Countries emerging from the difficulties of war, and those embarking on programs of development, insisted on so many exceptions to the general rules, against quantitative restrictions and in favor of low, nondiscriminatory tariffs, that the Congress of the United States judged the document worthless. The United States would be held to the general rule; other countries would claim avoidance under saving clauses.

The Department of State ultimately did not submit the treaty to the Senate for ratification. Instead, it concluded an executive agreement, not requiring congressional assent, the so-called General Agreement on Tariffs and Trade (GATT) that embodied the principal clauses of the ITO, and provided for a small staff to supervise operation of the agreement in Geneva. Under its aegis, a series of multilateral reductions of tariffs was negotiated in the postwar period, from the Geneva Round in 1949 to the Dillon, Kennedy and current Tokyo Rounds. The Kennedy Round negotiated after 1962 was particularly salient.

Help to developing countries was initially limited to the "development" aspect of the IBRD and Greek-Turkish aid. In his Inaugural speech of January 1949, however, President Truman included a Point IV aimed at this group of countries. This program initially consisted of technical assistance, especially in agriculture, education, and the planning of public works. As the 1950s wore on, it became increasingly evident that much more was needed, especially capital assistance. A euphoric mood developed that poor countries could all follow the development path of Britain, the rest of Western Europe, North America, and most recently Japan, and succeed in raising their standards of living. Needed were resolve on the part of local government and foreign aid in the form of goods, modern technology and effective management. Under the Republican regime of President Eisenhower, and later under Nixon, emphasis shifted from official aid to the role of American corporate investment in countries initially called "underdeveloped," then "less developed," and finally "developing." Both political parties put faith in the beneficent role of American food aid, under Public Law 480, designed to help developing countries and the American farmer, the latter by disposing of surplus stocks. Other groups were not slow in taking advantage of the opportunities afforded by foreign aid, shipping lines insisting on transporting it in American bottoms, suppliers that it be spent on or tied to American goods only. Even the Congress benefited through a provision that five percent of the local-currency counterpart derived from the sale of aid goods be set aside for American use, largely the building of embassies and the entertainment of junketing Congressmen.

Assistance was furnished through multilateral agencies and bilaterally. Under the former, there were U.N. programs: those of the IBRD and its subsidiaries—the International Development Association (IDA) for non-bankable projects, and the International Finance Corporation (IFC) to invest in private enterprise in developing countries. In time special regional banks were established, largely with American capital, in Latin America, Asia and Africa. In due course, aid to development was extended by other industrial countries after their recovery from the war. Development became an international concern of the Organization for Economic Cooperation and Development (OECD), which emerged under the Marshall Plan from the original Organization for European Economic Cooperation (OEEC)—enlarged to include the United States, Canada, Australia and Japan. Its Development Assistance Committee (DAC) gathered statistics, compared national efforts, and urged increased aid.

Foreign aid was assisted in the early stages by the cold war. South Korea, Taiwan and Israel were especially favored by U.S. aid because of their strategic importance. Cuba got no aid from the United States, a great deal from the Soviet Union. At the last minute Secretary of State John Foster Dulles backed away from building the Aswan Dam in Egypt and let the

Soviet Union take on the project. Bilateral aid was divided into military and economic, and the latter was often not that much different from the military aid in its implications for political alignment and support.

Discouragement with foreign aid set in during the 1960s. Economic development was stubbornly slow. Aid achieved little growth, less gratitude, few political objectives. The Hickenlooper Amendment, which required withholding aid when American property was nationalized without prompt, adequate and effective compensation, proved ineffective. Internationalists deduced from these circumstances that foreign aid should be multilateral, not bilateral. Those not so internationally minded thought there were better things to do with the money at home. Détente with the Soviet Union lessened the urgency of helping the developing countries. Aid still could be used in particular political impasses to grease a solution, help for both Egypt and Israel, or support for Rhodesia. But the moral commitment eroded.

Last in this catalog of areas of foreign economic policy was the monetary field. The IMF went into hibernation after the start of the Marshall Plan, except for a series of small operations, largely the furnishing of advice to developing countries, since the major financial needs of developed countries were covered by the Marshall Plan and by the substantial volume of dollars earned by Japan as a staging area for U.S. troops in Asia.

As recovery progressed, however, the countries of Europe and Japan began to accumulate foreign-exchange reserves, a process which continued after Marshall aid ceased. Some insignificant amounts of dollars were converted into gold in the 1950s. The greatest part was held in deposits in U.S. banks and in U.S. Treasury bills. The country became banker for the world, spending abroad, investing, lending, furnishing assistance in amounts which exceeded the dollars earned through exports of goods and services. Accumulation of dollars by foreign countries began to be regarded as a deficit in the balance of payments of the United States, and was a matter of concern to President Eisenhower in the closing days of his term of office, and to Presidents Kennedy and Johnson from 1960 to 1968. Gradually the country's economic preoccupations shifted from the rest of the world to the international position of the United States.

VI

Immediately after the war, the French economist François Perroux wrote of the United States as a dominant economy; i.e., its every action affected the rest of the world, but it was not in turn called upon to react to events outside.[10] A recent English observer, seeking to make an elusive distinction between "hegemony" and "leadership," characterized the role of the United States in international economic affairs in the 1950s and up to the middle of the 1960s as "hegemonic." [11] The decline in dominance was visible about 1960.

One view holds with hindsight that the shift from preeminent concern in foreign economic policy for the public international good began with the permanent exception sought by the United States in 1955 to the rule against quantitative restrictions in GATT for its agricultural products.[12] U.S. support for freer trade in agricultural products is highly selective: it favors freer trade in export products such as grain, oil seeds and meal, citrus fruit, poultry and tobacco; and opposes it in dairy products, meat, rice, sugar, cotton and wool, which are on its import list.[13] Farm groups have long had power in legislatures well beyond their economic significance, as a result of Engel's law and cultural or perhaps political lag. Engel's law—that food consumption as a proportion of expenditure declines as income rises—means that farm groups are in continuous decline in the proportion of national income produced, of persons employed, and in votes. Political lag—until the Supreme Court one-man, one-vote decision in 1962 required state legislatures to be reapportioned on a regular basis—meant that the states retained control of the decennial reapportionment process and that farmers dominated it. This fact and the seniority system kept them in effective control of key legislation far out of proportion to their numbers or economic importance. Where farm groups led the way in insisting on domestic special interests over the interest of the economic system on a world basis, other groups—trade unions, industries, shipping, large corporations and the like— did not tarry in asserting their own interests. The executive branch often fought a rearguard action, yielding slowly in watering down the successive trade legislation, for example, with escape clauses, peril point provisions, the application of export quotas abroad, anti-dumping provisions, and exceptions to freer imports in the interest of national defense.

The primary unraveling of the American dominance, hegemony or leadership in the world economic system, however, came in the monetary field, and had its roots in technical and political difficulties. The technical difficulties were those of understanding. The Bretton Woods system had strongly opposed flexible exchange rates on the basis of the 1930s experience of competitive depreciation. It permitted or encouraged control of international capital movements in the defense of a fixed exchange rate. At the end of the 1950s, members of the economics profession—prominent among them Yale Professor Robert Triffin—began to fear that the world money supply would prove inadequate. Gold production furnished only about $1.5 billion of additional reserves annually to the world, and much of this—ultimately all of it— went into private hands for industrial use and hoarding. Liquidity was furnished to the world by the U.S. balance-of-payments deficit, measured by the increase in dollar reserves by countries abroad. When the United States succeeded in correcting this deficit there would be insufficient liquidity to finance world production and trade. Observers like Jacques Rueff of France and Roy Harrod of Britain wanted to raise the price of gold; Robert Triffin recommended issuance of a new international money. Meanwhile, the United States sought unsuccessfully to correct its balance-of-payments "deficit" by halting capital exports through taxes on security issues, controls over bank lending, and restrictions on taking capital abroad by firms investing overseas—all to no or little avail. And countries like the United States and Germany conducted their monetary policies independently, without recognition that their money markets had been joined through the joining of each with the Eurocurrency market which had grown up outside the United States.

In retrospect it is clear that there were a number of errors of economic analysis in these views. First, it proved impossible to halt capital movements in most societies. Money is fungible and flows through many channels. To cut off one or two channels at a time will only increase the pressure on others and maintain the flow which, so long as there are enough conduits open, is impervious to the closing off of any one. Other temporizing devices worked out by the ingenious Under Secretary of the Treasury, Robert V. Roosa, such as issuing special bonds which guaranteed the buyer against exchange risk, or negotiating special offsets by Germany against American expenditure for the maintenance of its forces in Europe, were of little help, based as they were on the reasoning that the deficit in the U.S. balance-of-payments was a passing disturbance. Second, most of the deficit was a function of the fact that the United States was acting as banker to the world. Liquidity needs determined the deficit, rather than the deficit accidentally filling liquidity needs. This became less true in the final years of the Vietnam War after about 1968, and especially in 1970 and 1971, when the merchandise trade balance in the United States balance of payments turned adverse on an annual basis for the first time since 1894. The meaning of surplus and deficit in the balance of payments is different for a bank and for a bank customer. The United States was acting as a bank. The rest of the world represented customers. Third, when money markets are joined, as European markets were with those of the United States and Canada, monetary policies cannot be independently determined. In 1966 and 1969-70, U.S. attempts to tighten interest rates pulled a flood of money from Europe. The system ultimately collapsed in 1971 when the United States tried to achieve cheap money while Germany was seeking to raise interest rates. Dollars poured abroad and drowned the Bretton Woods system.

The Bretton Woods misconception about the possibilities of control of capital movements had another consequence. The IMF had been designed to fund cyclical—not persistent—balance-of-payments deficits on current accounts, not to handle capital flows. The amounts available were too small, even before postwar inflation, and provision of assistance was stretched out over time. The IMF was no help in a crisis on this score, and also because its decision-making procedures were time-consuming. A few steps were taken to modify IMF procedures to correct these disabilities. With convertibility in 1958, however, it proved necessary to provide a special fund for countries under speculative attack, called the General Arrangements to Borrow (GAB), organized by leading financial countries (the Group of Ten). A run on the pound sterling in March 1961 occurred while this machinery was being completed, and was met by an informal emergency loan to Britain on the part of a number of countries. This so-called Basel Agreement, led by the United States, was regularized in arrangements to swap claims on foreign central banks for foreign claims on domestic central banks, which were acti-vated in subsequent foreign-exchange crises in Canada in

1962, Italy in 1963, and Britain again in 1964 and 1967. As the largest supporter of the agreement, the United States found it of little help when the crisis affected the dollar.

In 1965, under President Johnson and Secretary of the Treasury Henry H. Fowler, the United States decided that it would be useful to adopt Triffin's suggestion of a new international reserve asset, but to do so in addition to gold and dollars, not as a substitute for them. The reason was that gold was going into hoarding and was not available for adding to world liquidity. The world had accumulated $25 billion or so of dollars and was wary of taking more. To increase world liquidity at some appropriate rate, therefore, it was believed necessary to add a third asset. Subconsciously, perhaps, the American authorities were more interested in restoring the U.S. ratio of reserve assets to foreign liabilities than they were in global liquidity. They failed to recognize that Special Drawing Rights for the United States meant SDRs for all.

An asymmetric or hierarchical system in which the United States acted as banker for the world; the ultimate provider, along with military security, of a market for distress goods; a source of goods in short supply, and of capital requirements; a monitor of the system of international money including the pattern of exchange rates; and a lender of last resort in crisis— such a system may be possible to contemplate in economic terms. By the 1970s it was no longer in the cards politically. Attacks on the system came from many sources: from within the United States where some industries, and most labor unions, joined farmers in asserting the primacy of their parochial interests over the international interest of the system; from radicals who insisted that U.S. professed action in the international interest was in fact a selfish imperialist one; from a stronger Europe, led by France and followed somewhat reluctantly by Germany, Britain and Italy, claiming an enlarged share of decision-making; and from the developing

[243]

countries. It was largely the domestic interests in the United States that led Secretary of the Treasury John Connally in August 1971 to insist on devaluation of the dollar, to break the pressure on import-competing industries, and which led President Nixon in August 1973 to embargo the foreign sales of soybeans, thus administering a second shock to Japanese economic interests and sensibilities. The French voice in international economic matters was larger than their economic specific gravity for a number of reasons: because they mobilized the European Economic Community (EEC) in support on occasion; because they were willing to exit—converting dollars to gold ostentatiously in 1965, withdrawing from NATO, refusing to vote in EEC until they got their way over agricultural prices.

The developing countries had organized themselves as the Nonaligned Nations at Bandung in 1955 and as the Group of 77 in the United Nations Conference on Trade and Development (UNCTAD) in 1964, and began gradually offering an alternative view of how the international economic system should be managed. In the United Nations, making effective use of a large majority because of the numbers of newly independent states, the developing countries gradually fashioned a position which differed from the free-market one professed by the United States in a long list of economic functions, from trade to commodity prices, assistance for balances of payments, foreign aid, the multinational corporation, and the issuance of international liquidity. They denounced the conception of a liberal system as neocolonialist, continuing economic subjection after political independence had been granted, and opposed it with a list of demands packaged as the New International Economic Order. The success of the Organization of Petroleum Exporting Countries (OPEC) in converting a political embargo into a drastic price rise in oil in December 1973 in the wake of the Yom Kippur

War raised expectations of the developing countries in their demand for a share of SDRs, and their demand for generalized preferences for manufactured exports of developing countries in industrialized nations. Secretary of State Henry Kissinger initially reacted to this importunism by ignoring it. Gradually, however, he began to take a hand, seeking a way to find an accommodation with the developing countries. After the Seventh Special Session of the General Assembly in September 1975, he went along with a proposal for a Committee of Twenty, to meet at Paris, with four committees, to prepare detailed plans. And during 1976 a genuine bargaining process seems to have been under way, in Paris, at the Jamaica meeting on monetary matters, at the UNCTAD Conference in Nairobi in May—as well as in the related area of the Law of the Sea Conference, where a deadlock between developed and developing countries persists on the issue of how to exploit and distribute the proceeds of the mineral resources of the ocean seabeds.

VII

Public goods are those the consumption of which by any one person or consuming unit does not diminish the amount available for the consumption of others. Short of some level of congestion, roads and parks furnish an example. Other types of public goods are law and order, clean streets, economic stability.

Public goods are difficult to get produced on a voluntary basis because it is in no one person's interest to undertake the expenditure of time, effort or money to do so. And, if they are going to be produced, the individual can enjoy them without payment, as a free rider. Hence, public goods are notoriously under-produced. They must be furnished by government, and even then sectional or group interests may politick against their production on the ground that *their* costs exceed *their* benefits.

In the international economy, there is no government to produce public goods. Certain international agencies are endowed with powers to discharge certain functions. For the most part, however, international public goods are under-produced unless some countries take on a leadership role, cajoling, persuading, arm-twisting other countries to take their appropriate shares of the cost. There can be stalemate: at the 1927 World Economic Conference under the auspices of the League of Nations, all countries, including the United States which attended as an observer, agreed to lower tariffs, but no country took action. All waited for a lead which was not forthcoming. At the World Economic Conference of 1933, no country was willing to abandon its national plans for recovery for the possibly illusory hope of a joint recovery effort.

Without leadership, international public goods are under-produced. With leadership there is the opposite danger that some country starts out believing that it is acting in the public or general interest and slips knowingly or unwittingly into serving its own ends exclusively.

The international economic system flourished, more or less, from 1870 to 1913 when Britain served as world economic leader. The public goods that it provided were a market for surplus or distress goods, a countercyclical source of capital, management of the gold standard that maintained a coherent set of exchange rates and coordinated macroeconomic policies, and the lender of last resort in crises. After 1913 Britain was unable to discharge these functions, and the United States was unwilling to. The Great Depression is largely ascribable to this gap.

Beginning about 1936 and with assurance during and immediately following World War II, the United States undertook to provide the public goods needed for world economic stability. Instead of the gold standard as cover, it had the United Nations and its specialized agencies. From the early 1960s, however, and increasingly from 1965 as the Vietnam War deepened, this country became less willing to act as a leader and the world became less ready to accept it in that role. Some of the U.N. agencies can go on without strong national initiatives, notably the IBRD. Most cannot. France is prepared to assert a claim to leadership, with the help of her EEC partners. It receives limited support. One or two voices have been raised in favor of a duumvirate or a triumvirate of the United States and Germany, or the United States, Germany and Japan. Quite apart from grave doubt as to whether the interests of such a pair or trio of countries could be harmonized sufficiently, there are questions first whether either Germany or Japan would be willing—up to now they prefer "loyalty" to "voice"—and whether the rest of the world would accede in such an arrangement. On all three counts, the prospects appear slim.

The New International Economic Order, calling for developed countries to accede to developing countries' demands on the ground of historical equity, seems to this observer utopian. Equally so is the possibility of negotiating on a long-run basis a giant "package deal" covering aid, preferences in trade, rights and duties of multinational corporations, international commodity stabilization, the "link" for the issuance of SDRs and the like. When principles are rejected, ad hoc arrangements may take their place but are unlikely to have much staying power. The universal historical record of failure in commodity agreements originates in the fact that while buyers and sellers may be content at any one time, at a later date when the agreement comes up for renewal, the price in the open market has changed and one or the other is dissatisfied. Complex package deals appeal to the diplomats, and the historical record contains a number—like the Congress of Vienna—that have demonstrated survival value. Most have not, nor have such deals in the economic field.

What then is ahead? Since 1971, despite inability to agree on the international economic system, the world has managed to avoid the beggar-thy-neighbor policies of competitive tariffs and competitive exchange depreciation which gave us the 1930s. Instability has been avoided though stability has not been assured. The nationalistic response to the oil embargo of November 1973—Operation Independence and end-runs to Tehran to assure national supplies of Iranian oil—has subsided without doing particular damage. But the world is far from agreement on a system, accepting it as legitimate, and responding to the cajoling or arm-twisting of a leader-enforcer. Moreover, the United States is the only candidate for the role visible on the horizon, and whether this country would be willing or acceptable—absent the charisma of a Roosevelt or a Kennedy—is very much in question.

What might such a system consist of? To a conventional liberal economist, the answer is relatively straightforward. It should be a market system on the whole, but with market solutions modified when they become intolerable, i.e., when goods are very scarce or so abundant as to threaten livelihoods. This does not mean commodity agreements so much as some provision for stocking grain against a repetition of 1974, some industrial materials stockpiling, but primarily international action to maintain world income in depression. Tariffs or quotas would be acceptable only on a disappearing basis, to moderate but not to forestall adjustment. A multilateral agency would be established on the multinational corporation, not to handle compensation for nationalization problems, on which no meeting of minds is likely, but to cope with questions of antitrust, trading with the enemy (whether the policies of one country in this area may intrude into another through foreign subsidiaries of domestic corporations), double taxation, tax

[248]

evasion, corruption and the like. The OECD is the obvious locus of such an agency today, but it should be open to other countries, as they perceive it in their interest. The OECD should also be the setting for coordination of macroeconomic policies, once discussed by Working Party No. 3, but lately fallen into desuetude. DAC in the OECD should continue to preside over aid, though the function needs a greater stimulus than the example-setting efforts of Sweden, Norway and Canada seem to provide.

The most sensitive area is that of money. At the moment, fixed exchange rates have been rejected in favor of flexible exchange rates, but sentiment seems to favor such management of flexibility as approaches fixity. A return to the dollar standard, a return to the gold standard, or the development of a full-blown SDR standard each seems unlikely. The Eurocurrency and the Eurobond markets are private organizations, escaping national and international restraint. Darwinian evolution seems inescapable in this field, and is perhaps superior to Bretton Woods planning. It is possible, and even probable, that ad hoc international management of the Eurodollar and Eurocapital markets through combined open-market operations, led perhaps by the Bank of International Settlements, will provide the stability needed. In any event, the evolution is toward the internationalization of monetary policy. Monetary autonomy, like national military security, is a will-o'-the-wisp in an interdependent world.

In all these matters, it is useful to think of normal management of the system, and crisis management. Those in trouble will think the system always in crisis. This view must be resisted. Yet the rules applicable to market forces, discrimination, exchange control, foreign aid and the like which hold in normal times may have to be set aside in a true crisis. This poses a dilemma. Readiness of the system to cope with crises reduces discipline in normal times and increases the frequency of trouble. The knife-edge must be negotiated.

[249]

The United States must be prepared to contribute to the public good of management of the international economic system in the long run, and to respond to crises, applying different rules and standards to each, striving not to let the one corrupt the other. That is difficult enough. This country must at the same time associate the other nations of the world in this task in ways that are not subject to entropy and decay. It is a tall order.

NOTES

1. Mancur Olson, *The Logic of Collective Action: Public Goods and the Theory of Groups,* Cambridge: Harvard University Press, 1965.

2. See Albert O. Hirschman, *Exit, Voice and Loyalty; Responses to Decline in Firms, Organizations and States,* Cambridge: Harvard University Press, 1970.

3. Frank W. Taussig, *Tariff History of the United States,* 8th ed., New York: G. P. Putnam's Sons, 1931, p. 15.

4. See Carlos F. Diaz Alejandro, "Direct Foreign Investment in Latin America," in *The International Corporation,* ed. C. P. Kindleberger, Cambridge: MIT Press, 1970, p. 321.

5. Paul P. Abrahams, "The Foreign Expansion of American Finance and its Relation to the Foreign Economic Policies of the United States, 1907-1921," Ph.D. dissertation, University of Wisconsin, 1967, p. 84. A somewhat premature expression of financial aggression is contained in a statement of the *New York Herald* in an 1857 issue: "Each panic has resulted in making the city of New York the centre of finance and trade for this continent. In 1837 it stood on a sort of struggling emulation with Philadelphia and Boston.... The rivalry between New York and other cities has ceased. The late struggle of 1857 was in great degree between New York and London, and has terminated in the advantage of the former

city. And the time must not ere long arrive, when New York, not London, will become the financial centre, not only of the New World, but also to a great extent, of the Old World." See D. Morier Evans, *The History of the Commercial Crisis, 1857-58 and the Stock Exchange Panic of 1859* (1859), reprinted New York: Kelley, 1969, pp. 113-14.

6. Stephen V. O. Clarke, *Central Bank Cooperation, 1924-31*, New York: Federal Reserve Bank of New York, 1967, pp. 60-67.

7. Milton Friedman and Anna Jacobson Schwartz, *A Monetary History of the United States, 1867-1960*, Princeton: Princeton University Press, 1969, pp. 298-99.

8. C. P. Kindleberger, *The World in Depression, 1929-39*, Berkeley: University of California Press, 1973, pp. 136-38.

9. See Joseph S. Davis, *The World between the Wars, 1919-1939: an Economist's View*, Baltimore: Johns Hopkins University Press, 1975, p. 421: "Personalities counted heavily and clashes of strong personalities were recurrent sources of intranational and international friction. There were never enough harmonizers (such as Morrow, Salter, D'Abernon, Stamp, Monnet and Stresemann) to help divergent minds meet."

10. François Perroux, "Esquisse d'une theorie de l'économie dominante," *Economie Appliquée*, No. 2-3, 1948.

11. Andrew Shonfield, "Introduction: Past Trends and New Factors," in *International Economic Relations of the Western World, 1959-71*, Vol. I, *Politics and Trade*, ed. Andrew Shonfield, London: Oxford University Press, 1976, p. 33.

12. T. K. Warley, "Western Trade in Agricultural Products," in Shonfield, *op. cit.*, pp. 345-47.

13. *Ibid.*, p. 322.